Freeing the First Amendment

FREEING THE FIRST AMENDMENT

Critical Perspectives on Freedom of Expression

EDITED BY
David S. Allen AND Robert Jensen

NEW YORK UNIVERSITY PRESS
New York and London

NEW YORK UNIVERSITY PRESS
New York and London

© 1995 by New York University

All rights reserved

Library of Congress Cataloging-in-Publication Data
Freeing the first amendment : critical perspectives on freedom of
expression / edited by David S. Allen and Robert Jensen.
p. cm.
Includes bibliographical references.
ISBN 0-8147-0637-1.—ISBN 0-8147-0638-X (pbk.)
1. Freedom of speech—United States. I. Allen, David S., 1955– .
II. Jensen, Robert, 1958– .
KF4772.F744 1995
342.73'0853—dc20
[347.302853]   95-4434
                          CIP

New York University Press books are printed on acid-free paper,
and their binding materials are chosen for strength and durability.

Manufactured in the United States of America

10 9 8 7 6 5 4 3 2 1

For Laura and Meg
—DAVID S. ALLEN

For Luke
—ROBERT JENSEN

CONTENTS

Part I. Free Speech and Ideology

1. Freeing the First Amendment: An Introduction   3
   DAVID S. ALLEN
2. The First Amendment As Ideology   10
   FREDERICK SCHAUER

Part II. Untangling Speech, Property, and Law

3. Some Thoughts on Free Speech, Language, and the Rule of Law   31
   THOMAS STREETER
4. A New Deal for Speech   54
   CASS R. SUNSTEIN
5. The Right Kind of Neutrality   79
   OWEN M. FISS

Part III. Private/Public, Workers/Citizens

6. The Supreme Court and the Creation of an (In)active Public Sphere   93
   DAVID S. ALLEN
7. Effective Voice Rights in the Workplace   114
   VICTORIA SMITH HOLDEN

Part IV. A Postmodern Turn

8. The "Popular First Amendment" and Classical Hollywood, 1930–1960: *Film Noir* and "Speech Theory for the Millions" — 143
   NORMAN ROSENBERG
9. Trigger: Law, Labeling, and the Hyperreal — 169
   SANDRA BRAMAN

Part V. Outsider Voices

10. Feminism and Free Expression: Silence and Voice — 195
    ROBERT JENSEN AND ELVIA R. ARRIOLA
11. Why Lesbians and Gay Men Need Traditional First Amendment Theory — 224
    PAUL SIEGEL
12. The Reality and Ideology of First Amendment Jurisprudence: Giving Aid and Comfort to Racial Terrorists — 253
    ROBIN D. BARNES
13. Speaking the Corn into Being — 278
    DIANE GLANCY

Part VI. Conclusion

14. Embracing Uncertainty/Facing Fear — 285
    ROBERT JENSEN

Contributors — 293

Index — 297

PART I
Free Speech and Ideology

ONE

Freeing the First Amendment: An Introduction

DAVID S. ALLEN

The title of this collection, *Freeing the First Amendment,* is likely to puzzle some readers. Why, some might ask, does the very document that is intended to ensure the freedom of citizens of the United States need to be freed? And from what does it need to be freed? While attempting to answer those questions, this book challenges the idea that the only "champions of free speech"[1] are traditional liberal theorists who oppose alternatives to the mainstream interpretation of the First Amendment. Too often those who question the reliance on free-and-open competition between "equal" individuals to produce free expression are labeled not as champions, but rather as enemies of free speech. We argue that these alleged enemies are or can be champions as well. Working from a recognition that all is not fair and equal, these critical scholars explore how gender, race, sexual orientation, economic status, and other factors limit participation in modern society. As a result, these scholars seek ways to free the First Amendment from its traditional narrow interpretation and address inequities in society.

It is from this interpretive battle over the definition of freedom of expression that this book takes its title. We begin from a seemingly simple question: In a society that prides itself on the most expansive legal guarantees of free speech in history, why are so many speakers so frustrated by the "system of freedom of expression" in the United States?[2] The pages that follow are an attempt to find answers to that question.

3

Talking vs. Understanding: Toward a New Paradigm

The origins of this book can be traced to a frustration with the level of discussion about what the First Amendment means. While there is much talk *about* freedom of expression, there is little understanding of it. The distinction is not a superficial one, but rather it is vital to understanding the problems that surround the issue of freedom of speech in society today. As J. M. Balkin has noted, increasingly some on the left of American politics are abandoning libertarian traditions, resulting in a "realignment of political beliefs and attitudes."[3] At least part of the reason for this realignment can no doubt be traced to the frustration of those on the left who fail to find within the framework of traditional free-speech thought answers to very difficult questions. For many, the more-speech-rather-than-enforced-silence argument has become intellectually bankrupt, having long ago been separated from its philosophical and pragmatic roots.

Much of the free speech discourse today has devolved into what Jürgen Habermas might call strategic action—that is, action where the goal is winning an argument or achieving some kind of victory, legal or otherwise.[4] If we want more than talk about the First Amendment, however, strategic action falls short of achieving understanding through any kind of public debate. Today's talk about free speech often reflects the desire to protect private interests—increasingly that seems to mean corporate interests[5]—at the expense of understanding what the purpose and mission of the First Amendment is all about.

While the opinions and the reasoning of the justices of the U.S. Supreme Court are not known to all people, the ideology that is at the heart of those decisions has become pervasive. Reduced to an admittedly simplistic definition, that ideology goes something like this: Hurtful speech might conceivably be of some value to society and therefore the proper answer to that speech is not censorship, but more speech. That dominant free speech frame contains many unanswered questions. For example, of what value is unpleasant speech? The answers vary from theorist to theorist. To identify but a few, unpleasant speech has been viewed as aiding in the discovery of truth,[6] creating a more tolerant society,[7] or protecting the antiauthoritarian nature in all of us.[8] While those ideas are often justifiable, we need to move to the next level of analysis to truly understand what is at the heart of freedom of expression. We need to ask why the speaker's rights are more important than the listener's, or the community of listeners'. We need to ask why the proper response to an insulting name is more speech rather than less speech. And we need to understand that while the First Amendment has been interpreted as articulating an equation for the protection of freedom of expression, that equation has little to say about the equality of speakers, especially when it comes to the use of resources.

Richard Delgado has labeled this dominant interpretation of the First Amendment the "formalist view of speech"—the idea that speech is the ideal way to test ideas and promote improvements for society.[9] Only recently have challenges arisen to that formalist view of the First Amendment. What we are seeing today, at least in the eyes of Delgado, is a paradigm shift, transforming how people look at the First Amendment. The new paradigm, with a "more nuanced, skeptical view" of speech, sees free speech as limited in scope, as a tool for legitimating the status quo, and suggests that speech can, at times, be used to harm people.[10]

In a way, Delgado's new paradigm calls for us to move from superficial talk about the First Amendment to a more in-depth analysis of the real power and limits of speech. In short, no longer is talk about free speech sufficient; in its place, we need understanding.

CHALLENGING SOME COMFORTABLE ASSUMPTIONS

Attempts to begin the discussion about the dominant formalist paradigm often result in failure. More often than not, First Amendment discourse that stays within that formalist paradigm goes unchallenged, while attempts to move beyond that paradigm encounter skepticism and hard questions at every turn. For example, when law professor Catharine MacKinnon and lawyer Floyd Abrams debated the meaning of the First Amendment in the pages of the *New York Times Magazine,* moderator-journalist Anthony Lewis quickly turned the debate into an examination of MacKinnon's ideas.[11] MacKinnon was repeatedly asked to justify her interpretation of the First Amendment; Abrams was never called upon to defend the principles upon which his First Amendment is constructed.

There is, of course, an easy explanation for this. It can be argued that the reason for that missing interrogation is that the ideas that ground Abrams's view of the First Amendment are ideas upon which we as a society have already agreed. There is little doubt that we are taught the values that underlie traditional First Amendment theory from an early age, both formally and informally. Whether we understand them, however, is another issue.

Those of us who teach First Amendment theory courses are all too familiar with the problem. Students have learned to respond to questions about freedom of speech with the correct answer. Their unemotional responses seem more reflective of a dead or dying set of ideas rather than a living document that is vital to the creation of a just society. It is as if they know the words and the tune to the song, but they have little understanding about why that song was written or how that song might be useful to their lived experiences. And when faced with tough questions, they look for easy legal answers rather than face the difficult ethical decisions, the latter requiring an understanding of the idea of freedom of speech that far exceeds what is often needed in the legal arena.

Lewis may have been entirely correct, then, not to challenge Abrams. To some extent, we all *do* have an understanding of Abrams's First Amendment. It has a familiar, comfortable, reassuring ring to it. So when Abrams says that only in the "rarest case do we even start down the road of saying, well this speech is so likely to cause harm of such extraordinary, provable, damaging nature that we won't allow it,"[12] we can all comfortably nod our heads in agreement. There is, however, a problem with being too comfortable. If the First Amendment is to remain a vital element of society, we need to continue to ask whether those "rarest cases" are indeed so rare, why they are special, and what types of speech deserve protection.[13] And, perhaps more importantly, we need to ask what kind of society we are attempting to create and what role freedom of expression can play in that creation. Unfortunately, in much of today's discourse about the First Amendment, it is difficult to find the answers to those questions.

The "Critical" First Amendment

The chapters that follow attempt to answer some of those questions. All, in their own way, are critical of the dominant view of the First Amendment that is so familiar to us all. The word "critical" is not intended to link the chapters of this book with any particular school of thought. Rather, we use "critical" to mean any approach that helps identify the conditions and constraints that restrict people from shaping their own lives. To paraphrase Max Horkheimer's classic definition of critical theory, the goal is the emancipation of people from the relationships that enslave them.[14] Put another way: This volume hopes to highlight the liberatory possibilities of expanded ideas about expressive liberty. The authors put forward revisions of liberal First Amendment theory that they hope will aid in the creation of a better, more just society.

This book is also guided by another idea that has links to critical theory—the idea of a functioning public sphere. While that term has been idealized and perhaps abused in much academic and nonacademic discourse, it is central to what this book is all about. In its broadest sense, the public sphere is envisioned as a place where individuals who are active members of society can engage in the discussion of policies and procedures that affect their lives.[15] It is important to note that in this vision of the public sphere, individuals do not cease to be individuals once they join the discussion, but rather that people begin to learn about and understand the role of individuals in the creation of society. Jazz is perhaps the most apt metaphor that can be found to describe the idea of a public sphere. As put forward by Sheldon Hackney, chairman of the National Endowment for the Humanities, jazz was "created from the bottom up, is non-hierarchical in both its performance and appeal ... and emphasizes the improvisation of individual performance within a group setting."[16]

This book obviously does not meet all the requirements of Hackney's jazz metaphor, nor can it be viewed as a public sphere. This volume is many things, for example, but it is certainly not nonhierarchical. The pages that follow are filled with writings by professors, some of whom work at major research universities. If anything, this book takes a small step, perhaps tentative at best, toward making the discussion about free speech more public. First Amendment theory is not the sole domain of lawyers and the legal profession. The ideas expressed in this work are not simply the views of law professors, although some join the discussion. They also reflect the views of those who work in the disciplines of communication, history, and literature. Most write in a style that will be familiar to many readers of articles and texts on the freedom of expression, but some challenge the traditional interpretation in writing style as well as ideas. Some of the authors call for what can be considered radical changes, suggesting interpretations that would give voice to marginalized groups in society and, in the process, provide less power for privileged groups. Others work more in the mainstream, tinkering with the institutions and interpretations that are so fundamental to changing and legitimating the First Amendment. Some write from a communitarian perspective, while others struggle to redeem liberal thought. It is our hope that this diversity of academic backgrounds and perspectives will help begin the discussion of freedom of speech. In the end, our goal is to give some life—some jazz, if you will—to the discussion of free speech.

Notes

1. The words "champions of free speech" are those of Nadine Strossen, president of the American Civil Liberties Union and professor of law at New York Law School. In 1993, Strossen wrote: "Although champions of free speech have been fighting a defensive battle in some segments of academe and the news media, so far we have prevailed." Strossen, "Legal Scholars Who Would Limit Free Speech," *Chronicle of Higher Education* (July 7, 1993): B2.

2. The words are identified with the work of Thomas I. Emerson. See *Toward a General Theory of the First Amendment* (New York: Random House, 1966) and *The System of Freedom of Expression* (New York: Random House, 1970).

3. J. M. Balkin, "Some Realism About Pluralism: Legal Realist Approaches to the First Amendment," *Duke Law Journal* (1990): 376.

4. Jürgen Habermas, *The Theory of Communicative Action, vol. 1*, Thomas McCarthy, trans. (Boston: Beacon Press, 1984), 101.

5. For a discussion of this point, see Balkin, 384.

6. See Zechariah Chafee, Jr., *Free Speech in the United States* (Cambridge: Harvard University Press, 1941), 35.

7. Lee C. Bollinger, *The Tolerant Society: Freedom of Speech and Extremist Speech in America* (New York: Oxford University Press, 1986).

8. Steven H. Shiffrin, *The First Amendment, Democracy, and Romance* (Cambridge: Harvard University Press, 1990).

9. Richard Delgado, "First Amendment Formalism Is Giving Way to First Amendment Legal Realism," *Harvard Civil Rights-Civil Liberties Law Review* 29 (Winter 1994): 170.

10. Delgado, 171–172.

11. *New York Times Magazine*, "The First Amendment, Under Fire from the Left" (March 13, 1994): 40–45, 56–57, 68, 71, 81.

12. *New York Times Magazine*, 81

13. For an interesting examination of this idea, see Frederick Schauer, "Must Speech Be Special?" *Northwestern University Law Review* 78 (December 1983): 1284–1306.

14. Max Horkheimer, as quoted in Seyla Benhabib, *Critique, Norm, and Utopia: A Study of the Foundations of Critical Theory* (New York: Columbia University Press, 1986), 3.

15. This view follows Habermas. See "The Public Sphere," in *Jürgen Habermas on Society and Politics: A Reader,* Steven Seidman, ed. (Boston: Beacon Press, 1989), 231–236.

16. Sheldon Hackney, "Organizing a National Conversation," *Chronicle of Higher Education* (April 20, 1994): A56.

TWO

The First Amendment As Ideology

FREDERICK SCHAUER

Not surprisingly, Learned Hand said it best. Writing for the Second Circuit in *International Brotherhood of Electrical Workers, Local 501 v. NLRB*,[1] he captured beautifully the paradox I wish to explore here:

> The interest, which [the First Amendment] guards, and which gives it its importance, presupposes that there are no orthodoxies—religious, political, economic, or scientific—which are immune from debate and dispute. Back of that is the assumption—itself an orthodoxy, and the one permissible exception—that truth will be most likely to emerge, if no limitations are imposed upon utterances that can with any plausibility be regarded as efforts to present grounds for accepting or rejecting propositions whose truth the utterer asserts, or denies.[2]

I do not want to focus on Hand's restatement of the standard marketplace-of-ideas principle that the value of freedom of speech lies in its instrumental value in (probabilistically) increasing the likelihood of identifying truth and rejecting falsehood. Much that I say here is not dependent on that theory, and is compatible with numerous different perspectives on the underlying rationale or rationales for freedom of speech and freedom of the press. Rather, I will train my attention on Hand's two-part claim: first, that the value of freedom of speech is itself an orthodoxy of the same type that the principles of free speech would otherwise refuse to countenance; and, second, that this orthodoxy is a permissible exception to the First Amendment's prohibition of orthodoxies. In what is to follow I will agree with the first part of Hand's claim and disagree with the second. I will argue that the view that a broadly protective understanding of the First Amendment is taken as an orthodoxy—or ideology, as I prefer to call it—in a large number of academic and professional environments, but that this is a phenomenon to be bemoaned and resisted rather than accepted or celebrated.

This is not an exercise in legal doctrine. In referring to the one permissible exception in *International Brotherhood of Electrical Workers,* Hand was not claiming that the First Amendment does not protect arguments against freedom of speech, nor was he urging a change in that state of affairs. With few exceptions,[3] no one has argued that the otherwise applicable principles of freedom of speech should be modified merely because the speaker urges the constriction or elimination of the free speech system itself. Undoubtedly, one who urges partial or even complete elimination of freedom of speech as we know it is fully entitled to the support of the First Amendment to provide legal immunity in making that claim.

Still, we owe to Mill the first observation that social intolerance of divergent opinion may at times be as much a source of concern as legal intolerance.[4] If, as Mill argued, positive value results from challenging received opinions, then a social or cultural environment in which such challenge is de facto difficult or impossible is as much to be condemned as an environment in which challenge to received opinion is prohibited by law.

I am concerned here with this form of inhibition of opinion. To put it more precisely, I want to focus on the social rather than the legal manifestation of Hand's statement and consequently address the question of whether a certain view of freedom of speech, or at the extreme, free speech itself, has become the orthodoxy, or ideology, and, if so, whether such a state of affairs is desirable.

What do I mean by "ideology"? The term is notoriously slippery and has numerous definitions in various domains. Under one definition, an ideology is "a prescriptive doctrine that is not supported by rational argument,"[5] but, at least at the outset, this is not what I am referring to here. Nor do I use the term "ideology" to refer simply to "any system of ideas and norms directing political and social action,"[6] or not nearly so simply to the concept of ideology in Marxist thought.[7] And I do not use the term as it is most often pejoratively employed in contemporary discourse, pursuant to which an "ideology" is something supported by an "ideologue," who seems to be someone adhering to ideas we believe are wrong, with about the same level of fervor we ourselves apply to the ideas we believe are right.

Still, I do intend to benefit from the word's pejorative connotations, such that for me an ideology is a prevailing idea existing within an environment in which adherence to the idea is more or less required, and challenge to the idea is more or less discouraged. In this sense I use "ideology" as something close to Hand's "orthodoxy," both of which are to be distinguished from "ideas" *simpliciter,* the latter suggesting nothing about the circumstances in which the idea is maintained. It is entirely consistent to say that freedom of speech is a very good idea, and at the same time to say that the idea that freedom of speech is a very good idea might be an ideology, a state of affairs that would not be nearly so good.

As should be clear from the foregoing definition, the notion of an ideology presupposes some population within which the relevant idea is treated as an ideology, and, as such, the idea of ideology is domain-dependent and domain-specific. It is thus incumbent upon me to specify the domain within which I believe an ideology exists and to specify as well the idea within which I believe that domain has assumed ideological status.

As to the first, the domain about which I wish to speak is, primarily, the domain I know best—the domain of American academic institutions in general and American law schools in particular. I will be making claims that I believe also apply with particular (and probably even greater) force to the world of journalism, including both practicing journalists and schools of communications and journalism, to the world of libraries, including both practicing librarians and schools of library and information studies, to the world of the arts, including artists and writers and their affiliated organizations and academic institutions, and to the world of publishing.

What these institutions share in common is a particular devotion to (and, arguably, need for) freedom of thought, freedom of inquiry, freedom of speech, and freedom of the press. It is, perhaps not surprisingly, within these institutions that an ideological view appears to have developed about freedom of thought, freedom of inquiry, freedom of speech, and freedom of the press. That is, these seem to be the institutions within which, despite their particular devotion to these freedoms, those freedoms are treated as implicitly inapt to discussion of the freedoms themselves. To put it more simply, there seems to be, within these domains, little free thought about free thought, little free inquiry about free inquiry, and little free speech about free speech.

Let me be somewhat more specific. My claim is that within these institutions the view prevails in ideological fashion that the appropriate amount of freedom of speech and press is somewhat greater than that now existing in the United States, or that now protected by the Supreme Court of the United States, or that protected by the Supreme Court of the United States in its periods of greatest protection, and that this view prevails as an ideology even though under any of these measures the degree of freedom of speech and press in the United States is substantially greater than that prevailing in any other country on the face of the earth.

This last comparative claim is important, for without it little distinguishes what I say about freedom of speech from what could be said about the desirability of equality, the undesirability of rape and torture, or the propositions that the Holocaust happened, that the earth is not flat, and that no American president has been a woman. With respect to these propositions, their virtually unanimous acceptance makes it difficult to distinguish the possibility that they might be held as ideologies from the possibility that they exist largely unchallenged simply because of the widespread and justified acceptance of their truth. Standard free speech theory would still maintain, correctly, that it would be unfortunate if conceivable challenges were stifled in one way or another, and a variant on standard free speech theory, one to which I will return presently, would maintain that it might still be important to generate challenges to these widely accepted views, however implausible such challenges might at first seem or might in fact be, just in order to attain the positive benefits of the challenge. Nevertheless, if one wanted to support an empirical claim about the existence of an ideological environment surrounding some correct proposition, it would be difficult to do so in a context in which the overwhelmingly accepted truth of the proposition made it empirically difficult to determine how much the lack of dissent was a function of truth and how much was a function of ideological pressure.

With respect to freedom of speech and press, this methodological difficulty is less severe. On almost every issue of free speech theory, doctrine, and practice, virtually every country on the face of the earth diverges from the United States, and diverges in the direction of lesser protection. No other country, for example, approaches American law in the extent to which factually untrue statements are protected against actions for defamation or their equivalent. To be more specific, I know of no country that would decide *Ocala Star-Banner Co. v. Damron*[8] or *Hustler Magazine v. Falwell*[9] the way in which they were decided here. So too with many other areas, including national security, in which *New York Times Co. v. United States*[10] (the case of the *Pentagon Papers*) represents a willingness to protect the publishers of arguably unlawfully obtained information in a way unreplicated anywhere else. And with respect to the operation of the judiciary, cases such as *Florida Star v. B. J. F.*,[11] *Smith v. Daily Mail Publishing Co.*,[12] *Nebraska Press Ass'n v. Stuart*,[13] and *Landmark Communications, Inc. v. Virginia*[14] are a few among many providing ample evidence of an approach that is uniquely American. The same phenomenon exists in other areas as well. Many other countries, including most Western democracies, have laws prohibiting the incitement of racial hatred, and both *Brandenburg v. Ohio*[15] and the *Skokie* cases[16] are far more exceptional than they are exemplary of international understandings, the best evidence being that some international human rights documents, such as the Universal Declaration of Human Rights[17] and the 1965 Convention on the Elimination of All Forms of Racial Discrimination,[18] which would *require* its signatories to have the kinds of laws against racist speech that are *prohibited* under current American constitutional law.[19] Similarly, the commercial speech cases[20] are a continuing source of astonishment to non-Americans and so too are many, many other cases.

All of this is possibly but an example of the unenlightened state in which the rest of the world exists, waiting for Americans to carry the white man's burden by introducing advanced American ideas to an unadvanced and largely uncivilized planet. But even if a uniquely American view about freedom of speech and freedom of the press is indeed the superior view despite its current uniqueness, the existence of such divergent views throughout the world, especially in politically stable, economically successful, and socially advanced societies, suggests at the least that, unlike some of the views I noted above, these are real issues, leading to genuinely plausible disagreements with existing American understandings.

The evidence from abroad, therefore, to say nothing of the evidence from other segments of current American society and from American understandings of as recently as thirty years ago, suggests that there are genuine sources of rational disagreement among reasonable people, areas of legitimate difference of not-presumptively preposterous opinion. If that is so, then the absence within some domains, especially within domains otherwise specially devoted to openness of thought, inquiry, discussion, and publication, of these nonpreposterous views might be reasonably strong evidence of the existence of an ideological environment preventing those views from being taken as seriously as they are in so many other environments.

Now that I have engaged in all of these clarifying preliminaries, it is time to turn to the evidence. Is there empirical support for the proposition that, within the domains I have specified, a broadly protective understanding of free speech and free press, generally broader than that espoused by the Supreme Court of the United States in even its most protective moments, functions as a prevailing ideology and exists within an environment such that a challenge to it is far more difficult than support of it?

Let me start with some anecdotal evidence. First, consider the experience that led to the writing of Leonard Levy's *Legacy of Suppression*.[21] As recounted in the preface to the revised edition,[22] Levy, already in 1957 a distinguished historian, was commissioned by The Fund for the Republic, Inc., later called The Center for Democratic Institutions, to prepare a study of the original meaning of the First Amendment.[23] The study was to be used at a series of conferences and published by The Fund. When Levy consulted the evidence, however, he came to believe, contrary to his prior beliefs, that the Framers had had a far narrower conception of the scope of the First Amendment's Speech and Press Clauses than was commonly understood. In particular, he came to believe that the Framers did not intend to eliminate the law of seditious libel and may not have intended to eliminate anything other than prior restraints on political speech.[24] When these conclusions (the truth of which I have neither reason nor expertise to affirm or deny) were incorporated into the study, The Fund's director, Robert M. Hutchins, among the most distinguished intellectuals of the time, refused to publish them, although he and The Fund were quite willing to publish Levy's considerably more politically sympathetic portions relating to the religion clauses. Levy wrote *Legacy of Suppression* as the indignant response of an author censored for daring to depart from the prevailing view about the history of censorship.

More recently, academics have found themselves accused of acting irresponsibly or unprofessionally (which is far different from and worse than being accused of being wrong) when they espouse a certain view about freedom of speech. Consider the following by Floyd Abrams, appearing in the *Harvard Law Review*:

> Although courts have thus far struck down those attempts [to pass laws restricting sexually oriented but non-obscene speech in cities, and regulations forbidding racist and sexist speech on college campuses], it is troubling that law professors actually have led the efforts to involve the government in limiting speech they deem to be offensive.[25]

Following the quotation was a footnote referring specifically to Catharine MacKinnon's *Feminism Unmodified: Discourses on Life and Law*[26] and to Charles Lawrence's article, "If He Hollers Let Him Go: Regulating Racist Speech on Campus."[27] Now why is this "troubling"? Certainly not because as law professors MacKinnon and Lawrence urged legal results inconsistent with existing doctrine. If that were the standard for condemnation, ninety percent of the legal professoriate would be at risk. Urging legal results at odds with the prevailing case law is much of (and in my view too much of, but that is for another day) what law professors do, and certainly Abrams could not be troubled by the fact that MacKinnon's and Lawrence's proposals were not supported by existing doctrine.

If that is so, then the source of the concern must be that their prescriptions for law reform go in one direction rather than another. If it is not troubling that law professors have "actually" suggested legal results inconsistent with, say, *Branzburg v. Hayes*,[28] *Hazelwood School District v. Kuhlmeier*,[29] or *Paris Adult Theatre I v. Slaton*,[30] then the only thing that "actually" makes it "troubling" that law professors such as Lawrence or MacKinnon have suggested legal results inconsistent with *Brandenburg v. Ohio*,[31] *Collin v. Smith*,[32] or *Miller v. California*[33] is that they have been on the side of lesser First Amendment protection rather than greater. This is not to say that MacKinnon and Lawrence are correct in their normative prescriptions, or that their normative prescriptions are not open to published attack. It is to say only that there is no evidence to indicate they have acted in any way less faithfully to the role of law professor than those whose views differ from theirs, and to so indicate seems some evidence of an ideology at work.

Similarly, and again Professor Lawrence is the target, Nadine Strossen has suggested that it is in some way specially incumbent upon the academic to avoid arguments of a certain kind:

> However, Professor Lawrence and other members of the academic community who advocate [restrictions on racist speech because the restrictions would make a symbolic contribution to racial equality] must recognize that educators have a special responsibility to avoid the danger posed by focusing on symbols that obscure the real underlying issues.[34]

This I am sure would be a surprise to those who have argued that one of the virtues of freedom of speech consists of the symbolic advantages a strong free speech system brings.[35] But if it is a violation of the special responsibility of the educator to focus on restrictions of speech for symbolic purposes, then presumably it is just as much a violation of that special responsibility to focus on protection of free speech for symbolic purposes. Because neither Lee Bollinger nor any other legal academic seems ever to have been accused of betraying the special responsibility of the educator in urging reliance on symbols in the service of greater freedom of speech, then it appears that the charge of violation of professional duty is deployed depending only on the viewpoint espoused.

Again, the mere fact of harsh criticism of the views of Lawrence or others would be no evidence of the presence of an ideology. But when the criticism takes the form of suggestions of violation of professional responsibility, and when the criticism is directed only against people who hold certain views, then it is beginning to appear that part of that professional responsibility is to have a certain view about freedom of speech.

My own observations and experiences lead me to believe that these three examples are far more typical than epiphenomenal, being but a few instances of many in which both the discourse used against and the treatment of those with restrictive views about freedom of speech are different in kind from that used with respect to those otherwise similarly situated, but whose views are protective rather than restrictive. Of course I certainly do not suggest that the phenomenon is universal. There are counterexamples to be sure (and I may be one of them). Still, I believe these examples represent rather than contradict a trend or tilt, and just as the presence of a bottle of dry German wine does not defeat the validity of the probabilistic generalization that German wine is sweet, and just as the presence of a stupid philosopher does not negate the probabilistic generalization that philosophers are clever, so too do I feel confident in the similarly probabilistic generalization that standards of evaluation and criticism are higher for those with less protective rather than more protective views about speech and press, and that the degree of social intolerance, to use Mill's term,[36] is considerably higher for those within the institutions of which I speak who have less protective rather than more protective views about freedom of speech and press, all other things being equal.

Some further support for this proposition appears to come from the periodical literature. Over the last ten years approximately 200 articles and student notes on free speech and free press have appeared in American law reviews each year. My own survey of titles, supported by randomly checking the articles themselves, indicates that in excess of ninety percent of these articles are prescriptive, urging certain doctrinal or theoretical approaches upon the courts (or sometimes legislatures), as opposed to those articles, generally historical or comparative, that are largely descriptive. Of this ninety percent, at least ninety-five percent of the prescriptions are in the direction of urging on courts or legislatures greater protection of the free speech or free press interests than the objects of the prescription currently recognize.

This casual empirical survey is potentially flawed, because a question about the baseline remains. Criticism of the Supreme Court is the generally prevailing mode of constitutional scholarship, and concluding that the Court was correct is not generally the way to fame, fortune, and tenure. Moreover, it is unlikely that American constitutionalists are representative of the political makeup of the country as a whole, and thus an appropriately controlled analysis would have to look at, for example, criminal procedure, due process, and equal protection doctrine in order to separate the question of speech-protective bias from liberal bias generally. Still, it does appear that this is the case, confirming not only what I believe to be the case about law journals, but also with respect to the journals in the other fields that are part of the relevant environment and with respect to symposia and other events that are also part of the activities of the environment.[37]

I may of course be wrong about all of this. Nevertheless, I want to proceed on the assumption that I am right, and that there exists an environment in which a range of seemingly plausible, even if not ultimately correct, nonprotective views about freedom of speech and press are stigmatized within the academy, within the world of journalism, within the world of the arts, within the world of libraries, and within the world of publishing, such that many sociological and psychological forces provide impediments to the articulation of those views—similar in effect to the impediments imposed by various more formal restrictions.

But is this state of affairs troubling? Here we might return to Mill, who argued in his treatment "Of the Liberty of Thought and Discussion"[38] that governmental or social restriction of ideas on the grounds of the supposed falsity of the ideas was unwise for three reasons. First, the suppressed opinion might be true. No matter how sure we are that it is false, such assertions of infallibility, Mill argued, are unwarranted, and without the assumption of infallibility we cannot conclude that there is no possibility that the opinion we believe false might not be true.[39]

In the context of freedom of speech and press, the arrogance of an assumption of infallibility can be exacerbated by an equally troubling assumption of American superiority. When the received opinion resembles the American view and the rejected opinion resembles the view held in many (or in this case all) other countries, tendencies towards nationalism may reinforce the belief that the rejected opinion cannot possibly turn out to be true.

Recognition of Mill's point, therefore, would counsel in the direction of caution before assuming too easily that a degree of freedom of speech greater than that now prevalent in the United States would be preferable, and a lesser degree would be dangerous. Moreover, because the rejected opinion, that less freedom of speech (or, conversely, more respect for other interests coming into conflict with freedom of speech) might be a good thing, could conceivably, according to Mill, be true, then it might be important to guard affirmatively and actively against the tendencies toward its suppression. If, as Holmes observed, "[p]ersecution for the expression of opinions seems . . . perfectly logical,"[40] then there is likely to be created an environment in which those with "no doubt of [their] premises or [their] power"[41] will employ what power they have to prevent articulation of the opposing opinion. If that power is the power to criticize as unprofessional, or the power to select participants for a symposium, or the power to choose articles for an academic journal, then there may very well be a use of that power to suppress the currently rejected opinion that less freedom of speech and freedom of the press might be a good thing.

Even if the received opinion is not false, Mill further argued, and even if the rejected opinion is not true, still in most cases the question of truth or falsity will be more complex. Even that which we are convinced is true is likely false in some respects, and even that which appears false may still contain a "portion of truth."[42] By allowing the challenge to that which we are certain is true, we have the tools available to refine that truth, discovering and eliminating partial errors and incorporating the best from views that are largely but not completely false.

Mill's argument was couched largely in terms of truth or falsity, but where social problems are concerned, the question is more likely to be one of soundness or unsoundness. Again, free speech itself provides a perfect example because a system of free speech is, first of all, highly complex, encompassing numerous legal doctrines, political and social institutions, popular understandings, and official practices. The more complex this array of practices, the more likely that some segment of this array might be in need of modification even while most of it is highly satisfactory, or that some doctrines will go "too far" while others might not go far enough. Moreover, most of these doctrines, practices, and institutions rest on empirical suppositions such as that embodied in ideas like the "chilling effect"; the belief that an act of suppression makes the suppressed idea more attractive; the belief that an act of suppression makes further and more dangerous acts of suppression likely; the belief that allowing the expression of hostile words has a cathartic effect, such that the expresser is consequently less likely to engage in hostile acts; and so on.

Again, it seems highly plausible that the basic ideas behind these and other empirical underpinnings of the idea of free speech are sound. But the more these ideas are empirical rather than logical in any technical sense, the more likely it is that any current understanding is somewhat, even if only slightly, off the mark. As a result, the more the ideas of free speech and free press are based on highly complex practices and contingent empirical understandings, the more likely it seems that the soundest ideas about free speech and free press will vary at least slightly from what we now think correct and incorporate at least some of what we now reject as false. If Mill is right in this part of his argument, then we approach the sounder understanding only by fostering an environment for discussion *of* free speech and free press that resembles the environment that the ideas of free speech and free press create for discussion of everything else.

Mill's third argument is perhaps the most intriguing. Even if the received opinion is completely true, he maintained, and even if the rejected opinion is completely false, challenges to the received opinion must be allowed or else the received opinion will turn into "dead dogma," learned by rote and not understood, and consequently over time impossible to defend against attacks upon it.[43]

Were Mill alive today and looking for just such a reflexively defended but rarely thought through principle, he would be hard pressed to find a better example than the principle of freedom of thought and discussion itself. With numbing frequency, the same platitudes and slogans substitute for argument whenever the subject of free speech arises within those institutions dependent on free speech for their existence. "The chilling effect." "Don't blame the messenger." "It's the first step on the slippery slope." "Suppression of opinion is what Stalin and Hitler did." "Speech is a symptom and not a cause." Some of these slogans may contain some truth. Still, the frequency with which they are used in place of argument, in place of analysis, and especially in place of empirical assessment of the empirical presuppositions on which they rest, may be a perfect example of the very "dead dogma" that Mill warned against.

If Mill is right that an unchallenged idea is at risk of being accepted only as dead dogma, and if he is right that an idea so accepted is less hardy in the long term than one that benefits from deeper understanding, then his insight provides much more than an argument against censorship. It provides an argument for furnishing a challenge to the received opinion even if none is "naturally" available. An argument against censorship is an argument against restricting an opinion that someone wants to offer. Arguments against censorship are classically liberal arguments, concerned with eliminating governmental intervention into the antecedently generated products of individual and social existence. Consequently, if it turns out that no one wants to offer such an opinion, then an argument against censorship has exhausted its utility. If, by contrast, an argument against censorship is but a component of a more encompassing argument for the positive virtues of even unsound opinions, and Mill's warning about dead dogma seems of just this sort, then the lack of an opinion to censor is still problematic, for the positive virtues remain unserved. If a challenge to received opinion is necessary in order that the received opinion not become dead dogma, then the absence of that challenge is troubling even if the absence is not attributable to an act of censorship.

Thus, even were the current unanimity of voice about freedom of speech and press (within the environments I am discussing) not the product of the very social censorship that Mill castigated, it would still be cause for concern, because it could still help to lessen serious understanding of the values of freedom of speech and freedom of the press; but here solutions seem at hand. First, those with the power to select, whether for journal articles, conference presentations, or projects to be funded, could engage in a form of affirmative action, taking the fact of a view's being currently underrepresented as a reason for selecting it. That reason need not be conclusive, but it could be a factor, such that the very challenge to the prevailing understanding would provide an additional argument in favor of the article, paper, presentation, or project.

In addition, a similar kind of affirmative action could pervade the scholarship of those who do endorse the received view. I take it as virtually self-evident that one earmark of intellectual honesty is confrontation of the best arguments for the opposing position. If this is so, then the absence of people actually making those arguments, or the fact of the arguments being made less persuasively than they could, is insufficient reason to relax the standards of intellectual honesty. Arguments in favor of strong free speech protection, therefore, must, to be honest, confront the best arguments for a lesser degree of protection. All too often, however, the confrontation is with the arguments that Senator Helms uses to attract votes or contributions, or with the silliest statements made by angry citizens at public meetings, or with a range of Orwellian caricatures. With spectacular frequency, the arguments for freedom of speech and freedom of press are, when not couched in the platitudes and slogans I mentioned above, contrasted only with some blend of Hitler, Mao, Stalin, the Ayatollah Khomeni, and the Cincinnati District Attorney's office, with the argument consisting of the proposition that the choice is only between American-style free speech and free press protection and the political programs of those I have just mentioned. Rarely do we see acknowledgment, let alone serious confrontation, of James FitzJames Stephen,[44] Willmoore Kendall,[45] Herbert Marcuse,[46] and many others whose arguments, whether sound or not, rise far above those of the most common targets.

Thus, if arguments for freedom of speech or arguments for some particular area in which free speech or free press could be greater are to satisfy this standard of intellectual honesty, they have an obligation either to find, or if necessary to create, the strongest argument for the contrary position. If the strongest argument is not strong enough, then what emerges does so because of its power as an argument, and will likely survive because of that very same power. If only weak arguments are dealt with, then there is no reason to believe that what emerges can defeat the best arguments, or will have the power to do so when they are actually made in the arena of public debate.

In the preceding section, and indeed in this entire article, I have been assuming that a broadly Millian argument about freedom of speech was sound, and I have been assuming as well that, if sound, it was fully applicable to freedom of speech itself. To be faithful to my own message, I must acknowledge that these assumptions themselves must be open to challenge. That is, it might be the case that Millian arguments about freedom of speech are false, and that as a result, there is no reason to apply them to free speech thinking. Or, more plausibly, it might be the case that good arguments for treating freedom of speech and freedom of the press as ideologies exist. Perhaps Learned Hand was right, and the orthodoxy of the First Amendment, contrary to what I have maintained here, is a permissible or even a necessary orthodoxy. That argument does not seem wholly implausible, although I remain doubtful, and I remain doubtful whether it can be accepted by someone purporting to be a scholar *of* the First Amendment. To deal with that question, however, would require dealing with the entire question of just what it is to be a scholar, and that inquiry is best left to others, or at least to other times.

Thus, I will conclude with the observation that the increasing presence of some number of genuinely repressive political forces is doubly unfortunate—first, because of the effects of those repressive actions; and, second, because the presence of Senator Helms and numerous others fuels the tendency of free speech scholars to think that because actual or potential censors are out there, the appropriate response is a call to arms rather than a concern about dealing with the best arguments that might be made for less free speech protection rather than more. Adopting this course might be more effective advocacy, but it is a course of action increasingly likely to be unfaithful to the very principles it seeks to defend. Without allowing as much free speech about free speech as free speech advocates urge about everything else, those advocates risk creating the impression that they are themselves unwilling to confront the assaults on their own belief systems that they demand be confronted by others. Even putting aside the question of the extent to which scholarship and advocacy are compatible, advocates whose own actions betray the very cause they advocate are likely in the long run to be less effective. When the environments that depend on free speech allow free speech about free speech within those environments, they then can with greater credibility urge the benefits of free speech on others.

Notes

This is the written version of a talk given at the Institute of Bill of Rights Law, Marshall-Wythe School of Law, College of William and Mary, on April 5, 1991, and to the Association for Education in Journalism and Mass Communication, in Boston, on August 6, 1991. A version of this article appeared in the *William and Mary Law Review* 33, no. 3 (Spring 1992): 853–869. I am grateful for the support of numerous friends and colleagues who over the years have endured my tediousness on this topic.

1. 181 F. 2d 34 (2d Cir. 1950), *aff'd,* 341 U.S. 695 (1951).
2. *Id.* at 40.
3. See, *e.g.*, Carl A. Auerbach, "The Communist Control Act of 1954: A Proposed Legal-Political Theory of Free Speech," 23 *U. Chi. L. Rev.,* 173 (1956). Some qualified support for this view can be found in Karl R. Popper, *The Open Society and Its Enemies,* 265 note 4 (London: Routledge, 4th ed. 1963), and in John Rawls, *A Theory of Justice,* 216–21 (Cambridge: Harvard University Press, 1971), both arguing that when the threat to political freedom is real, restricting those who would limit political freedom is permissible even as other forms of limitation of political activity are not.
4. John Stuart Mill, *On Liberty,* 31–34 (David Spitz ed., New York: W. W. Norton, 1975 [1859]).
5. D. D. Raphael, *Problems of Political Philosophy,* 17 (London: Macmillan, rev. ed. 1976).
6. Antony Flew, *A Dictionary of Philosophy,* 150 (New York: St. Martin's Press, 1979).

7. See generally David McClellan, *Ideology*, 10–20 (Minneapolis: University of Minnesota Press, 1986) (describing Marx's view of ideology as arising from rather than acting on the material, social, and economic relationships of the labor process).

8. 401 U.S. 295 (1971). I pick this case because, from among all of the Supreme Court defamation cases after *New York Times Co. v. Sullivan*, 376 U.S. 254 (1964), this one appears to have protected the greatest degree of journalistic negligence at the greatest apparent harm to the victim. I have discussed the case more extensively in Frederick Schauer, "Public Figures," 25 *Wm. & Mary L. Rev.*, 905, 910–13 (1984).

9. 485 U.S. 46 (1988) (denying public figure's emotional distress claim arising from a satire).

10. 403 U.S. 713 (1971) (per curiam).

11. 491 U.S. 524 (1989) (declaring unconstitutional an imposition of damages on a newspaper for publishing the lawfully obtained name of a rape victim).

12. 443 U.S. 97 (1979) (holding unconstitutional a West Virginia statute prohibiting newspapers from printing, without permission of juvenile court, the names of juvenile offenders).

13. 427 U.S. 539 (1976) (reversing a trial court order forbidding the press from publishing accounts of defendant's confessions prior to a highly publicized mass-murder trial).

14. 435 U.S. 829 (1978) (holding that a Virginia statute may not constitutionally bar the press from publishing truthful information from confidential proceedings of the Judicial Inquiry and Review Commission).

15. 395 U.S. 444 (1969) (per curiam) (reversing the conviction of a Ku Klux Klan leader prosecuted under an Ohio statute that punished mere advocacy of lawless action rather than actual incitement).

16. *Collin v. Smith*, 578 F. 2d 1197 (7th Cir.) (holding unconstitutional city ordinances that (1) prohibited the dissemination of materials promoting hatred toward persons based on their heritage; (2) prohibited the wearing of military uniforms during an assembly by members of a political party; and (3) required $300,000 in liability insurance before obtaining a parade permit when this requirement was used selectively to prevent certain parties from marching), *stay denied*, 436 U.S. 953, and *cert. denied*, 439 U.S. 916 (1978); *National Socialist Party v. Village of Skokie*, 434 U.S. 1327 (1977) (Stevens, J., as Circuit Justice, denying stay); *National Socialist Party v. Village of Skokie*, 432 U.S. 43 (1977) (per curiam) (declaring unconstitutional the denial of a stay of an injunction prohibiting the Nazi party from parading and displaying the swastika in the absence of strict procedural safeguards including immediate appellate review). The Skokie litigation is usefully contrasted with a series of recent Canadian cases denying freedom of expression protection under the Canadian Charter of Rights and Freedoms to a range of neo-Nazis, anti-Semites, and Holocaust-deniers. The

most prominent of these cases is *Regina v. Keegstra*, 3 S.C.R. 697 (1990) (denying constitutional protection to teacher prosecuted for expressing anti-Semitic beliefs to his students). To more or less the same effect are: *Regina v. Andrews*, 3 S.C.R. 870 (1990) (refusing to extend constitutional protection to leaders of a white supremacist group prosecuted for publishing a newspaper that expressed anti-Semitic beliefs, including the proposition that the Holocaust was a Zionist hoax); *Canadian Human Rights Comm'n v. Taylor*, 3 S.C.R. 892 (1990) (denying constitutional protection to a group and its leader prosecuted for operating a telephone service that played prerecorded messages denigrating the Jewish race and religion); *Regina v. Zundel*, 31 C.C.C. 3d 97, 111–28 (1987) (ruling on appeal of a convicted Holocaust-denier, and refusing to hold unconstitutional a statute criminalizing the willful and knowing publication of a false statement that is likely to cause injury to a public interest). For a discussion of the relevant German law, also substantially less speech-protective than that of the United States, see Eric Stein, "History against Free Speech: The New German Law against the *Auschwitz*—And Other—*Lies*," 85 *Mich. L. Rev.*, 277 (1986) (discussing additions to the German Criminal Code dealing with rising anti-Semitism).

17. "Universal Declaration of Human Rights," adopted Dec. 10, 1948, reprinted in 43 *Am. J. Int'l Supp.*, 127 (1949).

18. Dec. 21, 1965, 660 *U.N.T.S.* 195.

19. See Jordan J. Paust, "Rereading the First Amendment in Light of Treaties Proscribing Incitement to Racial Discrimination of Hostility," 43 *Rutgers L. Rev.*, 565 (1991); see also Mari J. Matsuda, "Public Response to Racist Speech: Considering the Victim's Story," 87 *Mich. L. Rev.*, 2320, 2345–48 (1989) (discussing various international and multinational acts that ban speech aimed at inciting racial hatred).

20. E.g., *Bates v. State Bar*, 433 U.S. 350 (1977); *Linmark Assocs., Inc. v. Township of Willingboro*, 431 U.S. 85 (1977); *Virginia State Bd. of Pharmacy v. Virginia Citizens Consumer Council, Inc.*, 425 U.S. 748 (1976).

21. Leonard Levy, *Legacy of Suppression: Freedom of Speech and Press in Early American History* (Cambridge: Harvard University Press, 1960).

22. Leonard Levy, *Emergence of a Free Press* (New York: Oxford University Press, 1985).

23. *Id.* at vii.

24. *Id.* at x–xix. On this possibility, see also *Patterson v. Colorado*, 205 U.S. 454 (1907) (Holmes, J.).

25. Floyd Abrams, "A Worthy Tradition: The Scholar and the First Amendment," 103 *Harv. L. Rev.*, 1162, 1171 (1990) (footnote omitted) (reviewing Harry Kalven, Jr., *A Worthy Tradition: Freedom of Speech in America*, Jamie Kalven, ed., 1988).

26. Catharine A. MacKinnon, *Feminism Unmodified: Discourses on Life and Law* (Cambridge: Harvard University Press, 1987).

27. Charles Lawrence, "If He Hollers Let Him Go: Regulating Racist Speech on Campus," 1990 *Duke L. J.*, 431.

28. 408 U.S. 665 (1972) (holding that First Amendment does not prohibit requiring news reporters to testify as to the criminal activities of confidential sources before state or federal grand juries); see, *e.g.,* Archibald Cox, "Freedom of Expression in the Burger Court," 94 *Harv. L. Rev.*, 1, 52–53 (1980) (arguing that perhaps the burden should be on the press when it claims First Amendment privilege not to reveal its confidential sources).

29. 484 U.S. 260 (1988) (holding that school officials could constitutionally exercise reasonable restrictions on content of speech in student paper).

30. 413 U.S. 49 (1973) (holding that state may constitutionally regulate obscene conduct on commercial premises in order to further legitimate state interests); see, *e.g.,* David A. J. Richards, "Free Speech and Obscenity Law: Toward a Moral Theory of the First Amendment," 123 *U. Pa. L. Rev.*, 45, 72–73 (1974) (arguing that the underlying contractual philosophy of liberty of the First Amendment renders all obscenity constitutionally protected).

31. 395 U.S. 444 (1969) (per curiam).

32. 578 F. 2d 1197 (7th Cir.), *stay denied,* 436 U.S. 953, and *cert. denied,* 439 U.S. 916 (1978).

33. 413 U.S. 15 (1973) (adopted a three-part test to determine whether a particular work is obscene and therefore subject to state regulation).

34. Nadine Strossen, "Regulating Racist Speech on Campus: A Modest Proposal?" 1990 *Duke L. J.*, 484.

35. See especially Lee Bollinger, *The Tolerant Society: Freedom of Speech and Extremist Speech in America*, 248 (New York: Oxford University Press, 1986).

36. Mill, *supra* note 4, at 32.

37. Note, for example, the contrast between the Supreme Court's unanimous decision in *University of Pennsylvania v. EEOC*, 493 U.S. 182 (1990), rejecting an academic freedom claim of privilege from disclosing information to an EEOC investigation, and the equivalently unanimous, but in the opposite direction, views articulated in "Symposium, Freedom and Tenure in the Academy: The Fiftieth Anniversary of the 1940 Statement of Principles," 53 *Law & Contemp. Prob.*, 1 (Winter 1990).

38. Mill, *supra* note 4, at 17–52.

39. *Id.* at 18–19.

40. *Abrams v. United States,* 250 U.S. 616, 630 (1919) (Holmes, J., dissenting).

41. *Id.*

42. Mill, *supra* note 4, at 50.

43. *Id.* at 35.

44. James F. Stephen, *Liberty, Equality, Fraternity,* 74–90 (R. J. White ed., Cambridge: Cambridge University Press, 1967) (arguing that Mill mistakenly believes removal of restraints invigorates rather than softens character by providing comfort rather than obstacles; also arguing that liberty, like fire, is only "good" or "bad" because of the time and place of its existence).

45. Willmoore Kendall, "The *Open Society* and Its Fallacies," 54 *Am. Pol. Sci. Rev.,* 972 (1960) (postulating that Mill's formula for the uninhibited exchange of ideas erroneously presumes that all people value the truth above all else, and will result in as much intolerance as tolerance).

46. Herbert Marcuse, "Repressive Tolerance," in Robert Paul Wolff *et al., A Critique of Pure Tolerance,* 81 (Boston: Beacon Press, 1969) (arguing that what passes for tolerance today is as much a "subversive" and oppressive practice as it was in the past).

PART II
Untangling Speech, Property, and Law

THREE

Some Thoughts on Free Speech, Language, and the Rule of Law

THOMAS STREETER

I. Introduction

This chapter discusses the relevance of research and reflection on language to recent critical trends in thinking on free speech. There is a tendency to interpret many of the recent revisionist approaches to free speech as if they were simply calls for exceptions to otherwise clear-cut rules and principles, as if, say, pornography or racism are so exceptionally evil that they fall outside the parameters of the kinds of speech that are "obviously" protected under the First Amendment. This misses the fact that the new approaches, with varying degrees of explicitness, involve theoretical and epistemological challenges to the underlying premises of free speech law in general; over the long run, what the new approaches are calling for are not exceptions but a restructuring of free speech law as a whole. The ideas driving this profound rethinking come from a variety of traditions, including various currents of feminism, literary theory, and theories of race and ethnicity. This chapter focuses on just one of those traditions: the complex twentieth-century theorizing of language, sometimes called the "linguistic turn" in twentieth-century philosophy. Although the linguistic turn is only one aspect of the new thinking about free speech, and although its importance and character are not agreed upon by all those advocating the new thinking, calling attention to it is useful because it highlights some conceptual difficulties of the traditional framework and because it helps differentiate the revisionist criticisms from social determinist and other subtly authoritarian criticisms of free speech.

On the one hand, this chapter argues that the linguistic turn involves some revelations about the nature of language and human communication that do not accord well with the understandings of language implicit in free speech law, particularly with the metaphor of the marketplace of ideas. On the other, it argues that part of what is at stake is the way American culture envisions the rule of law as a whole. In particular, important currents of the understanding of the rule of law suggest the possibility and necessity of constructing rules, procedures, and meanings that transcend or can be abstracted from context, whereas the linguistic turn suggests that this is impossible, that meanings can be determined only in relation to particular contexts. The final part of this chapter, therefore, suggests some avenues for exploring free speech in its historical and social context, as opposed to efforts to abstract it out of context.

II. The Power of Linguistic Style

In the course of a discussion of the campus hate speech controversy, literary critic Henry Louis Gates (speaking from an African American position) provided the following hypothetical examples of potentially "harmful" speech directed at a minority student:

> (A) LeVon, if you find yourself struggling in your classes here, you should realize it isn't your fault. It's simply that you're the beneficiary of a disruptive policy of affirmative action that places underqualified, underprepared and often undertalented black students in demanding educational environments like this one. The policy's egalitarian aims may be well-intentioned, but given the fact that aptitude tests place African Americans almost a full standard deviation below the mean, even controlling for socioeconomic disparities, they are also profoundly misguided. The truth is, you probably don't belong here, and your college experience will be a long downhill slide.
>
> (B) Out of my face, jungle bunny.[1]

Gates's point was that any reader can tell that the first statement would be much more alienating or "wounding" to a minority student, yet the typical campus hate speech code would only prohibit the second statement. But these two statements raise some interesting questions that Gates did not directly address: Why would the first statement seem more wounding, and why would our legal system be more amenable to penalizing the second?

Sociolinguistics offers an answer to the first question: the social phenomenon of linguistic style. It is not the content of the first statement that gives it force; the argument it makes is, at best, dubious and obfuscatory, whereas the second statement at least would communicate the true feelings of the speaker toward the hearer with considerable precision. The first statement's power comes from its style.

It is a well established fact that fluency in any language involves mastery, not just of a single "correct" version of a language, but of a variety of styles or codes appropriate to specific contexts.[2] Gates's first example is a case of the formal or "elaborated" style of contemporary English, which is highly valued in academic and professional settings. It is characterized by, among other things, Latinate vocabulary ("demanding educational environments" instead of "tough schools") and elaborate syntax. The second is an example of informal or restricted style, characterized by ellipsis (omitting "*You get* out of my face...") and colloquial constructions.

Linguists also have long insisted that, in an absolute sense, formal style is no more correct or better for communication than informal style. Scientifically speaking, what makes a style appropriate or inappropriate is the social context in which it is used: in an academic setting, the formal character of the first example gives the statement force, but in another context, say, a working-class bar, it might only elicit laughter and derision, whereas the second statement might have considerable impact. In the appropriate context, therefore, one can use informal style brilliantly and subtly, and conversely, it is quite possible to speak in a thoroughly formal style and yet be inept, offensive, or simply unclear.[3]

What style differences communicate, then, are not specific contents, but social relations between speakers and listeners, i.e., relations of power, hierarchy, solidarity, intimacy, and so forth. In particular, formal language suggests a relation of impersonal authority between speaker and listener, whereas informal language suggests a more intimate (though not necessarily friendly) relationship. You can petrify a child by interjecting into an otherwise informal conversation, "No, you may not." The shift to formal style (no ellipsis, "may not" instead of "can't") shows that the speaker is not just making a request, but is asserting his or her powers of authority as an adult over the child listener.

Gates's first example would be more wounding to a minority student, therefore, because, by couching itself in a formal, academic style, it is rhetorically structured as the expression of "impersonal," rational, and thus institutionally sanctioned, sentiments. It thereby invokes the full force of the authority of the university against the student's efforts to succeed in it. Gates's second example, with its informal style, suggests that one individual, the speaker, harbors racist ill will toward the listener. The first example, by contrast, suggests that, not just one individual, but the entire institution of the university in all its impersonal, "rational" majesty, looks upon the student as unfit.

III. The Traditional Framework: Problems with the Marketplace Metaphor

So why is it easier to penalize the second kind of statement than the first, when it is the first that is potentially more damaging (which is not necessarily to suggest that we should penalize the first kind of statement)? Contemporary law in general is insensitive to matters of linguistic style. Hollywood action movies have made a cliché of lampooning the incongruity of reading the highly formal, legalistic *Miranda* clause during arrests, which are typically emotional encounters between working-class cops and criminals, i.e., contexts where informal style would be appropriate.[4] In First Amendment jurisprudence, where language is not only the vehicle but the subject matter of the law, this insensitivity can lead to conceptual confusion. Linguistic style may be a fact of life, but traditional legal liberal ways of thinking about free speech, especially those encapsulated in the metaphor of the "marketplace of ideas," are strangely incapable of addressing it.

A. *The Arbitrariness of Language and Legal Indeterminacy*

The marketplace metaphor in free speech law involves imagining symbolic and linguistic phenomena as if they were analogous to market exchange, which implies a number of things about language. Most obviously, it implies that language is primarily an exchange, a transference of something (perhaps "information"), from one person to another. Hence, in linguistic exchanges what matters is the contents of the exchange, not the style or form in which it is "packaged," just as in real market exchanges it makes little difference if you pay by check or cash. Yet, as in Gates' example, in language the "package" can be everything. The marketplace metaphor, then, draws our attention away from the importance of just the kind of stylistic differences that sociolinguists say are central to the workings of everyday language.

The marketplace metaphor also tends to imply that the good that comes from unconstrained human speech comes from some neutral, universal, mechanical, and leveling process, a linguistic equivalent to the economist's invisible hand out of which will emerge truth, or at least some form of democratic justice. That neutral, mechanical process, furthermore, is contrasted in law with "arbitrary" government interference. And yet, in several ways, linguistics has taught that language itself is arbitrary at its core; in language, the boundary between "natural" processes and arbitrary ones is difficult, some would argue impossible, to discern.

Linguists say that language is "arbitrary" in the sense that meaning emerges, not from anything logically inherent in words or their arrangement, but from the specific conventions and expectations shared by members of a given speech community, conventions and expectations that can and do change dramatically from time to time and place to place. Aside from language in general and perhaps some very deep-level aspects of syntax, there is very little that is universal, neutral, or mechanical about human languages. This insight grew out of the observation that languages differ profoundly from one another, not only in terms of the meanings of specific words, but in terms of basic aspects of the ways those words are arranged: Some languages have only two or three words for color, for example, others have nothing English speakers would recognize as verb tenses. But it has also been bolstered by detailed analysis of the workings of language in general. Meanings are fixed neither by logic nor by some natural relation of words to things, but by the contextual and shifting system of interpretation shared by the members of a given speech community.

The arbitrariness of language presents two problems for traditional thinking about freedom of speech. One problem involves legal interpretation, the belief that properly trained judges and lawyers following the proper procedures can arrive at *the* correct interpretation of a dispute. Often described as the problem of the indeterminacy of law, the purely contextual character of meaning would suggest that legal decisions will always be forced to fall back on contingent values, social or political, to decide where the boundaries in the law lie.[5] It is in the character of language, in other words, that a judge will never be able to look at the text of the Bill of Rights and legal precedents to decide whether flag burning is protected by the First Amendment; she will always in one way or another be forced to make a choice about whether she thinks it *should* be protected, and will always be faced with the possibility that a reasonable person could plausibly disagree.

Indeterminacy should not be mistaken for the absurd assertion that any word can mean any thing, that there is no stability to meaning whatsoever. As deconstructionist literary critic Barbara Johnson puts it:

> [L]anguage cannot itself be entirely reduced to interpretability. This does not mean that language *never* means, but rather that beyond the apparent meaning, and even beyond the suppressed or hidden meanings (unconscious, poetic, ideological, counterdiscursive), there can always be a residue of functioning—which produces effects—that is not a *sign* of anything, but merely the outcome of linguistic rules, or even of "the absolute randomness of language." Not that language is always absolutely random, but that we can never be sure that it isn't.[6]

One can believe in indeterminacy, then, and yet say, "it makes sense to me, today," or even "it makes sense to us" that the text of the First Amendment means flag burning should be allowed. But in the face of the arbitrariness of language, it is no longer possible to coherently claim that "it will always mean that to any properly expert and rational person in any time, in any context."

B. The Inevitability of Context and the Impossibility of Formalism

A second problem suggested by the arbitrariness of language involves the impossibility of abstracting from context that is a linchpin of the formalist legal logic, which today dominates thinking about freedom of speech. According to some understandings of the rule of law, justice is best served when applied according to indisputable, clear rules of procedure and decision-making. Hence, the First Amendment protects Nazis marching in Skokie and flag burning, not because anything good is being accomplished in either case, but because the important thing is to uphold the rules impartially and unequivocally. And being impartial and unequivocal typically means that rules are upheld *regardless* of context.

A nonformalist might suggest, say, that the harm from Nazis marching in a Jewish suburb surely outweighs the value of protecting their speech, especially given the history of the Holocaust and the irrational and violent character of Nazi ideology. Or one might argue that flag burning is such an ineffectual form of political expression and so potentially offensive that nothing would be lost by restricting it. But the formalist does not try to address these matters of history and judgments about the effects of various forms of expression; the counterargument is not that Nazis and flag-burners do indeed have something to say, or that the effects of history are different. Rather, the argument is basically that we must not "blur" the boundaries, cross what lawyers call the bright lines, upon which our system of justice rests: The rules are more important than the context.

An important example of formalist reasoning is the *Bellotti* case, in which the Supreme Court struck down a Massachusetts law limiting corporate campaign donations. The Court reached its decision not simply by weighing the positive and negative effects of the law, nor by deciding that it was a good thing in this case to grant large corporations the same rights as private individuals, but rather based on the argument that even *considering* the source of the campaign donations (the "speech" in question) was inappropriate. Every individual has a right to unrestricted political speech, and even asking whether corporate "individuals" are as worthy of protection as ordinary individuals would blur the bright lines upon which the rule of law is based.[7] Another example would be *American Booksellers Association, Inc. v. Hudnut,* when the court threw out an antipornography ordinance. The court argued that even if pornography has negative effects the same might be said of other forms of protected speech. From this it concluded that "[i]f the fact that speech plays a role in a process of conditioning were enough to permit governmental regulation, that would be the end of freedom of speech," and thus negative effects do not justify restrictions. As Stanley Fish has pointed out, this is a peculiar logic: faced with facts that call into question the speech/action distinction that underlies the law, the court upholds the law against the facts that would undermine it. But it is a typically formalist logic: The point is to uphold the rule of law, i.e., abstract, neutral principles and procedures; if the coherence of those abstract principles is threatened by facts, you throw out the facts, not the principles.[8]

The problem is that, if the meanings of statements emerge from convention, from social context, then the insistence on *excluding* context, on divorcing rules and their enforcement from social and political complexities of a situation, is an impossibility. This is not simply an argument that it would be reasonable to sometimes include a little bit of context in legal decision-making, that First Amendment law should lean towards a more policy-oriented weighing and balancing of principles and rights in special circumstances, such as highly concentrated or technologically inaccessible media. Rather, the argument is that formalist arguments of free speech cannot be doing what they claim, that context is present in decisions in spite of claims to the contrary. Decisions that grant protection to marching Nazis and flag burning are *not* simply decisions that show a preference for bright line rules over context; on the contrary, such decisions are themselves a product of a particular social and historical context, and in turn contribute to the making of particular contexts.

C. The Speech/Conduct Distinction

The collapse of the boundary between "natural" speech and arbitrary interference with it implied by indeterminacy creates a further problem for First Amendment interpretation: the collapse of the distinction between speech and conduct or speech and action. The exercise of free speech, the "free marketplace of ideas," is imagined as a kind of neutral, free and equal exchange, contrasted with unfree or arbitrary coercion. What disappears in the face of the arbitrariness of language is the coherence of that contrast, the faith that there is an important categorical distinction between people talking and arguing and people coercing one another through some kind of action. It is now an axiom of sociolinguistics and many other schools of thought that language use is an important kind of social action, that words do not merely reflect reality or express ideas, they primarily are a way of doing things, a way of acting in the social world. Although J. L. Austin began his classic *How to Do Things with Words* by describing a limited category of statements that do things—"performatives"—he later enlarged the category and made its boundaries much less clear by acknowledging the frequency of "indirect performatives," i.e., statements that might appear to be merely descriptive but in context can be shown to be, in fact, doing something.[9] Some have since argued that in a sense all utterances are performatives.

None of which is to suggest that a subtle verbal snub is identical to punching someone in the nose. We do not call trespassing on someone's lawn and shooting them identical, though they are both categorized as violations, as coercive. When Fish argues that speech in everyday life should not be imagined as if it takes place in "the sterilized and weightless atmosphere of a philosophy seminar,"[10] or when Matsuda et al. argue that words can wound, the argument is not that every slight or insult ought to be treated as if it were assault and battery.[11] What they are criticizing is the belief that there is a fundamental, categorical dichotomy between speech and conduct, that the dichotomy is clear and generalizable enough to form one of the principle structures of our law and democracy.

D. Abstract Individualism vs. the Construction of Subjectivity

All this points to a deeper critique of the marketplace metaphor. The metaphor implies that linguistic exchanges, like market exchanges, take place between individuals who, in the absence of some outside interference, exist merely as individuals, not as persons in particular contexts with particular backgrounds. These are the famous abstract individuals of legal liberalism, the persons referred to as "A" and "B" in law school lectures on contracts: persons bereft, in legal liberalism's ideal world, of gender, class, ethnicity, history. People the world over, the marketplace metaphor suggests, all share the characteristics of being in essence rational, self-interested individuals, inherently active and desirous. Language use, then, is a matter of expressing preexisting interests; it is a tool used by individuals to buy cheap and sell dear in the marketplace of ideas. Language is something one uses.

But, according to at least some schools of linguistics and language philosophy, language is also something that happens to us. The "I" that speaks a language is itself a product of that language; in a sense, language "speaks us" as much as we speak it. Language is an inherently collective, social precondition to individuality. Most definitions of language exclude any notion of a language possessed by only one individual; for language to be language it must be shared. People do not choose, after all, their first language; in a sense it chooses people. And the particularities of the language that chooses people, many would say, in turn shapes their consciousness, their sense of what counts as reason, their perceptions of the world and their selves within it, even their desires.[12]

This is not to imply, however, some kind of simple social determinism. Here is where the linguistic turn in philosophy suggests something very different from the common assertion that individual behaviors are "caused" by social structures. For one of the central discoveries of linguistics and language theory is what Roland Barthes called "a paradoxical idea of structure: a system with neither close nor center."[13] Except for analytical purposes, linguistic structure does not exist outside of anyone's use of it. Language is certainly structured, in some sense of that word; linguistic grammar is the central example of structure, although scholars have brought to our attention many higher-level structures, like linguistic style. But that structure is not simply some kind of exterior constraint, a Hobbesian limit on individual action; it is not the "structure" of, say, Durkheimian sociology or orthodox Marxism. It is dynamic, changing, and creative. As Noam Chomsky pointed out, one grammatical system is capable of generating an infinite variety of sentences. And grammar is a practical, thoroughly collective human accomplishment, not an exterior system imposed upon individuals by a reified "society." It is enabling as well as constraining: Linguistic structure is a precondition of self-expression, not just a limit to it.

Language thus troubles *both* legal liberalism's happy vision of rational individuals *and* its dark side, its Hobbesian view of society as the basic constraint on individuals; it calls into question the marketplace metaphor's notions of both individual freedom *and* social order. The attraction of the marketplace metaphor in law is much the same as the attraction of marketplace theory itself: it posits a realm that is both free of arbitrary constraint, and yet ordered by the certain yet neutral and unequivocal rules of the marketplace. What the fact of linguistic structure calls into question is not merely the "freedom" of linguistic exchange but also its certainty, its divisibility from "arbitrary" external restraints and interference.

E. Summary: The Critique of Free Speech Is a Critique of Formalist Understandings of the Rule of Law

When MacKinnon argues that pornography is a form of action, not of speech, or when Matsuda argues that the context of racism and the subjective experiences of minorities in the United States ought to be a primary consideration in the creation and interpretation of hate speech laws, in the long run what motivates these scholars is not just a desire for specific *exceptions* to an otherwise intact First Amendment doctrine.[14] The suggestion is not simply that pornography is so damaging, or that the specific horrors of slavery and its legacy of racism so evil that unusual exceptions to free speech protection are called for (though the evils of rape-culture and racism very well might be the most urgent problems in the United States today). Rather, the suggestion, at least implicitly, is that the evils of rape-culture and contemporary racism force us, or should force us, to fundamentally reconsider how American law thinks about freedom, speech, and their regulation.

Furthermore, the critique of the oppositions that underpin free speech law, such as speech and action, rules and context, or politics and law, need not be read as a simple denial that any differences exist. It is obviously not the case that there is no difference between slighting someone with a racial epithet and hitting them in the head, or between decision-making in courts and decision-making in legislatures. The argument is rather that these differences are neither clear nor generalizable enough to coherently underwrite a system of decision-making that claims to be able to transcend context and achieve the neutrality that is the goal of law in the first place.

IV. Toward an Analysis of the Context of Free Speech: The Politics of the Rule of Law

Inquiry does not come to an end when one accepts the criticisms of the formalist First Amendment framework and acknowledges the inevitability of politics and context. Stanley Fish's quip notwithstanding, there is such a thing as free speech. If something is not what we think it is, it does not follow that it does not exist. Free speech is one of the major and most influential political and legal discourses of this century; for better or worse, it has helped make American society, our world, what it is. So the task is to rethink the character of free speech, to specify its historical context and political incidence. This is a large task; here I can only speculate about one aspect of the historical context of free speech, its relation to notions of the rule of law, and one aspect of its political incidence, its relations to social class.

The concept of a neutral, objective system of law that transcends politics is not just an abstraction important to lawyers and judges. (Lawyers and judges, in fact, are often acutely aware of just how political and unstable legal interpretation can sometimes be on a day-to-day basis.) A faith in the neutral rule of law is an important element of American culture, of the popular imagination. Evidence for this can be seen in the way that legal institutions and documents are more often celebrated, more often used to define American democracy, than political institutions and accomplishments. One might think, for example, that in an electoral democracy the most important historical event, the event most widely celebrated, would be the extension of the vote to the majority of the population. Yet most citizens do not know the amendment or the year in which the vote was extended to women, much less the history of the long political struggles that led to the passage of the nineteenth amendment in 1920. On the other hand, the Constitution is regularly celebrated in fora ranging from scholarly conferences to reverential Philip Morris ads, even though that hallowed document underwrote a legal system that upheld slavery for three quarters of a century, excluded women from voting for more than half a century after that, and did not come to rigorously protect political dissent until about fifty years ago. Nonetheless, American culture tends to worship the Constitution and remain ignorant of the history of universal suffrage. The story of the Constitution is a story of law, whereas the story of women's suffrage is a story of protracted political struggle. And in some ways, at least, mainstream American political culture worships the former more than the latter.

A. Free Speech and the Rule of Law: Two Legal Logics

What is the substance of this worship? What makes law neutral, and how does it support democracy? The short answer might be that if a society makes its decisions according to fixed rules instead of individual or collective whims, individuals will be less able to gain systematic advantage over others. The long answer would involve an extended and controversial discussion of a large chunk of the literature of legal theory and political science. But there is a mid-range answer based in historical observations, which suggests that in the United States two patterns of argument or logic have tended to shape legal decision-making, particularly in this century. One logic has been called alternately formalist, classical, bright line, rule-based, or simply legal justice; the other, standards-based, revisionist, policy oriented, realist, or substantive justice.[15]

Arguably, the First Amendment has become the centerpiece of the American faith in the rule of law in this century, and not coincidentally, First Amendment law is also highly formalistic. Formalism is not simply absolutism, a belief that there should be no exceptions. It is more a way of thinking about what law and legal interpretation are and how they work. (Describing the ACLU's position on the First Amendment as "absolutist" is thus a bit of a red herring.) In at least many of its variations, formalism involves the claim that law is apolitical and neutral because it rests on a rigid, formal model, based on an ideal of axiomatic deduction from rules and unequivocal, "bright line" legal distinctions. The role of law, then, is to locate and uphold clear boundaries—bright lines—between the rights of individuals and between individuals and the state. Legal language and legal expertise are thought valuable precisely because they provide fixed, rigorous meanings unsullied by the political and social winds of the moment. Given a certain set of legal rules and a certain legally defined situation, it is assumed, a properly trained judge or lawyer, within certain boundaries, can use expertise in legal language and reasoning to arrive at, or at least approximate, *the* correct interpretation, which is generally a matter of pinpointing exactly where the boundaries lie.

Policy-oriented decision-making, in contrast, tends to be context sensitive, accepting of blurry boundaries, functionalist, and messier. It is also much more common in legal decision-making than popular wisdom would suggest. In policy argument, justice is thought to be best served by subtle, well-informed analyses of particular contexts and judicial "balancing" of competing interests and principles; rights and values are treated not as hard rules distinguished by bright lines, but as general standards that can be differentially implemented according to context. Administrative law, such as that involved in enacting the Federal Communication Commission's public interest standard for broadcasters, is a classic example of policy-oriented decision-making. *Brown v. Board of Education* also includes some exemplary policy argument.

Policy-oriented decision-making sometimes is justified in terms of head-on attacks on formalism of the type associated with the critiques of free speech just discussed. Both in practice and in theory, the argument goes, the supposedly "bright line" distinctions upon which formalism is based are rarely if ever as bright as imagined. Fish's polemic, "There is no such thing as free speech," is a recent example of such a critique, but in some ways his position echoes, for example, Felix Cohen's legal realist argument earlier in the century, in "Transcendental Nonsense and the Functional Approach."[16]

It is important, however, that outside the academy policy-oriented legal decision-making has been justified less by theoretical criticisms of formalism as a whole and more by a sense that, in certain limited and specialized contexts, policy-oriented decision-making is simply practical. Formalism seems to be the place where our culture celebrates the ideal of the rule of law; policy argument seems to be the place where most of the detailed legal work of ordering society goes on. Policy argument dominates largely in domains unrelated to communication: the law of corporations, environmental law, urban planning, and so forth. The prominent example of policy logic in communication is probably government licensing of broadcast stations according to the public interest standard. Licensing was originally created because communication by radio waves was understood to be characterized by spectrum scarcity and other complicated and contingent technical matters, such as rapidly evolving technologies and strategic needs of the military. Treating broadcasters differently than newspapers was thus thought to be simply called for by context, not because there was thought to be a formal right or principle at stake such as the public's right of access to communication.

B. *The Political Need for Formalism and the Rise of Free Speech*

It is sometimes suggested that policy arguments began to replace formalist ones in legal argument somewhere around the turn of the century, and formalism was finally defeated with the end of the *Lochner*[17] era in 1937. On the level of legal metatheory, there may be truth to this, but it remains the case that in practice both logics remain today. Sometimes the two logics are associated with competing sides in a legal controversy. The argument that television violence ought to be censored because its measurably harmful effects on children outweigh considerations of free speech is a typical policy argument; arguing against such censorship because it would open the door to more serious restrictions of freedom of speech is to lean in a formalist direction. But the two logics are also often mixed in the context of any given argument. Conservatives argue that broadcast licensing violates free speech rights but also is inefficient in the context of new technologies; liberals argue that guaranteed citizen access to mass communications would be beneficial for industrial society but also should be treated as a "new First Amendment right."[18]

So it is perhaps the case that what has been changing over the years is not simply a shift from one kind of argument to the other, but a shift in the "mix" of the two, a shift in how the two kinds of argument have been used in which cases. And here the historical literature suggests that, gradually in this century, the focus of formalist argumentation has shifted from the realm of property and contract to free speech. Up through the late nineteenth century, during what Elizabeth Mensch calls the classical era of jurisprudence, property was the central, formal right; in theory, property was celebrated as the essence of legal liberalism, and in practice, it was used aggressively in a wide variety of areas. Property rights were invoked to justify bans on speaking in public parks, the picketing of factories during union drives, and turn-of-the-century social legislation. Gradually, this formalist application of property fell out of favor, and met its final demise in the 1937 overturn of *Lochner,* during the New Deal.[19]

Perhaps it is not entirely coincidental that, as formalist notions of property declined, the formalist understanding of free speech rose. In a familiar history, the First Amendment was gradually elevated to its current legal status, both in case law and in the popular imagination. What has triumphed in this period is not a policy-oriented understanding of free speech (in spite of the best efforts of a long line of scholars from Alexander Meiklejohn to Cass Sunstein) but a rigidly formalist one. So today, property rights advocates who would like to see a return to something like the *Lochner*-era interpretations of property, like Richard Epstein, argue that the rules applied to free speech should also be applied to property. Conversely, from somewhere toward the other end of the political spectrum, Sunstein has called for "A New Deal for Speech" wherein the 1930s revisions of property law be extended to communication.[20]

Why has formalism in legal discourse shifted from property and contract to free speech? At this point, I can only speculate. It's possible to put a cynical economic interpretation on the shift: Formal interpretations of property were abandoned because they became increasingly impractical in the face of the bureaucratic corporate form of business and other late nineteenth-and early twentieth-century economic developments. Conversely, the soap box speakers became sanctified in law precisely during the historical period in which they ceased being effective. In the nineteenth century, union organizers, pacifists, and other "radicals" all made good use of the soap box—of face-to-face speaking in public places—as a communicative tool, and were regularly arrested for doing so. In this century, however, the key to popular communication has become access to radio, television, and other expensive technology-based mass media, which have rendered the soap box increasingly irrelevant as an organizing tool. A formalist interpretation of the First Amendment grants symbolic protection to soap boxes while in practice protecting media corporations much more effectively than dissidents.

Such an account of the shift, however, risks a functionalist tautology (explaining historical events in terms of the needs they serve for the power bloc) and fails to account for the imaginative power of First Amendment formalism. So a more comprehensive explanation might add two observations. First, from a distance, formalism is satisfying to a legal liberal vision of the rule of law, whereas policy argument can appear as arbitrary, obscure, and haughtily technocratic. College sophomores have little trouble understanding why it might be good for the rule of law to protect Nazis marching in Skokie, but it takes a lot of effort to convince them of the grand principles at stake in, say, the regulation requiring TV stations to charge political candidates the same rate for advertising time they charge their most favored advertiser instead of their standard rates. Second, from up close, from the perspective of those involved in everyday, small legal decisions, formalism is frequently impractical, whereas policy-oriented decisions seem reasonable and pragmatic. Few suburban homeowners would take kindly to the suggestion that their neighbors should be allowed to raise pigs or let their lawns go to weed on the grounds that to do so would be to uphold the sanctity of formal property rights.

It seems to be the case, then, that the American polity seems to want a legal system that can satisfy *both* the desire for legitimacy provided by formalism *and* the "practical" effectiveness of policy-oriented decision-making. Perhaps, therefore, the formalist interpretation of the First Amendment became popular in part because it came to take property's place as a symbol of legal clarity and formal justice. In both the popular and legal imaginations, the image of the property-holding yeoman farmer was gradually supplanted by the soap box speaker as the central archetype and emblem of legally protected exercise of rights and freedoms in a democratic society.

C. The Class Context of Free Speech

1. Labor and Management. The polity, however, is not the public. The community of individuals who appreciate the formalist interpretation of free speech may include a wide range of people, such as lawyers, judges, politicians, journalists, professors, and many others in positions to directly or indirectly influence legal and political consciousness. And it includes a wide range of political positions: Liberals at the ACLU seem to have little trouble agreeing with conservatives on the Supreme Court that flag burning is protected speech. But it certainly does not include everyone. The majority of the American public has a hard time seeing the justice of protecting flag burning. And this may not mean simply that the public disdains free speech. The ACLU reports that the majority of the complaints it receives come from workers who feel their speech has been restricted by their bosses—a kind of speech that the Supreme Court and the ACLU agree is *not* protected.

Mensch has remarked that, although many formerly bright lines have been blurred in twentieth-century law, the boundary between capital and labor remains as bright and impermeable as ever.[21] The First Amendment, as it is currently interpreted, protects owners and managers more than individual speakers. It prevents government agencies from interfering with the speech of private agencies delineated by boundaries of ownership and management, not by individual human beings.

As a result, employees have basically no free speech rights with regards to their employers, including employees of media businesses. When a journalist is told by an editor to drop a story because it is politically inflammatory, the journalist can find little comfort in First Amendment law. Network program practices departments engage in systematic and thorough censorship of scripts for television series with all the zeal (if not the same principles) of Communist Party *apparatchiks.* Under law, there's a sense in which A. J. Liebling's *bon mot*—that the only freedom of the press in this country is for those who own one—is literally true.

For all that, Liebling's quip is an oversimplification. There are many limits on the power of media owners to influence content, such as the resistance of the community of professional journalists to owner manipulation on both ethical and self-interested grounds. Evidence suggests that, among some groups, there probably is a popular ethic of free speech in the United States that extends beyond the powers of owners and managers. When conservative newspaper tycoon Rupert Murdoch bought the left-wing *Village Voice* and tried to dismiss its editor, for example, the threat of a staff walkout forced him to back down, and he left the paper's editorial content alone thereafter.[22]

2. *Social Class and Linguistic Style.* Bringing "popular ethics" into the discussion, however, brings us back to the second question suggested by Gates' examples: Why does it seem easier to pass rules prohibiting direct racial epithets than elaborate, formal statements? It is well established that linguistic style is associated with social class. Sociolinguist Basil Bernstein demonstrated that children from middle and professional classes tend to do better in school than working-class students, in part because they speak more often and more fluently in formal style, or what Bernstein calls "elaborated code." Working-class students, in contrast, tend to be more comfortable, and are probably more fluent in, informal style, or what Bernstein calls "restricted code."[23]

One style is not better than the other. Rather, each style is an adaptation to specific patterns of life and work. Informal style has the effect of stressing membership within a group; it is useful for interactions among people who are familiar with each other and work with each other on a regular basis, and thus live in "dense" social networks, i.e., high levels of interaction with a limited number of people. It has a high proportion of ellipses and colloquialisms, not because such language is simpler, but because these take advantage of a higher degree of shared knowledge between speaker and listener. Similarly, it has a higher proportion of personal pronouns (you and they) and tag-questions soliciting agreement of the listener (nice day, isn't it?), because these express a sense of cooperation and solidarity.[24]

Formal style, in contrast, is for people whose social networks are less dense, who regularly deal with strangers and thus communicate in contexts in which ellipses and colloquialisms are more likely to generate confusion than solidarity. Similarly, formal style's high proportion of subordinate clauses, passive verbs, and adjectives (besides connoting high-mindedness through its echo of Latin grammar) are adaptations to the need to explain details comprehensively when speaker and listener do not share as much background knowledge and cannot easily rely on features of the extra-linguistic context. Interestingly, in spite of the frequency of passive verbs, formal style also contains a higher proportion of the pronoun "I." This has the effect of imposing the speaker's individuality on the utterance, of stressing her or his unique nature as a person, as opposed to expressing membership in a group. Some research suggests that formal style leads people to be judged as more intelligent, more educated, and less friendly and less likable than informal style.

It is not the case that working-class people use only informal style and middle-class people use only formal style. A garage mechanic will probably shift to formal speech when dealing with a customer irate over a bill, and only the most hopelessly pompous college professors use formal style when speaking with their friends and families. But mastery over the different styles is not evenly distributed. Bernstein's work suggests that middle- and professional-class students' relatively better skills and comfort with formal style functions as a form of what Pierre Bourdieu calls "cultural capital," enhancing their life prospects.[25] Given the relation of style to the character of work, moreover, fluency in formal style (though not accent) is probably associated with a person's present occupation, regardless of class background.

What does this have to do with free speech? James Carey has argued that the speech/action distinction in free speech law is an expression of distinctly middle-class values and sensibilities. Carey tells the story of a middle-class man who enters a working-class bar and not long thereafter comes flying out the plate glass window; the man then says with astonishment, "but all I did was use words!" Carey's point is that, to the working-class individuals in the bar, words have power. For them, the difference between insulting someone's mother and punching them in the nose is not as obvious or absolute as it is for the middle-class person.

Carolyn Marvin has elaborated on these contrasting sets of values in our culture in terms of what she calls "text" and "body":

> Text is traditionally the weapon of those whose cultural power and entitlement to participation in social life derive from educational and other textualizing credentials that exempt them from expending their bodies in pursuit of social resources. Those who command the text are most entitled to preserve their bodies and shield them from

physical effort and danger. The body, by contrast, is the emblem and resource of those without textual credentials, whose bodies are available to be used up by society and whose power and participation derive from whatever value their bodies have for cultural muscle-work.... *Text* and *body,* therefore, represent competing concentrations of economic and social power, characteristically different concepts and artifacts, and distinctive logics and frameworks of value ... Where the body is thought to be concrete, the text is considered abstract. Where the body is seen as particular, the text is described as universalizing.[26]

Those who celebrate the Bill of Rights, Marvin argues, are those who live text-oriented lives; yet as she points out, the Bill of Rights does not wave over the ballpark. The values of formalist free speech, then, are the values of what Marvin calls text: the abstract and universalizing values of people who do not have to "expend their bodies in pursuit of social resources," who lead a life that involves frequent contact with strangers, and who value a formal linguistic style. The point is not that those who value texts think words matter, and that those who value bodies think action matters. The point is that text and body represent different ways of conceptualizing the *relation between* words and actions. The dualism of speech and conduct, the sense that there is some fundamental, profound difference between talking and acting upon which one can base neutral, apolitical, and universally applicable rules for democracy, is an expression of the world view of people who make a living with words at relatively little expense to their bodies. Although it may be difficult for a text-valuing person such as myself to appreciate the point of view of a nontextual person, perhaps for those who work primarily with their bodies, words are simply an extension of bodily action.[27]

The First Amendment as currently interpreted is envisioned largely in terms of that which middle- and professional-class people have mastery over, abstract formal expression in speech and writing. This is why it is harder to censure Gates's first example than the second. Within the community of people who share those values, there *is* something equalizing about free speech. But it should not be surprising that, for people who do not make a living that way, for workers and other people whose bodies are the source of their value to society, formalist protection of free speech may not make sense, and might even appear as simply another way that people who have privileges (such as academics writing about free speech) exercise their power over people who don't.

V. Conclusion

The analyses and arguments of this chapter do not offer resolutions to all of the many important debates among nonformalist theorists of freedom of speech, such as those between Gates and Matsuda *et al.* over campus hate speech codes. But it does do two things. First, it tries to clarify some of the underlying principles and issues at stake today in debates over free speech, particularly the inevitability of context and the problems this poses for traditional formalist understandings of the rule of law. Second, it points in the direction of a rethinking of free speech *based* in context, and suggests two (among many possible) avenues to pursue: the historical shift of formalism from property to free speech and to matters of language and social class in both legal discourse and in nonlegal situations. Clearly, these examples of context-based analysis are intended only to be suggestive. But what they suggest, it is hoped, is that this kind of inquiry, if expanded into rich and subtle contextual analyses, might indeed help resolve some debates and contribute to a more fully democratic, substantive interpretation of the role of free speech in law and culture.

Notes

1. Henry Louis Gates, "Let Them Talk," *New Republic*, Sept. 20 & 27, 1993, 37–49: at 45.
2. "Style" is the generally accepted sociolinguistic term for language varieties that can be classified on a continuum from formal to informal. The word "code" is used by Basil Bernstein, *Class, Codes, and Control*, 2d ed. (Boston: Routledge & Kegan Paul, 1974).
3. William Labov, "The Logic of Nonstandard English," in Giglioli, ed., *Language and Social Context* (New York: Penguin, 1972), 179–216.
4. For a sociolinguistically informed analysis of the role of linguistic style during arrest and interrogation, see Janet E. Ainsworth, "In a Different Register: The Pragmatics of Powerlessness in Police Interrogation," *Yale Law Journal* 103 (November 1993): 259–322.
5. Mark Kelman, *A Guide to Critical Legal Studies* (Cambridge: Harvard University Press, 1987), 12 and *passim*.

6. Barbara Johnson, *A World of Difference* (Baltimore: Johns Hopkins University Press, 1987), 6.

7. *First National Bank of Boston v. Bellotti*, 435 U.S. 765, 776 (1978).

8. 771 F. 2d 323 (7th Cir. 1985), aff'd, 475 U.S. 1601 (1986), 329; quoted in Stanley Fish, "Fraught with Death: Skepticism, Progressivism, and the First Amendment," *University of Colorado Law Review* 64 (Fall 1993): 1065.

9. See Ainsworth, "In a Different Register," note 15: p. 265. "Austin initially adopts the intuitively appealing assumption that constative utterances, unlike performatives, are true or false. Having set up these opposing categories of performative and constative utterances, Austin ultimately deconstructs this dichotomy" with his analysis of indirect performatives.

10. Fish, "Fraught with Death," 1061.

11. Mari J. Matsuda, Charles R. Lawrence III, Richard Delgado, and Kimberle Williams Crenshaw, *Words that Wound: Critical Race Theory, Assaultive Speech, and the First Amendment* (Boulder, Colo.: Westview Press, 1993).

12. The classic and extreme version of this notion is the "Sapir-Whorf hypothesis" named after linguists Edward Sapir and Benjamin Whorf. For a poststructuralist variation of it, see Rosalind Coward and John Ellis, *Language and Materialism: Developments in Semiology and the Theory of the Subject* (London: Routledge & Kegan Paul, 1977).

13. Roland Barthes, *Image, Music, Text* (New York: Hill & Wang, 1977), 159.

14. Catharine A. MacKinnon, *Only Words* (Cambridge: Harvard University Press, 1993).

15. Elizabeth Mensch divides legal thought into classical and realist or revisionist forms. Duncan Kennedy talks of the distinction between rules and standards. Roberto Unger speaks of "legal justice" and "substantive justice." See Elizabeth Mensch, "The History of Mainstream Legal Thought," in David Kairys, ed., *The Politics of Law: A Progressive Critique* (New York: Pantheon, 1982), 18–39; Duncan Kennedy, "Form and Substance in Private Law Adjudication," *Harvard Law Review* 89 (1976): 1685, 1687–89; see also Roberto M. Unger, *Knowledge and Politics* (New York: Free Press, 1975), 91.

16. Stanley Fish, "There's No Such Thing As Free Speech and It's a Good Thing, Too," *Boston Review* (Feb. 1992): 3; Felix Cohen, "Transcendental Nonsense and the Functional Approach," *Columbia Law Review* 35 (1935): 809.

17. *Lochner v. New York*, 198 U.S. 45 (1905), overruled by *Day-Bright Lighting, Inc. v. Missouri*, 342 U.S. 421 (1952).

18. For example, Jerome A. Barron, *Freedom of the Press for Whom? The Right of Access to Mass Media* (Bloomington: Indiana University Press, 1973).

19. Jennifer Nedelsky, *Private Property and the Limits of American Constitu-*

tionalism: The Madisonian Framework and Its Legacy (Chicago: University of Chicago Press, 1990).

20. Cass R. Sunstein, chapter 4 in this volume and "Free Speech Now," *University of Chicago Law Review* 59 (Winter 1992): 255; Richard A. Epstein, "Property, Speech, and the Politics of Distrust," *University of Chicago Law Review* 59 (Winter 1992): 41.

21. Mensch, "The History of Mainstream Legal Thought," 26.

22. Alex S. Jones, "At Village Voice, A Clashing of Visions," *New York Times* (June 28, 1985): B5.

23. Bernstein, *Class, Codes, and Control*.

24. This survey of Bernstein's work relies heavily on Peter Trudgill, *Sociolinguistics: An Introduction to Language and Society* (London: Penguin Books, 1983, rev. ed.), 132–140.

25. Pierre Bourdieu, *Distinction: A Social Critique of the Judgment of Taste*, trans. R. Nice (London: Routledge & Kegan Paul, 1984).

26. Carolyn Marvin, "Theorizing the Flagbody: Symbolic Dimensions of the Flag Desecration Debate; or, Why the Bill of Rights Does Not Fly in the Ballpark," *Critical Studies in Mass Communication* 8 (June 1991): 120–121.

27. Social class is of course a complex construct, and is used here suggestively, not comprehensively or precisely. Marvin points out that the values of "body" in fact extend to and in many ways are exemplified by military personnel, a group which overlaps with but is not limited to working-class individuals (Marvin, "Theorizing the Flagbody").

FOUR

A New Deal for Speech

CASS R. SUNSTEIN

A New Deal is necessary for speech, one that would parallel the New Deal provided to property rights during the 1930s.[1] The goal of the New Deal should be to promote attention to public issues and diversity of view, and in this way to diminish the influence of money over the content of broadcasting.

To compress a long story:[2] Before the New Deal, the Constitution was often understood as a constraint on government "regulation." In practice, this meant that the Constitution often prohibited governmental interference with existing distributions of rights. On the pre–New Deal view, existing distributions marked the boundary not only between neutrality and partisanship, but inaction and action as well. The rallying cry "laissez-faire" of course captured such ideas. The fear and (more important) the very conception of "government intervention" did the same.

The New Deal reformers argued that this entire framework was built on fictions. Ownership rights were a creation of law. The government did not "act" only when it disturbed existing distributions. It was responsible for those distributions in the first instance. What people had, in markets, was partly a function of the entitlements that the law conferred on them. The notion of "laissez-faire" thus stood revealed as a conspicuous myth. Different forms of governmental ordering had to be evaluated pragmatically and in terms of their consequences for social efficiency and social justice. Markets would not be identified with liberty in any *a priori* way; they would have to be evaluated through an examination of whether they served liberty or not. This did not mean that markets would be rejected. Often, they are associated with liberty and productivity, and indeed with a form of equality. But interferences with markets—which are themselves made possible only by law—would be evaluated for what they did for human beings, and not taken as invalid per se.

These ideas have played little role in the law of free speech. For purposes of speech, contemporary understandings of neutrality and partisanship, or action and inaction, are identical to those that predate the New Deal. The category of government "intervention" is defined accordingly.

There is much good in the contemporary use of pre-New Deal understandings. Free speech absolutism—even if it is wildly simplistic, even if it fails to grapple with hard cases, even if it cannot survive reflection—is an important safeguard against myopic or oppressive legislation. But I think that recent First Amendment controversies in the area of broadcasting confirm the wisdom of the New Deal on this score, and they show that American constitutionalism, with respect to freedom of expression, has failed precisely to the extent that it has not taken that reformation seriously enough.

I do not mean to suggest that speech rights should be freely subject to political determination, as are, say, current issues of occupational safety and health. I do not mean to suggest that markets in speech are generally abridgments of speech, or that they usually disserve the First Amendment. I do not mean to say that government can favor some views over others, that free speech is a myth, or that the goal of "equality" ought to be balanced against the goal of "free speech." I do not mean to endorse command-and-control regulations. But I do mean that, at a minimum, what seems to be government regulation of speech might, in some circumstances, promote free speech, and should not be treated as an abridgment at all. I mean also to argue, though more hesitantly, that what seems to be free speech in markets might, on reflection, amount to an abridgment of free speech. Consider here Robert Hale's suggestion, capturing much of my argument, to the effect that "the power to set judicial machinery in motion for the enforcement of legal duties" should "be recognized as a delegation of state power."[3] This recognition—of prime importance in the area of broadcasting—is precisely what is missing from current free speech law.

A general clarification is necessary at the outset. It will be tempting to think that the argument to follow amounts to a broad and perhaps bizarre plea for "more regulation" of speech. Many of the practices and conditions that I will challenge are commonly taken to involve private action, and hence not to involve the Constitution at all. (Recall the state action doctrine, which means that private behavior is not subject to the Constitution.) The outcome of the "market" for expenditures on campaigns, and the practices of broadcasters and managers of newspapers, raise no constitutional question. It is "regulation" of "the market" that is problematic.

In fact there should be enthusiastic agreement that the First Amendment is aimed only at governmental action, and that private conduct raises no constitutional question. On this point the Constitution is clear. It seems clear, too, that to find a constitutional violation, one needs to show that governmental action has "abridged the freedom of speech." That action must usually take the form of a law or regulation.

But if the New Deal is taken at all seriously, it follows that governmental rules lie behind the exercise of rights of property, contract, and tort, not that the requirement of state action is unintelligible or incoherent. This is so especially when the law grants people rights of exclusive ownership and use of property—and emphatically when the law grants owners or speakers such rights. From this it does not follow that private acts are subject to constitutional constraint, or even that legally conferred rights of ownership violate any constitutional provision. To find a constitutional question, it is always necessary to point to some exercise of public power. And to find a constitutional violation, it is necessary to show that public power has compromised some constitutional principle. But a claim on behalf of new efforts to promote greater quality and diversity in broadcasting, for example, is a claim for a new regulatory system, not for "government intervention" where none existed before.

What I want to suggest here is, first and foremost, that legal rules that are designed to promote freedom of speech and that interfere with other legal rules—those of the law of property—should not be invalidated if their purposes and effects are constitutionally valid (a complex question that I will take up below). It may also follow that some existing rules may themselves be subject to constitutional objection, and in some surprising places, if and when such rules "abridge the freedom of speech" by preventing people from speaking at certain times and in certain places.

Thus far these remarks are uncomfortably abstract; I will give them much more specific content before long. Whether general or particular, they might seem unconventional. In fact, however, they have a clear foundation in no lesser place than *New York Times v. Sullivan*,[4] one of the defining cases of modern free speech law. There the Court concluded that a public official could not bring an action for libel unless he could show "actual malice," that is, knowledge of or reckless indifference to the falsity of the statements at issue. The *Sullivan* case is usually taken as the symbol of broad press immunity for criticism of public officials. Even more, *Sullivan* is often understood to reflect the conception of freedom of expression advocated by Alexander Meiklejohn[5]—a conception of self-government, connected to the American principle of sovereignty.

It is striking that in *Sullivan*, the lower court held that the common law of tort, and more particularly libel, was not state action at all, and was therefore entirely immune from constitutional constraint.[6] A civil action, on this view, involved a purely private dispute. The Supreme Court quickly disposed of this objection, as seems obviously right. The use of public tribunals to punish speech is conspicuously state action. What is interesting is not the Supreme Court's rejection of the argument, but the fact that the argument could be made by a state supreme court as late as the 1960s. How could reasonable judges perceive the rules of tort law as purely private?

The answer lies in the persistence of pre–New Deal understandings—to the effect that the common law simply implements existing rights, or private desires, and does not amount to "intervention" or "action" at all. The view that the common law of property should be taken as prepolitical and just, and as a refusal to use government power—the view that the New Deal repudiated—was the same as the view of the state supreme court in *Sullivan*. Reputation is of course a property interest, and just as in the pre–New Deal era, the protection of that interest did not appear to involve government action at all.

The Supreme Court's rejection of that claim seemed inevitable in *Sullivan* itself, and indeed this aspect of the case is largely forgotten. But many aspects of current law are based on precisely the same understandings as underlie the forgotten view of that obscure court. In fact, we might generalize from *Sullivan* the broad idea that protection of property rights, through the law, must always be assessed pragmatically in terms of its effects on speech. This idea has major implications. In a regime of property rights, there is no such thing as no regulation of speech; the question is what forms of regulation best serve the purposes of the free speech guarantee.

Consider, for example, the issues raised when people claim a right of access to the media, or seek controls on broadcasting in general. May broadcasters be required to be common carriers of local programming, as the 1992 Cable TV Act says? Suppose that most broadcasters deal little or not at all with issues of public importance, restricting themselves to stories about movie stars or sex scandals. Suppose, too, that there is no diversity of view on the airwaves, but instead a bland, watered-down version of conventional morality. A large part of the problem, for the system of free expression, is the governmental grant of legal protection—rights of exclusive use—to enormous institutions having huge resources with which to dominate communication. At least this is so if we assess our system of free expression by reference to two original constitutional goals: promotion of attention to public issues and opportunity to speak for diverse views. (I take up the issue of scarcity and its demise below.)

That grant of power—sometimes through the common law, sometimes through statute—is usually taken not to be a grant of power at all, but instead to be purely "private." Thus, the exclusion of people and views from the airwaves is immunized from constitutional constraint, on the theory that the act of exclusion is purely private; thus, rights of access to the media are thought to involve governmental intervention into the private sphere.

In *Sullivan,* the Supreme Court said, as against a similar claim, that legal rules should be inspected for their conformity with the overriding principle that government may not restrict freedoms of speech and press. "The test is not the form in which state power has been applied but, whatever the form, whether such power has in fact been exercised."[7]

We might apply this understanding to current problems. If the First Amendment is regarded as an effort to ensure that people are not prevented from speaking, especially on issues of public importance, then the commitments that currently dominate free speech law seem ill-adapted to current conditions. Above all, the conception of government "regulation" turns out to misstate important issues and sometimes to disserve the goal of free expression itself. With broadcasting, the "form" of the exclusion is rights of exclusion that prevent certain people from speaking, and that do so through law.

Some regulatory efforts, superimposed on current regulation through current property rules, may promote free speech, whereas the property rules may undermine it. Such efforts might not be "abridgments" of freedom of speech; they might increase free speech. To know whether this is so, it is necessary to understand their purposes and consequences. Less frequently, the use of property rules to foreclose efforts to speak might represent impermissible restrictions on speech. To know whether this is so, it is necessary to assess the effects of such rules in terms of their consequences for speech. In any case both reform efforts and the status quo must be judged by their consequences, not by question-begging characterizations of "threats from government."

It is tempting to understand this argument as a suggestion that the New Dealers were concerned about private power over working conditions, and that modern constitutional courts should be more interested in the existence of private power over expression or over democratic processes.[8] But this formulation misses the real point, and does so in a way that suggests its own dependence on status quo neutrality and pre–New Deal understandings. The major problem is not that private power is an obstacle to speech; even if it is, private power is not a subject of the First Amendment. Nor would it be accurate to say that employer power was the central concern for the New Dealers. The real problem is that public authority creates legal rules that restrict speech, that new exercises of public authority can counter the existing restrictions, and that any restrictions, even those of the common law of property, must be assessed under constitutional principles precisely because they are restrictions.

Consider a case in which a network decides not to sell advertising time to a group that wants to discuss some public issue or to express some dissident view. Under current law, the refusal raises no First Amendment question, in part because a number of the justices—perhaps now a majority—believe that there is no "state action."[9] But broadcasters are given property rights in their licenses by government, and the grant of such rights is unambiguously state action. To be sure, it is generally good to have a system in which government creates ownership rights or markets in speech, just as it is usually good to create rights of ownership, and markets, in property. The key point here is that a right of exclusive ownership in a television network is governmentally conferred; the exclusion of the would-be speakers is backed up, or made possible, by the law of (among other things) civil and criminal trespass. It is thus a product of a governmental decision.

A system in which only certain views are expressed or made available to most of the public is a creation of law. The constitutional question is whether reforms eliminating exclusive ownership rights—or, more precisely, eliminating an element of such rights by conditioning the original grant, perhaps by creating common carrier obligations—are consistent with the First Amendment, or whether the government grant of exclusive ownership rights violates the First Amendment. We cannot answer such questions merely by saying that ownership rights are governmental. We need to know the purposes and effects of the grant. That question cannot be answered a priori, or in the abstract. We need to know a lot of details.

It might be tempting to respond that the Constitution creates "negative" rights rather than "positive" ones, or at least that the First Amendment is "negative" in character—a right to protection against the government, not to help from the government. So stated, the claim certainly captures the conventional wisdom. Any argument for a New Deal for speech must therefore come to terms with the view that the Constitution does not create positive rights, and should not be understood to do so.

There are two responses to this view. The first and most fundamental is that no one is asserting a positive right in these cases. Instead, the claim is that government sometimes cannot adopt a legal rule that imposes a (negative) constraint on who can speak, and where they can do so. When someone with view X is unable to state that view on the networks, it is because the civil and criminal law prohibits him from doing so. Negative liberty is indeed involved.

This is the same problem that underlies a wide range of familiar constitutional claims; consider a ban on door-to-door soliciting. An attack on content-neutral restrictions of this kind is not an argument for "positive" government protection. It is merely a claim that legal rules that stop certain people from speaking in certain places must be reviewed under First Amendment principles. In fact, the response that a New Deal for speech would create a "positive right" trades on untenable, pre–New Deal distinctions between positive and negative rights.[10]

The second point is that the distinction between negative and positive rights fails even to explain current First Amendment law. There are two obvious counterexamples. The Supreme Court has come very close to saying that when an audience becomes hostile and threatening, the government is obligated to protect the speaker. Under current law, reasonable crowd control measures are probably constitutionally compelled, even if the result is to require a number of police officers to come to the scene.[11] The right to speak thus includes a positive right to governmental protection against a hostile private audience.

Or return to the area of libel. By imposing constitutional restraints on the common law of libel, the Court has held, in effect, that those who are defamed must subsidize speakers, by allowing their reputation to be sacrificed to the end of broad diversity of speech. Even more than this, the Court has held that government is under (what might be seen as) an affirmative duty to "take" the reputation of people who are defamed in order to promote the interest in free speech. The First Amendment requires a compulsory, governmentally produced subsidy of personal reputation for the benefit of speech.[12]

Cases of this sort reveal that the First Amendment, even as currently conceived, is no mere negative right. It has positive dimensions as well. Those positive dimensions consist of a command to government to take steps to ensure that the system of free expression is not violated by legal rules giving too much authority to private persons. In the hostile audience case, government is obliged to protect the speaker against private silencing; in the libel cases, government is obliged to do the same thing, that is, to provide an extra breathing space for speech even though one of the consequences is to infringe on the common law interest in reputation.

In any case, a constitutional question might well be raised by a broadcasting system in which government confers on networks the right to exclude certain points of view. In principle, the creation of that right is parallel to the grant of a right to a hostile audience to silence controversial speakers, subject only to the speakers' power of self-help through the marketplace (including the hiring of private police forces). In the hostile audience setting, it is insufficient to say that any intrusion on the speaker is private rather than governmental. It is necessary instead to evaluate the consequences of the system by reference to the purposes of the First Amendment—just as it is necessary to evaluate the consequences of any system in which property rights operate to hurt some and benefit others.

None of this demonstrates that the creation of property rights in broadcasting fails to produce broad diversity of views and an opportunity to speak for opposing sides. Especially in a period without much scarcity, we might expect a great deal of diversity and a great deal of attention to public issues. If we have these things, the market system created by law is constitutionally unobjectionable. But it is surely imaginable that a market system will have less fortunate consequences.

We might look in this connection at the Court's remarkable opinion in the *Red Lion* case.[13] There, the Court upheld the fairness doctrine, which required attention to public issues and a chance to speak for opposing views. (At least it required these in theory; it was rarely enforced in practice.)[14] In the *Red Lion* opinion, the Court actually seemed to suggest that the doctrine was constitutionally compelled. According to the Court, the fairness doctrine would "enhance rather than abridge the freedoms of speech and press," for free expression would be disserved "by unlimited private censorship operating in a medium not open to all." The Court suggested that

> [A]s far as the First Amendment is concerned those who are licensed stand no better than those to whom licenses are refused. A license permits broadcasting, but the licensee has no constitutional right to be the one who holds the license or to monopolize a radio frequency to the exclusion of his fellow citizens. There is nothing in the First Amendment which prevents the Government from requiring a licensee to share his frequency with others and to conduct himself as a proxy or fiduciary with obligations to present those views and voices which are representative of his community and which would otherwise, by necessity, be barred from the airwaves.

Thus, the Court emphasized that

> the people as a whole retain their interest in free speech by radio and television and their collective right to have the medium function consistently with the ends and purposes of the First Amendment. It is the right of the viewers and listeners, not the right of the broadcasters, which is paramount. It is the purpose of the First Amendment to preserve an uninhibited marketplace of ideas in which truth will ultimately prevail, rather than to countenance monopolization of that market, whether it be by the Government itself or a private licensee. It is the right of the public to receive suitable access to social, political, esthetic, moral, and other ideas and experiences which is crucial here. That right may not constitutionally be abridged either by Congress or by the FCC.[15]

Compare this suggestion from the head of the FCC in the 1980s: "It was time to move away from thinking about broadcasters as trustees. It was time to treat them the way almost everyone else in society does—that is, as businesses. [T]elevision is just another appliance. It's a toaster with pictures."[16]

The *Red Lion* vision of the First Amendment stresses not the autonomy of broadcasters (made possible only by current ownership rights), but instead the need to promote democratic self-government by ensuring that people are presented with a broad range of views about public issues. I do not mean to defend the fairness doctrine itself, about which we need not be enthusiastic. But in a market system, basic democratic goals may be compromised. It is hardly clear that "the freedom of speech" is promoted by a regime in which people are permitted to speak if and only if other people are willing to pay enough to allow them to be heard.

PRACTICE

A core insight of the *Red Lion* case is that the interest in private autonomy from government is not always the same as the interest in free speech through democratic self-governance. To immunize broadcasters from legal control may not promote quality and diversity in broadcasting. It may be inconsistent with the First Amendment's own commitments. The question, then, is what sorts of regulatory strategies have the most beneficial effects for the system of free expression.

We might be able to generate a First Amendment "New Deal" with many proposals for legal reform. Begin with the fact that for much of its history, the Federal Communications Commission (FCC) has imposed on broadcast licensees the so-called "fairness doctrine." As noted, the fairness doctrine requires licensees to spend some time on issues of public importance, and it creates an obligation to allow access by people of diverse views.

The last decade has witnessed a mounting constitutional assault on the fairness doctrine. Technology allows numerous stations; indeed, there are far more radio and television stations than there are major newspapers. Under President Reagan, the FCC concluded that the fairness doctrine violates the First Amendment, because it involves an effort, by government, to tell broadcasters what they may say. On this view, the fairness doctrine represents a form of impermissible government intervention into voluntary market interactions. It is for this reason a violation [17] of the government's obligation of neutrality, reflected in respect for market outcomes. Influential judges and scholars have reached the same conclusion.

The Constitution does forbid any "law abridging the freedom of speech." But is the fairness doctrine such a law? To its defenders, the fairness doctrine promotes "the freedom of speech" by ensuring diversity of views on the airwaves, diversity that the market may fail to bring about. Actually, the FCC's attack asserts, without a full look at the real-world consequences of different regulatory strategies, that the doctrine involves governmental interference with an otherwise purely law-free and voluntary private sphere. We might adopt a presumption against rigid, command-and-control approaches of the kind exemplified by the fairness doctrine without thinking that the doctrine or alternatives violate the First Amendment.

Those entrusted with interpreting the Constitution should deal with the fairness doctrine by exploring the relationships among a market in broadcasting, alternative systems, and the goals, properly characterized, of a system of free expression. On the one hand, it seems clear that a market will provide diversity in available offerings, especially in a period with numerous outlets. So long as the particular view is supported by market demand, it should find a supplier. The broadcasting status quo is far preferable to a system of centralized government regulation, at least if such a system sharply constrains choice. Markets do offer a range of opinions and options. The enormous expansion of technology means that the number of stations may be close to infinite for all practical purposes. Perhaps people will be able to see whatever they want. A government command-and-control system, if it restricted diversity of view and attention to public affairs, would indeed abridge the freedom of speech. Nothing I have said argues in favor of governmental foreclosure of political speech.

We should therefore distinguish among three possible scenarios. First, the market might itself be unconstitutional if it produces little political discussion or little diversity of view. For reasons suggested below, courts should be cautious here, in part because the issue turns on complex factual issues not within the competence of courts. Second, government regulation of the market might well be upheld, as against a First Amendment challenge, if the legislature has made a considered judgment, based on a record, that the particular regulation will indeed promote free speech goals, understood to include attention to public issues and opportunity to speak for diverse views. (For reasons taken up below, this judgment may be right even in a period in which scarcity is not a problem.) Such a judgment is least objectionable if there is a problem of monopoly. Third, regulation of the market should be invalidated if it discriminates against certain viewpoints, or if it can be shown that the regulation actually diminishes attention to public affairs or diminishes diversity of view. On this latter, highly factual question, the legislature is entitled to a presumption of constitutionality.

Importantly, a market will make it unnecessary for government officials to oversee the content of speech in order to assess its value. The fact that a market removes official oversight surely counts strongly in its favor. The restrictions of the market are content-neutral, in the sense that the content of the speech is not directly relevant to the application of property law. But the restrictions of the fairness doctrine, or any similar alternative, are content-based, in the sense that any such doctrine would have to be applied with government attention to the content of the speech.

On the other hand, a market in communications could create many problems. Take first the case of a natural monopoly. If cable companies have a natural monopoly—a complex question—government "access rights" might well be justified on the simple ground of ensuring an outcome closer to that which would be provided by a well-functioning competitive system. It follows that the Supreme Court should uphold the "must carry" rules. Those rules are viewpoint-neutral; they do not favor any particular standpoint. The Court lacks the expertise to second-guess a plausible legislative judgment that a natural monopoly exists, even if that judgment is ultimately wrong. (Of course an implausible legislative judgment would be invalid.) If, then, we have a reasonable legislative judgment of monopoly, and a viewpoint-neutral response, there should be no constitutional difficulty.

But suppose that there is no monopoly, but instead a property rights regime with a well-functioning competitive system. Even under these circumstances, the constitutional issue would not be at an end. To paraphrase Justice Oliver Wendell Holmes: A system of competitive markets is not ordained by the First Amendment to the Constitution. Imagine, for example, if someone proposed that the right to speak should be given to those people to whom other people were willing to pay enough to qualify them to be heard. Suppose, in other words, that the allocation of speech rights was decided through a pricing system, like the allocation of soap, or cars, or candy. It would follow that people would be prevented from speaking if other people were not willing to pay enough to entitle them to do talk.

Surely this would be a strange parody of democratic aspirations—the stuff of science fiction, rather than self-government. It would be especially perverse insofar as it would ensure that dissident speech—expression for which people are often unwilling to pay—would be foreclosed. But in many respects, this is precisely what a competitive system would produce, and indeed it is the system we now have to the extent that it is competitive. Broadcasting licenses and speech opportunities are allocated very much on the basis of private willingness to pay.

In one respect our system is even worse, for programming content is produced not merely by consumer demand, but also by the desires of advertisers. Viewers are in this way the product as well as its users. This introduces some large additional distortions. In any case, the First Amendment issues must depend in part on the details.

Some Facts

Much information has now been compiled on local news, which began, incidentally, as a direct response to the FCC's fairness doctrine. In fact very little of local news is devoted to genuine news. Instead, it deals largely with stories about movies and television and with sensationalized disasters of little general interest. "The search for emotion-packed reports with mass appeal has led local television news to give extensive coverage to tragedies like murders, deaths in fires, or plane crashes, in which they often interview survivors of victims about 'how they feel.'"[18]

During a half-hour of news, no more than eight to twelve minutes involves news at all. Each story that does involve news typically ranges from twenty to thirty seconds. Even the news stories tend not to involve issues of government and policy, but instead focus on fires, accidents, and crimes. Government stories are further de-emphasized during the more popular evening show. And even coverage of government tends to describe not the content of relevant policies, but instead sensational and often misleading "human impact" anecdotes. In addition, there has been greater emphasis on "features" dealing with popular actors, or entertainment shows, or even stories focusing on the movie immediately preceding the news. Economic pressures seem to be pushing local news in this direction even when reporters would prefer to deal with public issues in a more serious way.

With respect to network news, the pattern is similar. In 1988, almost 60 percent of the national campaign coverage involved "horse race" issues—who was winning, who has momentum—while only about 30 percent involved issues and qualifications. In the crucial period from January to June 1980, there were about 450 minutes of campaign coverage, of which no fewer than 308 minutes dealt with the "horse race" issues.[19]

It is notable in this regard that for presidential candidates the average block of uninterrupted speech fell from 42.3 seconds in 1968 to only 9.8 seconds in 1988. A statement of more than 10 seconds is therefore unlikely to find its way onto the major networks. There is little sustained coverage of the substance of candidate speeches. Instead, attention is placed on how various people are doing.

There has been an increase as well in stories about television and movies, and a decrease in attention to public questions. In 1988, there was an average of thirty-eight minutes per month of coverage of arts and entertainment news; in the first half of 1990, the average was sixty-eight minutes per month.[20] According to one person involved in the industry, "By the necessity of shrinking ratings, the network news departments have had to, if not formally then informally, redefine what is news." According to the Executive Producer of NBC's *Nightly News,* "A lot of what we used to do is report on the back and forth of where we stood against the Russians. But there is no back and forth anymore. I mean nobody is talking about the bomb, so you have to fill the time with the things people *are* talking about." Note the problem of circularity here: What people are talking about is in part a function of what sorts of things are presented in the popular media.

There is evidence as well of advertiser influence over programming content, though at the moment the evidence is largely anecdotal.[21] No conspiracy theory will have plausibility. But some recent events are disturbing. There are reports, for example, that advertisers are having a large impact on local news programs, especially with respect to consumer reports. In Minneapolis, a local car dealer responded to a story involving consumer problems with his company by pulling almost one million dollars in advertisements. He said: "We vote with our dollars. If I'm out trying to tell a good story and paying $3000 for 30 seconds, and someone's calling me names, I'm not going to be happy." Consumer reporters have increasingly pointed to a need for self-censorship. According to one, "We don't even bother with most auto-related stories anymore"; according to another, "I won't do the car repair story, or the lemon story . . . It's not worth the hassle."[22]

Educational programming for children simply cannot acquire sponsors. It is for this reason that such programming can be found mostly on PBS.[23] A revealing recent episode involved the effort by Turner Broadcasting Systems (TBS) and the Audubon Society to produce a program dealing with the "spotted owl" controversy between loggers and environmentalists in the Pacific Northwest. Believing that the program was biased, members of the logging community did not want it to be aired; all of the eight advertisers (including Ford, Citicorp, Exxon, and Sears) pulled their sponsorship of the program. TBS aired the program in any event, but was forced to lose the $100,000 spent on production.[24] NBC had severe difficulties in finding sponsors for its television movie "*Roe v. Wade.*" Fearful of boycotts by religious groups, hundreds of sponsors solicited by NBC refused to participate.[25] It seems highly unlikely that advertisers could be found for any program adopting a "pro-life" or "pro-choice" perspective.

We might look as well at children's television. On ordinary commercial networks, high-quality television for children has been practically unavailable. Instead, children's television has been designed largely to capture attention and to sell products. In the 1960s, the FCC issued recommendations and policy statements calling for "programming in the interest of the public" rather than "programming in the interest of salability." In 1974, it concluded that "broadcasters have a special obligation to serve children," and thus pressured the industry to adopt codes calling for educational and informational programs. In 1981, the new FCC Chair, Mark Fowler, rejected this approach.

Shortly thereafter, network programming for children dramatically decreased, and programs based on products took its place. Thus it is that children's television became "a listless by-product of an extraordinary explosion of entrepreneurial life forces taking place elsewhere—in the business of creating and marketing toys."[26] In 1983, cartoons based on licensed characters accounted for fourteen programs; by 1985, the number rose to over forty. It has increased since.

Most of the resulting shows are quite violent, and the violence increased in the period after deregulation. Statistical measures will of course be inadequate, but it is at least revealing that before 1980, there were 18.6 violent acts per hour for children's programs, whereas after 1980, the number increased to 26.4 acts per hour. Children's daytime weekend programs have been consistently more violent than prime-time shows. Few of these shows have educational content.

More generally, there is a high level of violence on television.[27] Seven of ten prime-time programs depict violence; during prime time in 1980, there was an average of between five and six violent acts per hour. By 1989, the number increased to 9.5 acts per hour. In 1980, ten shows depicted an average of more than 10 acts of violence per hour; by 1989, the number was 16. The high mark was in 1985, with 29 such shows. Violence on children's television has been found to increase children's fear and also to contribute to their own aggression.[28]

Potential Correctives—and the First Amendment

Regulatory strategies cannot solve all of these problems, but they could help with some of them. Some such strategies should not be treated as abridgments of the freedom of speech.

At this point it might be suggested that in an era of cable television, the relevant problems disappear. People can always change the channel. Some stations even provide public affairs broadcasting around the clock. Both quality and diversity can be found in light of the dazzling array of options made available by modern technology. In this light, a concern about the broadcasting market might seem to be a puzzling, even bizarre rejection of freedom of choice. Ought not government foreclosure of expressive options be thought to infringe on freedom of speech?

There are several answers. First, and most simply, we may have a situation of natural monopoly, at least with respect to cable. If government is responding to such a situation, there should be no constitutional problem.

Second, information about public affairs has many of the characteristics of a "public good," like national defense or clean air.[29] It is well-known that if we rely entirely on markets, we will have insufficient national defense and excessively dirty air. The reason is that both defense and clean air cannot be feasibly provided to one person without simultaneously being provided to many or all. In these circumstances, each person has inadequate incentives to seek, or to pay for, the right level of national defense or clean air. Acting individually, each person will "free ride" on the efforts of others. No producer will have the right incentives. The result will be unacceptably low levels of the relevant goods.

Much the same is true of information, especially with respect to public affairs. The benefits of a broad public debate, yielding large quantities of information, accrue simultaneously to many or all people. Once information is provided to one person, or to some of them, it is also provided to many others, too, or it can be so provided at minimal cost. The production of information for one or some person thus yields large additional benefits for other people as well. But—and this is the key point—the market provides no mechanism to ensure that these benefits will be adequately taken into account by those who produce the information, in this case the newspaper and broadcasting industries.

At the same time, the benefits of informing one person—of making him an effective citizen—are likely to accrue to many other people as well, through that person's contribution to multiple conversations and to political processes in general. But these additional benefits, for each person, will not be taken into account in individual consumption choices.

Because of the "public good" features of information, no single person has sufficient incentive to "pay" for the benefits that she receives. The result will be that the market will produce too little information. Reliance on free markets in information will therefore have some of the same problems as reliance on markets for national defense or environmental protection. For this reason, a regulatory solution, solving the public good problem, is justified.[30]

So much for the public good issue. The third problem with reliance on the large number of outlets is that sheer numbers do not explain why there is a constitutional objection to democratic efforts to increase quality and diversity by ensuring better programming on individual stations. Even with a large number of stations, there is far less quality and diversity than there might be. Of course people can change the channel. But why should the Constitution bar a democratic decision to experiment with new methods for achieving their democratic goals?

Fourth, it is important to be extremely cautious about the use, for constitutional and political purposes, of the notion of "consumer sovereignty." Consumer sovereignty is the conventional economic term for the virtues of a free market, in which goods are allocated through consumer choices, as these are measured by how much people are willing to pay for things. Those who invoke the notion of free choice in markets are really insisting on consumer sovereignty. But Madison's conception of "sovereignty" is the relevant one. That conception has an altogether different character.

On the Madisonian view, sovereignty entails respect not for private consumption choices, but for the considered judgments of a democratic polity. In a democracy, laws frequently reflect those judgments, or what might be described as the aspirations of the public as a whole. Those aspirations can and often do call for markets themselves. But they might also call for intrusions on markets—a familiar phenomenon in such areas as environmental law, protection of endangered species, social security, and antidiscrimination law. Democratic liberty should not be identified with "consumer sovereignty." And in the context at hand, the people, acting through their elected representatives, might well decide that democratic liberty is more valuable than consumer sovereignty.

Finally, private broadcasting selections are a product of preferences that are a result of the broadcasting status quo, and not independent of it. In a world that provides the existing fare, it would be unsurprising if people generally preferred to see what they are accustomed to seeing. They have not been provided with the opportunities of a better system. When this is so, the broadcasting status quo cannot, without circularity, be justified by reference to the preferences. Preferences that have adapted to an objectionable system cannot justify that system. If better options are put more regularly in view, it might well be expected that at least some people would be educated as a result. They might be more favorably disposed toward programming dealing with public issues in a serious way.

It is tempting but inadequate to object that this is a form of "paternalism" unjustifiably overriding private choices. If private choice is a product of existing options, and in that sense of law, the inclusion of better options, through new law, does not displace a freely produced desire. At least this is so if the new law has a democratic pedigree. In that case, the people, in their capacity as citizens, are attempting to implement aspirations that diverge from their consumption choices. I do not suggest that preferences should be ignored. I do not say that as a matter of policy, government should disregard preferences for broadcasting fare. But I do suggest that democratic judgments that are viewpoint-neutral, but inconsistent with consumption choices, should not be per se invalid under the Constitution, so long as they are based on a plausible record and represent an effort to promote attention to public issues or diversity of view.

For those skeptical about such arguments, it may be useful to note that many familiar democratic initiatives are justified on precisely these grounds. As against the two-term rule for the president, it is hardly decisive that voters can reject the two-term president in individual cases if they choose. The whole point of the rule is to reflect a precommitment strategy. And to those who continue to be skeptical, it is worthwhile to emphasize that a Constitution is itself a precommitment strategy, and that this includes the First Amendment itself.

What strategies might emerge from considerations of this sort? Here, we should be frankly experimental. Flexible solutions, supplementing market arrangements, should be presumed preferable to government command-and-control.[31] In circumstances of natural monopoly, "must carry" rules are unobjectionable, at least insofar as they are designed to promote attention to public issues, even if these are local ones. There is also a strong case for public provision of high-quality programming for children, or for obligations, imposed by government on broadcasters, to provide such programming. Regulation of violence on children's television ought not to be thought objectionable, so long as the regulation is both narrow and clear.[32] The FCC should begin with advice and recommendations, and hope that these will be sufficient; but if self-regulation fails, narrow and clear guidelines and even mandates ought not to be invalid, at least if they are protective of children. Moreover, the provision of free media time to candidates would be especially helpful, simultaneously providing attention to public affairs and diversity of view, while overcoming the distorting effects of "sound bites" and financial pressures.

More generally, government might award "points" to license applicants who promise to deal with serious questions, or provide public affairs broadcasting even if unsupported by market demand. A point system might well be adapted as a more flexible means of promoting the policies of the "must carry" rules. Or government might require purely commercial stations to provide financial subsidies to public television, or to other commercial stations that agree to provide less profitable but high-quality programming. It is worthwhile to consider more dramatic approaches as well, such as rights of reply, reductions in advertising on children's television, content review of such television by nonpartisan experts, or guidelines to encourage attention to public issues and diversity of view.

Of course, there will be room for discretion, and abuse, in making decisions about quality and public affairs. There is thus a legitimate concern that any governmental supervision, of the sort I have outlined, would pose risks more severe than those of the status quo. The market, surrounded by existing property rights, will indeed restrict speech. But at least it does not entail the sort of substantive approval or disapproval, or overview of speech content, that would be involved in the suggested "New Deal." Surely it is plausible to say that the relative neutrality of the market minimizes the role of public officials, in a way that makes it the best of the various alternatives.

There are two responses. The first is that the current system is worse than imperfect; it creates extremely serious obstacles to a well-functioning system of free expression. The absence of continuous government supervision should not obscure the point. With respect to attention to public issues, and diversity of view, the status quo badly disserves democratic goals.

The second point is that it seems plausible to think that the key decisions can be made in a nonpartisan way, as is currently the case for public television. Regulatory policies have helped greatly in the past. They are responsible for the very creation of local news. They have helped increase the quality of children's television. Public television, which has a wide range of high-quality fare, needs government help. We have no basis for doubting that much larger improvements could be brought about in the future. If the regulatory policies do show bias, or if they fail in practice, they should be changed or even invalidated.

How might all this bear on the constitutional question? It seems quite possible that a law that contained regulatory remedies would promote rather than undermine "the freedom of speech," at least if we understand that phrase in light of the distinctive American contribution to the theory of sovereignty. The current system does not plausibly promote that understanding, but instead disserves and even stifles citizenship.

QUALIFICATIONS AND CONCLUSIONS

I have not argued that government should be free to regulate broadcasting, whether network or cable or something else, however it chooses. There remain hard policy and legal questions. At the legal level, regulation designed to eliminate a particular viewpoint would, of course, be out of bounds. All viewpoint-discrimination would be banned. Government could not say that feminists or the religious right must be represented; it must be neutral on this count. The "must-carry" rules are neutral in this way, as is the fairness doctrine. This is a necessary condition for constitutional validity.

Moreover, many viewpoint-neutral but content-based restrictions would be unacceptable. For one thing, more draconian controls than those I have described—for example, a requirement of public affairs broadcasting around the clock—would raise quite serious questions. For another, some content-based restrictions would suggest illegitimate motivations. Consider a requirement of attention to the problem of homelessness, or to the issue of national defense, or to the problem of AIDS. Requirements of this kind would suggest a governmental effort to focus public attention in its preferred fashion. Such efforts should not be permitted.

At the policy level, there are serious risks of elitism and futility. Regulation should not be designed to cater to the interests of a self-appointed elite with, for example, special interest in classical music or English television shows. Moreover, any efforts must be monitored for efficacy. If public affairs programming is required, little will be gained if people simply change the channel. Aspirational efforts may not work at all. The possibility of failure is real, and if existing policies do not succeed, they should be changed.

None of this, however, defeats the case for a New Deal for speech (unaccompanied by the New Deal's enthusiasm for centralized bureaucracies). At the very least, natural monopoly may be regulated on a viewpoint-neutral basis. Only slightly more ambitiously, government may control the power of advertisers over programming content. Slightly more ambitiously still, government may protect children through incentives designed to require high-quality broadcasting and to diminish violence. My most controversial suggestions involve democratic goals—most notably the interest in attention to public issues and in exposure to diverse views. It is here that I think that common carrier obligations are least objectionable, because they conform so closely to some of the basic goals of the First Amendment itself. Viewpoint-neutral controls on broadcasters, designed to promote those goals, fit well with the purposes of the free speech guarantee, however much they might conflict with principles of neoclassical economics. It would be most ironic, and most unfortunate, if the First Amendment itself were to be invoked to prevent experimentation of this kind.

Notes

This essay draws on my *Democracy and the Problem of Free Speech* (New York: Free Press, 1993).

1. Something of this general sort is suggested in Onora O'Neill, "Practices of Toleration," in *Democracy and the Mass Media*, Judith Lichtenberg, ed. (Cambridge, Mass.: Cambridge University Press, 1990), 155; T. M. Scanlon, "Content Regulation Reconsidered," in Lichtenberg, 331; Owen Fiss, "Free Speech and Social Structure," *Iowa Law Review* 71 (1986): 1405; Fiss, "Why the State?" *Harvard Law Review* 100 (1987): 781; J. M. Balkin, "Some Realism About Pluralism," *Duke Law Journal* (1990): 375.

Many of the concerns expressed here were set out long ago in Commission on Freedom of the Press, *A Free and Responsible Press* (Chicago: University of Chicago Press, 1947). That Commission, headed by Robert Hutchins and Zechariah Chafee, included among its members John Dickinson, Harold Lasswell, Archibald MacLeish, Charles Merriam, Reinhold Niebuhr, and Arthur Schlesinger. It did not recommend legal remedies for the current situation, but it suggested the need for private measures to control novel problems. "The press has been transformed into an enormous and complicated piece of machinery. As a necessary accompaniment, it has become big business.... The right of free public expression has therefore lost its earlier reality. Protection against government is now not enough to guarantee that a man who has something to say shall have a chance to say it. The owners and managers of the press determine which persons, which facts, which versions of the facts, and which ideas shall reach the public" (Commission, 15–16).

2. Details can be found in Sunstein, chapter 7, "The Partial Constitution" (1993).

3. Robert Hale, "Force and the State," *Columbia Law Review* 36 (1935): 149, 197.

4. 376 U.S. 254 (1964).

5. See Alexander Meiklejohn, *Free Speech and Its Relation to Self-Government* (New York: Harper & Brothers, 1948), 14–19. The link is made explicitly in William J. Brennan, "The Supreme Court and the Meiklejohn Interpretation of the First Amendment," *Harvard Law Review* 79 (1965): 1.

6. *New York Times v. Sullivan*, 273 Ala. 656, 144 So. 2d 2540 (1962). It is notable here that in *Sullivan*, the government was not a party—something that

distinguishes the case from most others in which First Amendment objections had been raised. But to see this as meaning that there is no state action is simply another version of the problem discussed in the text.

7. *Sullivan,* note 19, p. 265.

8. It is sometimes so argued. See David A. Strauss, "Persuasion, Autonomy, and Freedom of Expression," *Columbia Law Review* 91 (1991): 334, 361–68.

9. *Columbia Broadcasting System v. Democratic National Committee,* 412 U.S. 94, 114–210 (1973). There, only three justices said that there was no state action. But those three justices may now represent the majority view. See *Flagg Bros. v. Brooks,* 436 U.S. 149, 163 (1978).

10. To say this is not to say that the distinction itself is untenable. We can understand a positive right as one that requires for its existence some act by government, and a negative right as one that amounts merely to an objection to some such act. There is nothing incoherent about this distinction. The argument in the text is directed against the view that an objection to rights of exclusive ownership is a call for a positive right; in fact that objection is mounted against something that government is actually doing.

11. See, for example, *Kunz v. New York,* 340 U.S. 290, 294–95 (1951); *Edwards v. South Carolina,* 372 U.S. 229, 231–33 (1963); *Cox v. Louisiana,* 379 U.S. 536, 550 (1965); *Gregory v. City of Chicago,* 394 U.S. 111, 111–12 (1969). See also Scanlon, "Content Regulation Reconsidered," 338–39, and Fiss, *supra* note 1, both discussing this point.

12. A qualification is necessary here. To decide whether there is a subsidy, one always needs a baseline. To see reputation as part of the initial set of endowments is to proceed under the common law baseline, and the social contract version of this idea (the state must protect certain rights in return for the decision of citizens to leave the state of nature) might support it. But it would of course be possible to say that on the right theory, people do not have such a right to reputation and that, therefore, no subsidy is involved in the libel cases.

13. *Red Lion Broadcasting Co. v. FCC,* 395 U.S. 367 (1969).

14. See Robert Entman, *Democracy without Citizens* (New York: Oxford University Press, 1989), 104–06.

15. 395 U.S. at 389–90 (citations omitted, including a reference to the Brennan article referred to earlier). See also Commission on Freedom of the Press, p. 18: "To protect the press is no longer automatically to protect the citizen or the community. The freedom of the press can remain a right of those who publish only if it incorporates into itself the right of the citizen and the public interest."

16. Mark Fowler, former chairman of the Federal Communications Commission, quoted in Bernard D. Nossiter, "The FCC's Big Giveaway Show," *Nation,* October 26, 1985, 402.

17. The key decision is *Syracuse Peace Council v. Federal Communications*

Commission, 2 FCCR 5043, 5055 (1987). See also Lucas A. Powe, Jr., *American Broadcasting and the First Amendment* (Berkeley and Los Angeles: University of California Press, 1987).

18. Phyllis Kaniss, *Making Local News* (Chicago: University of Chicago Press, 1991), 110, on which I draw for the material in this and the succeeding paragraph.

19. See James Fishkin, *Democracy and Deliberation* (New Haven: Yale University Press, 1991), 63.

20. J. Max Robins, "Nets' Newscasts Increase Coverage of Entertainment," *Variety,* July 18, 1990, 3, 63, on which I draw for the material in this paragraph.

21. The best discussion is C. Edwin Baker, *Advertising and a Democratic Press* (Princeton, N.J.: Princeton University Press, 1994).

22. "Consumer News Blues," *Newsweek,* May 20, 1991, 48.

23. Statements of Bruce Christensen, President of the National Association of Public Television Stations, before the *Hearing on Children and Television,* 98th Cong., 1st Sess. (March 16, 1983), 36–37.

24. "Advertisers Drop Program on Logging," *New York Times,* Sept. 23, 1989, 37.

25. Verne Gay, "NBC v. Sponsors v. Wildman RE: Telepic *Roe v. Wade,*" *Variety* (May 10, 1989): 71.

26. See Engelhardt, "The Shortcake Strategy," in *Watching Television,* Todd Gitlin, ed. (New York: Pantheon Books, 1986). See generally Amy Gutmann, *Democratic Education* (Princeton, N.J.: Princeton University Press, 1987): 241–244, on the subject of children's television.

27. See George Gerbner and Nancy Signorielli, "Violence Profile 1967 through 1988–89: Enduring Patterns," *Broadcasting* 117 (Dec. 4, 1989): 97.

28. See Jerome L. Singer, Dorothy G. Singer, Wanda S. Rapaczynski, "Family Patterns and Television Viewing as Predictors of Children's Beliefs and Aggression," *Journal of Communication* 24 (Spring 1984): 87–88.

29. See Daniel Farber, "Free Speech without Romance: Public Choice and the First Amendment," *Harvard Law Review* 105 (1991): 554, 558–562. Information is not a pure public good, for it is often feasible to provide it to those who pay for it, and copyright and patent laws can guarantee appropriate incentives for its production. But it does have much in common with pure public goods.

30. It might be thought that the distinctive characteristics of the broadcasting market provide at least a partial solution. Because advertisers attempt to ensure a large audience, viewers are commodities as well as or instead of consumers. In these circumstances, it is not as if individual people are purchasing individual pieces of information. Instead, advertisers are aggregating individual preferences in seeking popular programming and, in that sense, helping to overcome the collective action problem.

The problem with this response is that the advertisers' desire to attract large audiences does not adequately serve the goal of overcoming the public good problem with respect to information about public affairs. A program with a large audience may not be providing information at all; consider most of network television. As we have seen, advertisers may even be hostile to the provision of the relevant information. Their economic interests often argue against sponsorship of public service or controversial programming, especially if the audience is relatively small, but sometimes even if it is large. The external benefits of widely diffused information about politics are thus not captured in a broadcasting market. The peculiarities of the broadcasting market do overcome a kind of collective action problem, by providing a system for aggregating preferences, but they do not overcome the crucial difficulty.

31. See Sunstein, *After the Rights Revolution* (Cambridge: Harvard University Press, 1992); David Osborne and Ted Gaebler, *Reinventing Government* (Reading, Mass.: Addison-Wesley, 1992).

32. Narrow and clear regulation of "indecent" or sexually explicit speech should also be upheld, though it is not easy to draw up an acceptably limited standard.

FIVE

The Right Kind of Neutrality

OWEN M. FISS

Imagine a community that has been traditionally all white. A black family moves into the community. They purchase a house. Some of the neighbors are upset about the arrival of this new family. Most are content to show their displeasure by snubbing the new arrivals, but soon the situation changes for the worse. One night, someone places a cross on some public property in front of the black family's home, and the cross is set afire.

Afterward, the perpetrators are apprehended and prosecuted for violating a local statute that prohibits expressive activities (including cross-burning) that cause anger, alarm, or resentment to individuals who are singled out on the basis of their race, religion, or gender. The perpetrators defend themselves on the ground that the statute violates their First Amendment rights.

In 1992, in *R.A.V. v. City of St. Paul, Minnesota*,[1] the Supreme Court was faced with an analogous case and, in an opinion written by Justice Scalia, declared the challenged statute unconstitutional. That ruling, one of the most important pronouncements of the Rehnquist Court on free speech, caused an enormous stir within constitutional circles and divided many of those who have long viewed themselves as friends of the First Amendment.

The focus of the Court in the St. Paul case was not on the act of cross-burning. Justice Scalia did not suggest that cross-burning itself is constitutionally protected or immune from state regulation. Rather, the

Court objected to the specific statute under which the individuals were prosecuted. The Court held the statute unconstitutional on its face and ruled that it could not be applied to anyone, whether accused of burning a cross or engaged in any of the other prohibited activities.

In its entirety, the St. Paul ordinance provided: "Whoever places on public or private property a symbol, object, appellation, characterization or graffiti, including, but not limited to, a burning cross or Nazi swastika, which one knows or has reasonable grounds to know arouses anger, alarm or resentment in others on the basis of race, color, creed, religion or gender commits disorderly conduct and shall be guilty of a misdemeanor."[2]

In enacting this measure, the city was trying to regulate the kinds of symbols that could be placed on public or private property and, by way of specific enumeration, mentioned one of the most notorious racist symbols in America—a burning cross, a symbol long associated with the Ku Klux Klan, typically used to convey the view that blacks are not welcome in the community. Clearly, the St. Paul ordinance could be characterized as a regulation of expression.

In judging the validity of this law, Scalia wisely avoided an approach—once heralded by Justice Black—that would have condemned the ordinance simply because it is a regulation of expression or speech. The First Amendment provides "Congress shall make no law abridging the freedom of speech," and, laying the foundation for his absolutism, Black insisted again and again that "no law" means "no law."[3]

Once a loyal New Deal Democrat in the Senate, Black was placed on the Court by President Roosevelt during the 1930s and from the very beginning, was determined to avoid the ways of *Lochner v. New York*[4] and other decisions of the Supreme Court that wreaked havoc on the New Deal. At the core of Black's judicial philosophy was an aversion to "substantive due process" and the kind of discretion that it provided to judges to strike down laws they found "arbitrary" or "unreasonable."[5] As a result, the Justice rejected any constitutional interpretation that would force the Court to make such open-ended judgments. He sought refuge in literalism, looking for the plain and simple meaning of constitutional provisions, and in the domain of free speech, this approach gave rise to an absolutism.

Black's First Amendment absolutism never received the support of a majority of the Court. For one thing, it was obvious that his literalism was selective, for he read the word "Congress" to embrace both the

Executive and the Judiciary. A selective literalism must presuppose some theory to explain which phrases should be given their ordinary meaning, and which ones should not, and thus could not itself be a form of literalism. Moreover, the kind of judgment Black so feared would necessarily have to be exercised in determining whether some forms of human behavior constituted "speech" rather than "action." Surely, he would want the First Amendment to protect, as the Court indeed has held, not just verbal utterances, "speech" as it is ordinarily understood, but also films, novels, parading, and even waving a flag.

Justice Black made a great deal out of the phrase "no law," but was less focused in delineating what were those laws the First Amendment prohibits. This was no trivial oversight. As Alexander Meiklejohn emphasized, what the First Amendment prohibits is law that abridges "the freedom of speech," not the freedom *to* speak.[6] The phrase "the freedom of speech" implies an organized and structured understanding of freedom, one that recognizes that the state's power over speech is limited but not denied altogether. In contrast to Black's view, the approach of the Court—in R.A.V. and elsewhere—has been to permit regulations of speech but to confine them to the smallest domain necessary to enable the state to conduct its other vital functions.

By its very terms, the St. Paul ordinance seemed to reach very broadly, perhaps too broadly. The Minnesota court was aware of this and, in an effort to bring the ordinance within the scope of regulation traditionally allowed the state, construed the ordinance to be confined to "fighting words." This phrase refers to a category of expression that is likely to provoke an immediate violent reaction by the persons to whom the words are addressed and that also conveys little by way of ideas and thus makes only the most limited contribution to public debate. For these reasons, in a very early decision, the Supreme Court of the United States held that "fighting words" are unprotected or, to put it another way, within the power of the state to suppress.[7]

This narrowing interpretation of the St. Paul ordinance did not eliminate the First Amendment problem altogether, for as Justice Scalia stressed in R.A.V., "fighting words" are still words. "Fighting words" may be subject to state regulation or may even be suppressed, but because they are a means for conveying an opinion or advancing a position and thus part of the rough-and-tumble of public discourse, one must be sensitive to the *way* they are regulated.

What Scalia found objectionable with the way St. Paul proceeded in this regulation of speech arose from the partiality of the law. Initially, this may seem puzzling since in one sense the St. Paul ordinance was comprehensive. It covered the expressive activities of racists of all persuasions that might arouse alarm or anger in their targets, whether those activities be aimed at whites or blacks. On the other hand, the statute did not cover the activities of those fighting racism—the antiracists. Obviously, those fighting racism are not about to burn crosses to promote their ideas, but they have their own symbols or appellations that may cause anger, alarm, or resentment in others—their own "fighting words." For example, they might place graffiti on public property accusing their opponents of being Nazis or they might burn the American flag in front of the houses of those they believe harbor racist views. The St. Paul ordinance did not, by its very terms, cover those activities, and from this omission or limitation on its coverage Justice Scalia concluded that the law discriminated on the basis of viewpoint and thus ran afoul of one of the governing principles of the First Amendment. As Justice Scalia wrote: "St. Paul has no ... authority to license one side of a debate to fight freestyle, while requiring the other to follow Marquis of Queensbury Rules."[8]

Underlying the principle banning viewpoint discrimination is a view of the First Amendment, now almost axiomatic in the profession, that treats that law as an instrument of democratic self-government. According to this view,[9] the purpose of the First Amendment is to protect the sovereignty of the people to decide how they wish to live their lives. The state is not to make that choice for the people. Nor is the state allowed to manipulate public debate in a way that determines that choice. The state must remain neutral between competing viewpoints. In Justice Scalia's eyes, St. Paul breached its obligation to remain neutral when it enacted a measure limiting the expressive activities of racists but not those fighting racism.

Many of those who have criticized Scalia's decision acknowledge the non-neutrality of the St. Paul ordinance, but justify this differential treatment in terms of the substantive value underlying the state's intervention: equality.[10] It is perfectly permissible, so they say, for the city to favor the antiracists because the Constitution, as represented by the Thirteenth, Fourteenth, and Fifteenth Amendments, as well as all the statutes enacted under those provisions, condemns racism. Those fighting racism could be viewed as furthering the egalitarian goals of the

Constitution—they are the soldiers of the Constitution—and should be allowed certain advantages in public debate over the proponents of racism. True, the city is not being neutral, but since it is favoring a position that is itself favored by the Constitution, there is no reason for concern.

This defense of the St. Paul ordinance raises far-reaching questions about the limits of self-governance. Should an individual be able to urge action inconsistent with one of the organizing values of our constitutional order, and should the First Amendment protect his or her right to do so? There is a tradition in the First Amendment, perhaps best illustrated in the modern period by the hostile reaction of liberals to the anti-Communist crusade of the 1950s, that conceives of the right of self-governance in the broadest terms and answers this question in the affirmative. Everything is up for grabs, even first principles. It is almost as though the First Amendment gives rise to a right of revolution.

The Communists were charged with advocating the violent overthrow of government—a repudiation of the Constitution in its entirety—and liberal critics of McCarthyism argued that this option should be presented to the people, if only so it could be subject to scrutiny and duly rejected. In the end, the Court embraced the liberal position,[11] and paradoxically those decisions might lend support to *R.A.V.* On Scalia's behalf, some might well insist that the First Amendment protects the advocacy of racism or, even further, the denunciation of the Civil War amendments and all the statutes enacted under them. No matter what the issue, the state must not take sides or, more to the point, tilt the debate one way or the other.

Over the years, the Supreme Court has struck a delicate balance between preserving the state's neutrality in public debate and enabling the state to fulfill its police power function. As a result, even at its most liberal moments, the Supreme Court has been measured in its protection of subversive advocacy. Communists were allowed to engage in the general advocacy of revolution, but the Court drew the line when advocacy turned into incitement. Similarly, it could be argued that though racists should be able to advocate on behalf of inequality—they can write a book urging repeal of the Civil War amendments or hold a rally on the green proclaiming theories of racial superiority—they should not be entitled to express their views by burning a cross in front of a black family's house at night. Such an expressive activity might be considered a "threat" or "harassment" and treated as comparable to an "incitement"—a speech act that is temporally proximate to a harm that the state has an unquestioned right to restrict. To deny the state the power to interfere with such a speech act is to deny it the power to prevent the harm.

All of this is true, yet it is worth emphasizing again that the Court in *R.A.V.* was making a judgment about the ordinance, not the activity; it may well be that the state has to have the power to suppress crossburning as part of a comprehensive regulation of threats, harassment, or "fighting words." Nothing in *R.A.V.* precluded that possibility. What the decision turned on was the fact that the St. Paul ordinance was a partial regulation of speech, that it covered the "fighting words" of racists, but not comparable expressions of those opposed to racism. It would be as though the state sought to regulate the incitements of communists but not capitalists.

The liberal position on the Communist cases, and Scalia's objection to the partiality of the St. Paul ordinance, is premised on a view that accords a very privileged position to free speech. In effect, Scalia is saying that debate on all public issues must be uninhibited and wide open, even when it puts a constitutional value such as equality in jeopardy. The critics of the *R.A.V.* decision have insisted that such an ordering of constitutional values remains unjustified—in the conflict between liberty and equality, it is not clear why liberty should prevail. Such an ordering of values may well accord with classical liberal philosophy, with its exclusive devotion to individual liberty, but contemporary liberalism, especially as forged by the civil rights struggles of the 1960s, is defined by a duality of commitments—liberty and equality.

The major premise of *R.A.V.* is vulnerable on this score. Yet those who criticize *R.A.V.* on this ground are on ground no more secure in their premises than Scalia's—in the conflict between liberty and equality, they assert the priority of equality, without much more by way of justification. The upshot is an impasse, liberals divided among themselves, one group asserting the priority of liberty, the other the priority of equality, without any principled basis for deciding among them. No wonder disputes over hate speech—and perhaps a number of other free speech controversies that so dominate the headlines today, such as pornography[12] and campaign funding[13]—are so intractable. It occurred to me, however, that it might be possible to allow Justice Scalia, at least for purposes of argument, his major premise—assume the firstness of the First Amendment—and yet find the partiality of the St. Paul regulation acceptable.

This approach is predicated on the view that cross-burning does not merely insult blacks and interfere with their right to choose where they wish to live. It also interferes with their speech rights. It discourages them from participating in the deliberative activities of society. They feel less entitled and less inclined to voice their views in the public square, and withdraw unto themselves. They are silenced as effectively as if the state intervened to silence them.

Seen from this perspective, the intervention of St. Paul might be analogized to that of a parliamentarian trying to protect the integrity of public debate. The city is trying to insure that the speech rights of black citizens are protected; the ordinance is partial because the city has made the judgment that racists do not require such protection, and indeed that certain of their speech activities—for example, burning a cross, but perhaps not publishing a book or walking down Main Street in white hoods or Nazi uniforms—have to be curbed in order to protect the expressive activities of blacks in the community. St. Paul is silencing some to allow others to speak.

In intervening in this manner, the state may be protecting the speech rights of the blacks, but it can do so only by restricting the range of speech acts in which racists are allowed to engage. In favoring the speech rights of blacks in this way, the state is not making a judgment about the merit—constitutional or other—of the views both sides are likely to express, through "fighting words" or otherwise, but only that this sector of the community must be heard from more fully if the public is to make an informed choice about an entire range of issues on the national agenda, like affirmative action, education, or welfare policy. The state is acting as a parliamentarian trying to end a pattern of behavior that silences one group and thus distorts or skews public debate. The state is not trying to usurp the public's right of collective self-determination but rather to enhance its capacity to properly exercise that right.

Admittedly, such intervention is likely to have an effect on the choices of the people. Every regulation of process affects outcome. But this impact on outcome is comparable to the effect on outcome that arises when a parliamentarian insists that both sides be heard. While participants in a meeting may vote differently when they hear both sides of the debate rather than one, this is something to applaud, rather than condemn. The principle of democratic self-governance enshrined by the First

Amendment does not simply protect choice by citizens, but rather a choice made with adequate information and under suitable conditions of reflection.

In an earlier period, First Amendment theorists such as Alexander Meiklejohn and Harry Kalven—the architects of the liberal position on free speech—often used the metaphor of the parliamentarian to define an appropriate role for the state regulation of speech.[14] They conceived of society as one gigantic town meeting, and within this framework defended "time, place and manner" regulations and explained why the "heckler's veto" was so objectionable. Recently, Professor Robert Post has criticized this use of the notion of a "town meeting" and the further conclusion that the state could be viewed as a parliamentarian on the grounds that such a view ultimately rested on antidemocratic assumptions.[15]

According to Post, while actual town meetings take place against a background in which the participants agree to the agenda—sometimes implicitly and informally—no such assumptions could be made about civil society. In civil society no one is ever out of order. Civil society, he argued, could be thought of as a town meeting only if it too had an agenda, but that would require a certain measure of dictatorial action by the state and a disregard of democratic principles, which require that citizens set the agenda and always be free to reset it.

The notion of a town meeting does indeed presuppose an agenda—there must be some standard of relevance—but agendas, either of actual town meetings or the more metaphoric type, need not be set by the deliberate action of the participants or imposed by an external force, such as the state. They could evolve more organically. In democratic societies, there is always an agenda that structures public discussion—one week, nuclear proliferation; the next, health care—even though that agenda is not set by anyone in particular.

Of course, the role I envision for the state as parliamentarian is arguably more ambitious than that contemplated by Kalven and Meiklejohn. For the most part they assumed that the state could discharge its duty as a parliamentarian simply by following something akin to Robert's Rules of Order: a predetermined method of proceeding that does not turn on the substance of what is transpiring or what is being said in the debate, but rather on some universal procedural principle like temporal priority. Indeed, it was Kalven, writing in the early 1970s, who did so much to place the rule against content regulation—the rule invoked by Scalia—at the foundation of the First Amendment tradition.[16] I doubt Kalven would have reified it in the way the Court has since he wrote, but in any event, it seems clear today that the state should not be confined to Robert's Rules of Order when acting as a parliamentarian. A fair-minded parliamentarian must be sensitive to the excesses of advocacy and the impact of such excesses on the quality of debate. Ugly, hateful speech may force some participants to withdraw and may be as destructive to a full airing of an issue as speaking out of turn.

In conceiving of the state as a parliamentarian, and suggesting that the cross-burning ordinance be seen as an instrument to further the robustness of public debate, I do not mean to ignore or slight the additional impact that cross-burning or similar expressive activities have upon the social standing of various groups. Indeed, I will even acknowledge the possibility that this was the motivating force behind the legislation. However, as some of the most honored cases teach, what is crucial for constitutional analysis is not the actual motive, but the possible justifications.[17] Regardless of the factors that subjectively moved the legislators, a law should be allowed to stand if it can be objectively justified—if it serves legitimate purposes. While standard First Amendment doctrine requires that the purpose of a regulation have special urgency (heightened scrutiny), and also that the fit between means and ends be more precise than usual (the least restrictive alternative), validity still turns on what might be said in defense of the law, its objective effects, not the subjective motives of the legislators.

Clearly, this mode of analyzing the St. Paul case depends upon specific facts and context. It turns upon a judgment as to whether the speech that is being regulated has a silencing effect and whether the robustness of public debate will be advanced by the state choosing the side that it does. On this score, it is hard to make blanket judgments. Even if the statute is limited to a narrow category of hateful speech, say "cross-burning," certain applications of the statute may be unconstitutional because the speech is aimed at someone who would not be silenced, as indeed might be the case if the target is not a member of a disadvantaged group. Then the hate speech may not be having a silencing effect, and St. Paul may be unable to justify the ordinance on the ground that it is acting like a parliamentarian. The silencing effects of words do not simply depend on their content, but also the intended audience.

For this reason, the result in *R.A.V.* might be correct, but not the underlying theory. The majority never attended to the consequences of hate speech upon discourse itself and thus never made the empirical inquiry my approach requires. Seeing only a conflict between liberty and equality and determined to proclaim the priority of liberty, the Court struck down the statute on its face because it was partial. The Court did not understand that it was confronted not simply with a conflict between liberty and equality, but also with a conflict within liberty, and that in such conflicts a certain measure of partiality might be acceptable.

Notes

The author gratefully acknowledges the contribution of Richard St. John and Olivier Sultan to this essay.

1. 112 S. Ct. 2538 (1992).

2. St. Paul Bias-Motivated Crime Ordinance, St. Paul, Minn. Legis. Code §292.02 (1990).

3. See, e.g., *New York Times Co. v. United States*, 403 U.S. 713, 714–20 (1971) (Black, J., concurring); Hugo L. Black, "The Bill of Rights," *New York University Law Review* 35 (1960): 865–81.

4. 198 U.S. 45 (1905).

5. See Tinsley E. Yarbrough, *Mr. Justice Black and His Critics* (Durham, N.C.: Duke University Press, 1988), 50–51. For two of the more passionate formulations of this view, see *Griswold v. Connecticut*, 381 U.S. 479, 513 (1965) (Black, J., dissenting), and *Goldberg v. Kelly*, 397 U.S. 254, 276–77 (1970) (Black, J., dissenting).

6. See Alexander Meiklejohn, "The First Amendment Is an Absolute," *Supreme Court Law Review* 1961: 245–66, at 255.

7. *Chaplinsky v. New Hampshire*, 315 U.S. 568 (1942).

8. 112 S. Ct. at 2548. Scalia also objected to the subject covered—that it dealt with racial antagonisms but not, for example, with animosity addressed to organized labor. That objection is more akin to the kind of partiality present in *Police Dep't v. Mosley*, 408 U.S. 92 (1972), which held a ban on picketing unconstitutional because it exempted labor picketing from its coverage, but seems less central to his decision and the First Amendment principles.

9. See generally Owen M. Fiss, "Why the State?" *Harvard Law Review* 100 (1987): 781–94.

10. See, e.g., Cass R. Sunstein, *Democracy and the Problem of Free Speech* (New York: Free Press, 1993), 193. Professor Amar faults the Court for ignoring the Civil War amendments, principally using the Thirteenth as the source of the equality value, but stops short of accusing the Court of having erred in its choice

of values. Akhil R. Amar, "The Case of the Missing Amendments: *R.A.V. v. City of St. Paul*," *Harvard Law Review* 106 (1992): 124–61, at 151–61.

11. See *Noto v. United States*, 367 U.S. 290 (1961); *Scales v. United States*, 367 U.S. 203 (1961); *Yates v. United States*, 354 U.S. 298 (1957). For a general discussion of these cases, see Harry Kalven, Jr., *A Worthy Tradition* (New York: Harper & Row, 1988), 211–26. See also *Brandenburg v. Ohio*, 395 U.S. 444, 447 (1969) (proscriptions against advocating force only unconstitutional when advocacy has become an incitement to imminent lawless action).

12. See Owen M. Fiss, "Freedom and Feminism," *Georgetown Law Journal* 80 (1992): 2041–62.

13. See Owen M. Fiss, "Free Speech and Social Structure," *Iowa Law Review* 71 (1986): 1405–25.

14. See Alexander Meiklejohn, *Political Freedom: The Constitutional Powers of the People* (New York: Oxford University Press, 1965), 24–28; Harry Kalven, Jr., "The Concept of the Public Forum," *Supreme Court Review* 1965: 1–32, at 23–25.

15. See Robert Post, "Meiklejohn's Mistake: Individual Autonomy and the Reform of Public Discourse," *Colorado Law Review* 64 (1993): 1109–37, at 1113–19; Morris Lipson, "Autonomy and Democracy," *Yale Law Journal* 104 (1995): 2249–75.

16. See generally part one of Kalven, *A Worthy Tradition*.

17. See, e.g., *Katzenbach v. Morgan*, 384 U.S. 641, 653 (1966).

PART III
PRIVATE/PUBLIC, WORKERS/CITIZENS

SIX

The Supreme Court and the Creation of an (In)active Public Sphere

DAVID S. ALLEN

In 1972, Justice William O. Douglas touched on one of the fundamental dilemmas facing modern American society: How can citizens rule if they are remote, either physically or intellectually, from the sources of power? Justice Douglas, dissenting in the landmark case *Branzburg v. Hayes*,[1] criticized the majority for not recognizing the press's constitutional claim for a right to protect its sources. But in articulating his differences with the majority, he defined the conditions of "public" life in the modern welfare state:

> The people who govern are often far removed from the cabals that threaten the regime; the people are often remote from the sources of truth even though they live in the city where the forces that would undermine society operate. The function of the press is to explore and investigate events, inform the people what is going on, and to expose the harmful as well as the good influences at work.[2]

The story that Justice Douglas puts forward tells us much about the assumptions that are made by members of the Supreme Court about mass society and the public sphere. Within that story, we are confronted with an inactive public composed of individuals who have become isolated from their political institutions. It is a public that has been separated from political life—a public that rarely enters the political arena and, when it does, lives that political life through the institutional press.

It also casts doubt on the citizen's ability to gather information. Even if an inquiring citizen decided to seek information, Justice Douglas's portrait of public life raises doubts about the probable success of that citizen's efforts.

The trouble with Justice Douglas's short story is not that it is wrong, but rather that it might be a more accurate portrait of modern society than many would care to admit. But more importantly, Justice Douglas's story illustrates what I believe to be a central problem in the popular interpretation of the First Amendment: a confusion between an informed public and an active public.

In most current discourse about the First Amendment and modern society, the two terms are often used interchangeably. However, there is a qualitative difference between the two, a distinction that is often lost as we collapse the meaning of the word "democracy." Justice Douglas's story tells of an informed public sphere—a group of people who are isolated and inactive, but nonetheless informed about political life by society's institutions. Individualism, not community, is at the core of an informed public. It is concerned with protecting the rights of individuals to receive information. The citizen in an informed public achieves her or his goals in relative isolation, requiring only the aid of information-providing institutions.

An active public, on the other hand, assumes a very different type of citizen. At its center is the creation of community. It requires or is constituted by citizens who are active in political life and who possess a shared sense of community. An active public has developed or is in the process of developing avenues that will make that sense of community a reality. Acting is primarily a social activity and a central part of political life, requiring other members of society to make that action relevant. As Hannah Arendt writes, a life without speech and action "is literally dead to the world; it has ceased to be a human life" because it no longer has ties to community.[3]

The distinction between an informed public and an active public aids in understanding how the decisions of the U.S. Supreme Court can aid or hinder the formation of a functioning public sphere. This essay will begin by arguing that much of First Amendment theory, through its link with the idea of an informed public, devalues political action. In the ideas of such writers as Arendt and Jürgen Habermas can be found the importance of political action to democratic theory. It will conclude by illustrating how the Supreme Court has favored an informed public over an active public by looking at the Court's decisions in two areas: the right of citizens to travel and receive mail from communist countries, and the right of citizens and the press to have access to jails and prisons in the United States. It will ultimately be argued that in order to revitalize the public sphere, the Court needs to take seriously the idea of an active public and recognize the distinction between the different kinds of publics. The Court needs to recognize that certain kinds of action are essential to the creation of an active public sphere.

AN INFORMED PUBLIC IN FIRST AMENDMENT THEORY

Broadly speaking, First Amendment theory tends to revolve around either of two basic ideas: It articulates a way to protect an individual's right to speak or publish or, failing that, it grants broad protection to an institution, such as the press, that serves as a stand-in for individuals. What mainstream theory fails to do is recognize the importance of the First Amendment in the creation of an active public.

The desire to separate expression from conduct in First Amendment theory has a long history. As early as 1911, the Supreme Court was attempting to draw a distinction between "normal speech" and "verbal acts."[4] In that vein, the Supreme Court has concentrated on attempting to determine when speech crosses the magical line and becomes conduct that government has the right to prohibit. Much of First Amendment theory is based on the idea that expression is protected, but not conduct. As Thomas Emerson puts it: "A majority of one has the right to control action, but a minority of one has the right to talk."[5]

Where the line is drawn between expression and conduct, of course, varies from theorist to theorist, from court to court. However, the expression-conduct heuristic provides the parameters for our discussion about First Amendment freedoms in the United States. When questions are raised about whether to allow some type of activity, be it closer to speech or action, theorists and judges attempt to fit it into that expression-conduct framework. In short, the expression-conduct debate has become part of the ideology of the First Amendment.

The problem with the expression-conduct dichotomy is that over time it ceases to be a guide to thinking about problems of expression and instead becomes a method of categorizing difficult cases. Action is cast as something that is not to be valued or, at the very least, that is of less value to society than expression. Those theorists who do find some value in action often elect to label that action as expression. For example, Emerson, an influential theorist in the expression-conduct formulation, has argued that burning a draft card is really expression, but blocking a street or building is unprotected action.[6] To label one as expression and the other as action ignores the fact that both are physical, not verbal acts. In effect, when Emerson elects to grant burning a draft card expression status, he is making a political choice.

If the truth were to be told, there is good expression and bad expression, just as there is good action and bad action. Just as there is expression that is central to the formation of the public sphere, so is there action that is central to that formation. Action can include anything from setting a house on fire to attending a city council meeting. One is to be valued and protected, the other clearly is not.

If the goal is an informed public, the expression-conduct heuristic might be a workable option. It protects the individual's right to speak and to *receive* information from institutional sources, such as the press or governmental bodies. In that regard, the metaphor of the "free flow of information" provides an apt image of an informed public—messages flowing downstream to consumers. However, rivers only flow in one direction, providing few outlets for citizens to convert those messages into action.

If the goal is an active public, that expression-conduct heuristic falls short. Using the model of an active public, the focus is placed on the exchange of information between equal members of a community. Citizens are encouraged to collect information and share that information and their opinions with other citizens. Under mainstream First Amendment theory, however, the individual collection of information is often viewed as unprotected conduct. In a democracy that takes seriously the desire to create an active public sphere, the right to gather information should be protected. In that regard, the ultimate choice that needs to be made is not between expression and conduct, but rather between an informed and an active public sphere.

Valuing Political Action

Much of democratic theory is an attempt not to find a way to increase citizen action, but rather to find a way to accommodate an inactive public. Theorists are faced with the problem of either admitting that the United States is not a democracy because of an apathetic public, or finding a way to account for that apathetic public in their theories.[7] The latter option is more frequently used, as institutions are treated as proxies for an inactive public. Often lost in that struggle, however, is the very question of the value of political action to democratic life—a question that for many seems irrelevant or hopelessly idealistic in a country as large and diverse as the United States.

To dismiss the possibility of an active public, however, is to give up on what some believe to be a central component of democratic life. Arendt, for one, argues for the importance of political action. In her classic work *The Human Condition,* she admits to the loss of community in modern society, but struggles to hold on to its relevance for society. As she writes, "What makes mass society so difficult to bear is not the number of people involved, or at least not primarily, but the fact that the world between them has lost its power to gather them together, to relate and to separate them."[8]

Arendt finds political action to be a fundamental part of the creation of community.[9] And while her view of action is somewhat limited, she sees political action as being primarily speech and is willing to make a distinction between words and deeds.[10] Nevertheless, the importance that she is willing to grant to her narrowly defined idea of political action is unique.

For Arendt, the decline of action as an important part of public life can be traced to the decline of the Greek city-state. Action, in the period following the city-state, was gradually replaced by contemplation as the defining element of citizenship.[11] Modern society, in the eyes of Arendt, excludes the possibility of action. She writes, "Instead, society expects from each of its members a certain kind of behavior, imposing innumerable and various rules, all of which tend to 'normalize' its members, to make them behave, to exclude spontaneous action or outstanding achievement."[12]

One of the contradictions of modern life is that the very institutions that were once identified with political action, such as the news media, are viewed by some today as actually inhibiting active citizenship. The problem is clearly reflected in a question asked by Richard Sennett: How is it "the mass media infinitely heighten knowledge people have of what transpires in the society, and they infinitely inhibit the capacity of people to convert that knowledge into political action?"[13]

This contradiction did not escape the attention of sociologists Paul Lazarsfeld and Robert Merton, who in the 1940s drew attention to what they called the "narcotizing dysfunction" of the mass media. They theorized that the mass media were serving as a social narcotic, turning the body politic into an "apathetic and inert" citizenry.[14] Lazarsfeld and Merton argued that people have intellectualized democracy, substituting knowledge about a situation for action.

Despite the decline, the importance of political action to the creation of democracy has been recognized by others. Sara Evans and Harry Boyte, for example, have argued for the need of "free spaces" in society—"settings between private lives and large-scale institutions where ordinary citizens can act with dignity, independence, and vision."[15] It is important to note that for Evans and Boyte, free spaces are not simply places where people can increase their knowledge, but rather the place where people transform that knowledge into action. Evans and Boyte argue that democratic movements change people. They write: "They discover in themselves and in their ways of life new democratic potentials. They find out new political facts about the world. They build networks and seek contacts with other groups of the powerless to forge a broader group identity."[16]

Those who see action as a centerpiece of democracy remain in the minority. Most tend to dismiss the idea of action as either hopelessly unrealistic, unworkable, or misleading. But if it is true that action has always been a fundamental part of the human condition, the question that remains is how the importance of action has been purged from our ideas about the First Amendment and democracy.

Democratic Theory and an Active Public

While the idea of democracy is fundamental to our society, Americans tend to use the word in a very loose manner. There does not seem to be any one definition of what we mean by the word democracy. When talking about democracy, many retreat to the words of the Constitution. But as Martin Edelman and others have noted, the Constitution does not articulate a theory of democracy so much as it details republican values. As such, the goal of the writers of the Constitution was to establish a representative, working government.[17] The fact that we live with no formal, articulated theory of democracy is not, of course, necessarily bad. At the very least, the lack of a formal theory creates an opening for the discussion of different ways to organize society.

Having no official theory of democracy does not mean that Americans lack a shared meaning of the word. Political scientists have found agreement among citizens on certain abstract democratic principles.[18] In that same vein, the democratic ideals that guide policy are linked closely with traditional liberal beliefs of the primacy of the individual. Ignored are the variants of democracy that emphasize the creation of an active, vital community of citizens. At the root of most liberal thinkers is not an attempt to find a way to activate citizens, but rather to find a way to educate citizens so that they might be able to indirectly participate in democracy.

This, of course, is not a new development. The roots of that movement lie in the classic, liberal theory of such men as James Madison, James Mill, and Jeremy Bentham. David Held labels them as putting forward theories that are best called "protective democracy," where government primarily exists to protect individuals from powerful groups or other individuals in society.[19]

In liberal theory can be found a fear of giving too much power to those "other" individuals, and specifically to the community. For example, John Stuart Mill opposed the creation of an all-powerful state. For Mill, society had sadly become too large, too complex for such romantic versions of democracy to work.[20] Instead, Mill proposed a representative government, where people would exercise their power through their elected deputies. His hope was that through the election process, citizens would become educated about public affairs.[21]

It is out of the liberal idea of protecting the individual and the creation of representative government that we can see the current tension that exists in the United States: either admit that Americans are not living up to the standards of democratic citizenship, or conclude that America is not a true democracy. Out of that puzzle, political theorists instead created a new democratic theory—a theory that, in the words of Michael Margolis, emphasized the "particular institutional features, which sufficed to make up for the individual citizen's shortcomings."[22] While it has many different variants, frequently this idea is referred to as the theory of democratic elitism. Under its auspices, citizens are replaced by a bureaucracy that is intended to manage government. The operation of society has, in essence, been turned over to the hands of experts and technology. The role of citizens is reduced to deciding by which elite group of experts they wish to be ruled. For theorists such as Joseph Schumpeter, whose work influenced much of the theory in this area,[23] political questions had no reality for citizens.

> In fact, for the private citizen musing over national affairs there is no scope for such a will and no task at which it would develop. He

is a member of an unworkable committee, the committee of the whole nation, and this is why he expends less disciplined effort on mastering a political problem than he expends on a game of bridge."[24]

Theorists such as Schumpeter questioned the possibility of an active citizenry. It was not simply a question of population and physical distance, although they were of importance; it had more to do with the decline of citizenship. Citizens were increasingly not living up to their end of the deal in democracy. As Peter Bachrach notes in his critique of democratic elitism: "All elite theories are founded on two basic assumptions: first, that the masses are inherently incompetent, and second, that they are, at best, pliable, inert stuff or, at worst, aroused, unruly creatures possessing an insatiable proclivity to undermine both culture and liberty."[25]

The idea of an informed public has a clear connection with the ideas put forward in the theory of democratic elitism. While we cling to the idea that a nation of informed citizens is a good worth pursuing, many have no expectation that it can be achieved, or that information will be transformed into action. Instead, the best that can be achieved is the creation of institutions that will act in the country's best interests, and citizens who are knowledgeable about public affairs.

Toward Deliberative Democracy

Democratic elitism provides an instrumental justification for democracy. It seeks to make democracy more efficient, more manageable. Lost, however, is the intrinsic value of democracy—the hope of generating and creating citizenship.[26] Habermas's work can be viewed as an attempt to find a compromise between the two worldviews—the attempt to maintain the functional aspects of the state, yet provide citizens with the ability to steer action through public opinion. Habermas seeks to "erect a democratic dam against the colonializing *encroachment*" of bureaucratic knowledge on the public sphere.[27] But perhaps more importantly, Habermas attempts to rekindle political action in democratic theory.

Habermas has been criticized for not putting forward a theory of democracy, but rather a theory of social interaction.[28] And while he has generally stopped short of providing a structural model of a new democratic society, his ideas have provided at the very least a starting point to begin thinking about how to revitalize the public sphere.

Habermas addresses a crucial question: While the scope of the public sphere has been expanding impressively for nearly the last century, why has its function been steadily declining?[29] The development of the bourgeois public sphere can be linked to the development of trade capitalism that changed the relationship between citizens and government. No longer did the word "public" mean "state-related," but rather "public" was linked to individuals cultivating their reason through public discussion and rational communication.[30] Often, this cultivation took place in coffeehouses and salons, where, in Habermas's words, "the mind was no longer in the service of a patron; 'opinion' became emancipated from the bonds of economic dependence."[31]

The openness of the bourgeois public sphere as described by Habermas has been called into question.[32] But perhaps more important to Habermas is his attempt to trace the decline of elements of the public sphere. As capitalism became more organized, "the contours of the bourgeois public sphere eroded," and the public sphere's political function began to decay.[33] In the words of Arendt, the political realm was replaced by the social realm.[34] Public functions were transferred, often through state intervention, to private corporate bodies. For example, in some areas "company towns" were created where industries helped citizens purchase homes, educate students, and organize theater performances.[35] The public sphere, having been depoliticized, lost its reason for being.

The role of public readings and meetings to discuss issues of public concern has been reduced in modern society. Public debate continues, but it takes the form of a commodity, something to be bought and sold. Debates about public issues are no longer truly public debates, but discussions organized through the political or economic apparatus. In the United States, this idea is best illustrated by the emergence of political talk shows, both on television and radio, where experts discuss current affairs. The result is the formalization of public discussion. As Habermas writes on this transformation: "[Y]ou had to pay for books, theater, concerts, and museums, but not for the conversation about what you had read, heard, and seen and what you might completely absorb only through this conversation. Today the conversation itself is administered."[36]

While Habermas's early work can be seen as providing a starting point for a critique of the modern welfare state, he takes his ideas a step further by attempting to show how the emancipatory interest of the public sphere can be recaptured. He has linked much of this project to his ideas about the force of communicative action, the ability to achieve understanding through the use of the well-reasoned argument. In his view, communicative action is the heart of the lifeworld, of which the public sphere is a part. The lifeworld is a part of modern society where tradition, culture, and language are "intersubjectively shared."[37] Action, understanding, and meaning are embedded in the lifeworld, but they are functionally organized in the lifeworld's counterpart, the system. It is in the system, the area of strategic action controlled by the market and the bureaucratic state, that the material needs of the lifeworld are maintained.[38] However, the goal of the system is not the achievement of understanding, but rather the goal is winning.

Relying on that formulation, Habermas argues that in the modern welfare state the lifeworld, which includes the public sphere, is no longer vital for coordinating action in society. Habermas writes, "[T]he lifeworld is both uncoupled from and made dependent upon increasingly complex, formally organized domains of action, like the economy and state administration."[39] Political decisions that could once be at least traced to the lifeworld now cannot be traced beyond formal institutions. James Bohman sums up this occurrence:

> [M]arkets and the defense bureaucracy have come to determine, more and more, the questions and methods of scientific research; universities are increasingly becoming integrated into the occupational system; and finally, the insurance industry is increasingly dictating the nature of medical practice.[40]

The result of what Habermas terms the colonization of the lifeworld is that the public sphere loses much of its reason for being. Much of his project is an attempt to find a way to offset the structural advantages enjoyed by those in power. Habermas notes that they have the advantage of "definitional power to establish which goals are going to count as collective ones."[41] In its place, Habermas calls for what can perhaps be best described as deliberative democracy.[42] Relying on Joshua Cohen's description of deliberative democracy, Habermas puts forward a model of democracy that values public argument and deliberation in the formation of basic institutional goals and plans.[43]

Habermas holds open the possibility that "novel institutional arrangements" can be developed to stimulate the public sphere.[44] And while he apparently recognizes the importance of constitutional guarantees, the political public sphere needs the cultural support of a "populace accustomed to freedom."[45]

Creating an Active Public

Habermas's articulation, however sketchy, provides a framework from which to analyze the problem presented in this chapter. If Habermas is correct in arguing that the public sphere has become increasingly depoliticized, we can see the importance of emphasizing the need for an informed public over that of an active public. In Habermas's articulation, the system still relies on the public sphere to provide legitimacy to its actions. People express their policy preference, either formally through elections or informally through public opinion polls, but their choices are bureaucratically selected. Under such a top-down system of democracy, the best that can be hoped for or achieved is an informed citizenry. The need and the avenues for action—for the formation of truly public opinion—have been cast aside, as either redundant or inefficient.

If the responsibility of guiding and influencing policy decisions is removed from the public sphere, an active citizenry is no longer required. In fact, an active public sphere, under elitist formulations of democracy, can be more of a detriment than an aid to the efficient operation of government.

If it is true that current interpretations of democracy are actually hindering the creation of an active public, then we need to identify avenues that will allow citizens to become active players in democracy. It has been argued that one of the ways to secure that public space is through the law. As Arendt writes: "Before men began to act, a definite space had to be secured and a structure built where all subsequent action could take place, the space being the public realm of the *polis* and its structure the law."[46]

It seems clear that the law, at least to some degree, is important for the creation of a public sphere. Law professor James Boyd White argues that law establishes roles and relationships in society. In that regard, the law is a "method of constructing a world, a self, and a life."[47] The decisions of the Supreme Court are an important element of that creation. In its decisions can be found guides for citizens about how to act or behave in society. This is not to say that the Supreme Court is determinative. By itself, it cannot create an active public sphere. Having said that, however, it is not too much to say that the Court does play some role in the creation of public life. And its decisions can help, or hinder, the formation of that public life.

Activating Citizens: Two Cases

The argument that the Supreme Court plays a role in the creation of a certain kind of public, be it informed or active, will be examined by looking at two particularly illustrative groups of cases. First will be two cases from the 1960s involving the ability of citizens to collect information from foreign countries and second will be a series of cases that established whether the public and press could have access to jails and prisons in the United States. Both, I hope to show, are illustrative of how the Supreme Court has come to value the idea of an informed public over that of an active public.

Travel and the Mail

In 1965, the Supreme Court decided two cases that helped shape the rights of private citizens to collect information. In the first, *Zemel v. Rusk*,[48] the Court ruled that the government could refuse to grant a passport to a citizen wishing to travel to a country with which the United States had broken diplomatic ties. The Court refused to recognize a citizen's First Amendment right to travel and gather information. In the second, *Lamont v. Postmaster General*,[49] the Court ruled that the First Amendment did protect a citizen's ability to receive information, including "communist propaganda." The Court found rules that required citizens to officially register with the post office before receiving information to be unconstitutional.

In *Zemel*, at issue was the U.S. State Department's ability to restrict travel to Cuba. On January 16, 1961, the U.S. broke ties with Cuba. In 1962, Louis Zemel requested authorization to travel to Cuba "to satisfy my curiosity about the state of affairs in Cuba and make me a better informed citizen."[50] The government refused to grant him permission, which Zemel claimed violated his constitutional rights. Past decisions by the Court, such as *Kent v. Dulles*,[51] had suggested that the right to travel overseas might be protected by the First Amendment. However, the

Supreme Court, through Chief Justice Earl Warren, upheld the State Department's decision, noting that it was not based on Zemel's political beliefs (as was the decision in *Kent*) "but rather because of foreign policy considerations affecting all citizens."[52]

The Court relied on the expression-conduct distinction in making its decision. Chief Justice Warren admitted that the government's action in this case is an inhibition of Zemel's rights, but noted that it is "an inhibition of action," not speech.[53] Restrictions on action can decrease the flow of information, but Warren did not see that argument as justifying an "unrestrained right to gather information." He argued that prohibiting unauthorized entry into the White House diminishes the flow of information, but that does not mean that entry into the White House is a First Amendment right.[54]

Justice Douglas, in his dissenting opinion, strongly defended the value to citizenship that might result from Zemel's travel. While admitting there were areas where the government could legitimately restrict travel, such as war zones, "the only so-called danger present here is the Communist regime in Cuba." Douglas suggested that travel to communist countries is one way of keeping "intellectual intercourse between opposing groups" alive.[55]

Still, even Justice Douglas reduced the debate over travel to the familiar expression-conduct typology. Douglas argued that the right to travel is at best on the "periphery of the First Amendment, rather than at its core." Travel, in the eyes of Douglas, is more than speech: "it is speech brigaded with conduct." In the end, travel should not be restricted unless there is some "clear countervailing national interest."[56]

Less than a month later, the Supreme Court ruled on another case that established parameters for the government's ability to control the collection of information by citizens. At issue in *Lamont* was whether the Postal Service could require citizens to officially register before receiving "communist political propaganda."[57] Dr. Corliss Lamont, who was in the business of publishing and distributing pamphlets, filed suit after the Postal Service detained a copy of *Peking Review* #12 in 1963.

A unanimous Supreme Court, through Justice Douglas, found the Postal Service's rules to be an unconstitutional restriction on "the unfettered exercise of (Lamont's) First Amendment rights." At least indirectly, Douglas attempted to draw a connection between the use of the mails and speech. Quoting from Justice Holmes's dissenting opinion in *Milwaukee Publishing Co. v. Burleson*,[58] Douglas noted that while government controls the mail service, it is "as much part of free speech as the right to use our tongues."[59] In fact, Justice Douglas found that if there was any unconstitutional conduct to be found in this case, it was on the part of the government—"the actor."[60] It is governmental conduct the Court is restricting, thereby protecting the ability of citizens to receive information.

Justice William Brennan, in a concurring opinion, finds the case easy to decide because the concern is not the First Amendment rights of the senders.[61] Justice Brennan admitted there was no First Amendment right of access to receive publications, but that access does make the guarantees of the Bill of Rights "fully meaningful." As Brennan noted, "It would be a barren marketplace of ideas that had only sellers and no buyers."[62]

Put into the expression-conduct framework, Brennan noted that even if the Court did accept the idea that the Postal Service was only limiting the exercise, not the content of speech, there must be some governmental interest to sustain the action.[63] And in the end, Brennan can find no governmental need for the action.

The *Zemel* and *Lamont* cases illustrate how the expression-conduct test is generally of little help in sorting out First Amendment rights. Despite coming to different conclusions, the Court offers little explanation for why a citizen traveling to a communist country to gather information is not of value, while staying at home and collecting information from a communist country is of value. Looked at from the perspective of the differences between an informed and active public, perhaps some rationale can be found. In both *Zemel* and *Lamont,* the Court operates from the perspective of an informed public, where the primary question is whether government has the right to impede the receipt of information by citizens. But the larger question of allowing citizens to gather information as an aid in the creation of an active public sphere is ignored. Framing the question as whether the act is closer to expression or conduct strips that act of its political nature. Instead of asking whether the act has value for the public sphere, the Court asks whether government has the right to restrict the act. As a result, freedom of expression issues revolve around questions of government, not the public sphere.[64]

The Prison Access Cases

In the 1970s, the Supreme Court was asked to decide whether the press and, in turn, the public had a constitutional right of access to collect information on the conditions of jails and prisons in the United States. In the three cases, *Pell v. Procunier*,[65] *Saxbe v. Washington Post*,[66] and, *Houchins v. KQED*,[67] the Court ruled that the press enjoyed no constitutional right of access greater than that of the public. The opinions expressed by the Court, however, are important far beyond that limited ruling. The opinions also say something about how the Court views the public sphere.

The expression-action test is essential to Justice Potter Stewart's majority opinions in both *Pell* and *Saxbe*. In *Pell*, Stewart argued that limitations on press interviews within California prisons were only established after a violent episode that prison officials had "at least partially" attributed to "face-to-face prisoner-press interviews."[68] Justice Stewart argued that allowing certain prisoners the right to speak to the press turns those prisoners into "virtual public figures," allowing them to gain "a disproportionate degree of notoriety and influence among their fellow inmates."[69] In that sense, expression, which by itself might be allowed, could be restricted because certain prisoners "espoused a practice of noncooperation with prison regulations" and eroded "the institutions's ability to deal effectively with the inmates generally."[70] In a sense, the threat of violence turns protected expression into unprotected conduct.

Justice Stewart attempted to argue that on the question of access to information, the press and the public are equal before the Court. Stewart wrote: "[N]ewsmen have no constitutional right of access to prisons or their inmates beyond that afforded the general public."[71] There is, however, more to Stewart's narrow opinions in both *Pell* and *Saxbe*. He noted that while the press cannot obtain access to prisoners by using the First Amendment, there is nothing wrong with prison officials continuing to grant reporters special privileges in others areas.[72] Stewart noted that reporters are allowed to visit maximum-security and minimum-security areas and to stop and speak to inmates they encounter. Journalists are allowed to observe group sessions and interview randomly selected inmates for interviews. As Stewart wrote: "In short, members of the press enjoy access to California prisons that is not available to other members of the public."[73]

Stewart advocated a minimum standard of equal access. And while he found no constitutional support for increased access by the press to prisons, he also saw nothing wrong with giving the press special privileges. Justice Stewart is, in effect, setting a minimum standard for public access and claiming that press access must be equal to or greater than that of the public. As Stewart wrote: "[T]he total access to federal prisons and prison inmates that the Bureau of Prisons accords to the press far surpasses that available to other members of the public."[74]

Stewart attempted to accommodate "the practical distinctions between the press and the general public."[75] Reporters do not tour jails for their "own edification," Stewart noted in his concurring opinion in *Houchins*. Rather, they do so to enlighten society.[76] Justice Stewart's minimum standard puts the institutional press above the public in the ability to gather information. As Stewart wrote: "[T]erms of access that are reasonably imposed on individual members of the public may, if they impede effective reporting without sufficient justification, be unreasonable as applied to journalists who are there to convey to the general public what the visitors see."[77]

The dissenting opinions, while differing from the majority in the power they would grant to the press, offer much the same interpretation of the role of the public. Justice Lewis Powell, in his dissenting opinions in *Pell* and *Saxbe*, believed the majority's decision restrains the press from conducting its constitutional function "of informing the people on the conduct of their government."[78] Powell argued that the press does not have constitutional rights superior to those of the public, but in order to make the right to publish meaningful, privileges must be extended.[79] Powell wrote:

> No individual can obtain for himself the information needed for the intelligent discharge of his political responsibilities. For most citizens the prospect of personal familiarity with newsworthy events is hopelessly unrealistic. In seeking out the news the press therefore acts as an agent of the public at large.[80]

Justice Douglas offered much the same assessment in his dissenting opinion in *Pell*. Douglas, arguing that press rights in the end are the people's rights, called the majority's decision an unconstitutional infringement on the "public's right to know protected by the free press guarantee of the First Amendment."[81] Justice Douglas defended an image of the press as a stand-in for the public, writing: "The average citizen is most unlikely to inform himself about the operation of the prison system by requesting an interview with a particular inmate with whom he has no prior relationship. He is likely instead, in a society which values a free press, to rely upon the media for information."[82]

In the end, the Supreme Court's decisions in the prison access cases articulate a clear vision of an informed public. The idea of giving citizens access to information for the sake of their own enlightenment or, for that matter, if they want to share that information through interpersonal networks, is not something to be nurtured and valued. Giving citizens the avenue to collect and distribute their own information—information that is not presorted by institutional sources—is part of an active citizenry. It is interesting that Justice Powell, in his *Saxbe* dissent, noted the value of personally witnessing an event to understand it. As Powell wrote, "correspondence is decidedly inferior to face-to-face discussion as a means of obtaining reliable information about prison conditions and inmate grievances."[83] However, Powell reserves the value of that face-to-face discussion for members of the institutional press. The unanswered question is why those face-to-face discussions are not of equal value to citizens.

If we follow Justice Stewart's reasoning, the press can be granted special privileges because it does not seek access for its own edification. Continuing that line of reasoning, citizens who want to tour jails and prisons to increase their knowledge of the criminal justice system are not encouraged.

This is not to argue that authorities should throw open the gates of prisons to the general public. Rather, it is to suggest that in the prison access cases we can see how the Court has appointed an institution, in this case the press, to serve as the legitimate representative of an inactive public sphere. The Court's decisions effectively use the public as the baseline against which all access to information is measured. Members of the public are at the bottom of the scale, looking up at their institutional representatives. In the end, the Supreme Court in the prison access cases protects the public's right to receive information, an essential element of an informed public, but not the public's right to *actively* gather information for themselves.

Conclusion

By framing the debate over the meaning of the First Amendment in the terms of informed and active public, rather than expression or conduct,

I hope that we can begin to see the value of political action to our society. Action has long been central to the meaning of freedom of expression in the United States, even if that interpretation has eroded in recent years. As David Kairys reminds us, the fight for freedom of expression in its early years was not a legal battle, but a political battle.[84] It was fought not with words, but with action. Group demonstrations, strikes by labor groups, and speeches, to name only a few, were the weapons of choice. Writers such as Arendt, Habermas, and others show the importance of action to a democratic society, but we as citizens need to recognize the value of political action.

The Supreme Court, as we all do, needs to ask what kind of society our system of freedom of expression is intended to create. The answer to that question is central to how we decide what we mean by First Amendment freedoms.

NOTES

1. 408 U.S. 665 (1972).
2. *Branzburg v. Hayes*, 722.
3. Hannah Arendt, *The Human Condition* (Chicago: University of Chicago Press, 1958), 176.
4. *Gompers v. Bucks Stove & Range Co.*, 221 U.S. 418 (1911).
5. Thomas I. Emerson, *The System of Freedom of Expression* (New York: Random House, 1970), 8.
6. Emerson, 85–89.
7. This point is made by Michael Margolis, "Democracy: American Style," in *Democratic Theory and Practice*, ed. Graeme Duncan (Cambridge: Cambridge University Press, 1983), 117.
8. Arendt, 52–53.
9. Arendt, 22.
10. Arendt combines speech and action (Arendt, 176). Arendt writes, "Speechless action would no longer be action because there would no longer be an actor, and the actor, the doer of deeds, is possible only if he is at the same time the speaker of words" (Arendt, 178–179). For a critique of Arendt's distinction, see George Kateb, *Hannah Arendt: Politics, Conscience, Evil* (Totowa, N.J.: Rowman & Allanheld, 1984), 14–15.
11. Arendt, 14.
12. Arendt, 40.
13. Richard Sennett, *The Fall of Public Man: On the Social Psychology of Capitalism* (New York: Vintage Books, 1978), 283.

14. Paul F. Lazarsfeld and Robert K. Merton, "Mass Communication, Popular Taste, and Organized Social Action," in *Mass Communications,* ed. Wilbur Schramm (Urbana: University of Illinois Press, 1960), 501.

15. Sara M. Evans and Harry C. Boyte, *Free Spaces: The Sources of Democratic Change in America* (New York: Harper & Row, 1986), 17.

16. Evans and Boyte, 188.

17. See Martin Edelman, *Democratic Theories and the Constitution* (Albany: State University of New York Press, 1984), 14–18.

18. James W. Prothro and Charles M. Grigg, "Fundamental Principles of Democracy: Bases of Agreement and Disagreement," *Journal of Politics* 22 (1960): 276–294.

19. David Held, *Models of Democracy* (Stanford, Calif.: Stanford University Press, 1987), 67.

20. Held, 93.

21. John Stuart Mill, *Considerations of Representative Government* (London: Parker, Son, & Bourn, 1861). For a discussion of this point, see Carole Pateman, *Participation and Democratic Theory* (Cambridge: Cambridge University Press, 1970), 29–30.

22. Margolis, 117.

23. Pateman, 3.

24. Joseph A. Schumpeter, *Capitalism, Socialism, and Democracy,* 2d ed. (New York: Harper & Brothers, 1947), 261.

25. Peter Bachrach, *The Theory of Democratic Elitism: A Critique* (Boston: Little, Brown & Co., 1967), 2.

26. David Miller, "The Competitive Model of Democracy," in *Democratic Theory and Practice,* ed. Graeme Duncan (Cambridge: Cambridge University Press, 1983), 151.

27. Habermas, "Further Reflections on the Public Sphere," in *Habermas and the Public Sphere,* ed. Craig Calhoun (Cambridge: MIT Press, 1992), 444 (emphasis in original).

28. See Carol C. Gould, *Rethinking Democracy* (Cambridge: Cambridge University Press, 1988), 17. Gould argues that Habermas includes nothing about decision-making or the organization of government in his work, in effect taking it out of the realm of democratic theory.

29. Habermas, *The Structural Transformation of the Public Sphere,* trans. by Thomas Burger (Cambridge: MIT Press, 1989), 4.

30. *Structural Transformation,* 18.

31. *Structural Transformation,* 33–34.

32. See Nancy Fraser, *Unruly Practices* (Minneapolis: University of Minnesota Press, 1989). Habermas has acknowledged that his view of society as being a unified totality, as presented in *Structural Transformation,* was questionable. See Habermas's "Further Reflections on the Public Sphere," in Calhoun, 443.

33. Habermas, *Structural Transformation*, 140.
34. Arendt, 69.
35. Habermas, *Structural Transformation*, 154.
36. *Structural Transformation*, 164.
37. Habermas, *The Theory of Communicative Action*, vol. 1, trans. Thomas McCarthy (Boston: Beacon Press, 1981), 12–13.
38. Habermas, *The Theory of Communicative Action*, vol. 2, trans. Thomas McCarthy (Boston: Beacon Press, 1987), 153–155.
39. Habermas, vol. 2, 305.
40. James Bohman, " 'System' and 'Lifeworld': Habermas and the Problem of Holism," *Philosophy and Social Criticism* 15 (1989): 381–382.
41. Habermas, vol. 2, 271.
42. The label deliberative democracy has been used in many different ways. James Fishkin has called for a form of democracy based on deliberative public opinion polls—representative citizen juries would meet to discuss ideas and topics and the decisions the juries reach will count as public opinion. Fishkin, *Democracy and Deliberation: New Directions for Democratic Reform* (New Haven: Yale University Press, 1991). Cass Sunstein recently has argued for a deliberative democracy to "ensure discussion and debate among people who are genuinely different in their perspectives and position, in the interest of creating a process through which reflection will encourage the emergence of general truths." Sunstein argues that deliberation is the basis of Madisonian republicanism. See Sunstein, *Democracy and the Problem of Free Speech* (New York: Free Press, 1993), 241.
43. Joshua Cohen, "Deliberation and Democratic Legitimacy," in *The Good Polity*, eds. Alan P. Hamlin and Philip Pettit (New York: Blackwell, 1989), 12–24.
44. Habermas, "Further Reflections," 450.
45. "Further Reflections," 454.
46. Arendt, 194–195.
47. James Boyd White, *When Words Lose Their Meaning* (Chicago: University of Chicago Press, 1984), 289.
48. 381 U.S. 1 (1965).
49. 381 U.S. 301 (1965).
50. *Zemel*, 4.
51. 357 U.S. 116 (1958).
52. *Zemel*, 13.
53. *Zemel*, 16.
54. *Zemel*, 17.
55. *Zemel*, 25.
56. *Zemel*, 26.
57. The government defined political propaganda as publications that were

"issued by or on behalf of any country with respect to which there is in effect a suspension or withdrawal of tariff concessions or from which foreign assistance is withheld pursuant to certain specified statutes" (*Lamont*, 302–303).

58. *Milwaukee Publishing Co. v. Burleson*, 255 U.S. 407, 437 (Justice Holmes dissenting).
59. Quoting Holmes, *Lamont*, 305.
60. *Lamont*, 306.
61. *Lamont*, 308.
62. *Lamont*, 308.
63. *Lamont*, 308–309.
64. Of course, this is hardly surprising based on the wording of the First Amendment and the related concept of state action. However, a different interpretation of the ideas that underlie the First Amendment could serve to empower the public sphere. For example, interpreting the First Amendment as articulating a positive right rather than a negative right might shift the Court's attention. This is not to suggest that the government should go unchecked, but rather that the emphasis in the area of freedom of expression should be less on what government does and more on what the public sphere needs to sustain itself.
65. 417 U.S. 817 (1974).
66. 417 U.S. 843 (1974).
67. 438 U.S. 1 (1978).
68. *Pell*, 831.
69. *Pell*, 832.
70. *Pell*, 832.
71. *Pell*, 834.
72. *Pell*, 830–831.
73. *Pell*, 830–831.
74. *Saxbe*, 849.
75. *Houchins*, 16.
76. *Houchins*, 17.
77. *Houchins*, 17.
78. *Pell*, 835.
79. *Saxbe*, 859.
80. *Saxbe*, 863.
81. *Pell*, 841.
82. *Pell*, 841.
83. *Saxbe*, 854.
84. David Kairys, "Freedom of Speech," in *The Politics of Law: A Progressive Critique*, ed. Kairys (New York: Pantheon, 1982), 156.

SEVEN

Effective Voice Rights in the Workplace

VICTORIA SMITH HOLDEN

Most Americans spend a substantial portion of their lives at their jobs, often working for someone else. Yet the fundamental rights Americans enjoy as citizens—rights such as freedom of speech, press, assembly, and association—vanish when citizens assume their roles as workers. As David Ewing of the Harvard Business School puts it, "Once a U.S. citizen steps through the plant or office door at 9 a.m., she is nearly rightless until 5 p.m., Monday through Friday."[1]

This condition stems in part from the U.S. Constitution's "state action" requirement, which holds that the constitutional guarantees in the Bill of Rights and subsequent amendments apply primarily in the public sphere of government and politics. With the notable exception of the Thirteenth Amendment (which, without reference to the state, forbids enslavement of any person by another), the Constitution protects individuals against actions by government, not by private agents. Thus, as workers, American citizens are not free to assert constitutional rights against employers, and the private workplace is generally allowed to operate as democratically or autocratically as employers choose. Historically, the main exception to this arrangement has been the protection afforded by labor unions and labor law, which, since the 1930s, have "brought the First Amendment to private employment," in the words of one labor law scholar.[2] Labor unions have been the main hedge against the abuse of corporate power in the United States. They have also served as an important vehicle or protection of individual rights in the workplace, a fact that relates to a key assumption in this essay: Labor unions exist to amplify individual voice and power and, thus, labor expression should be seen as a form of individual, rather than corporate or collective, expression.

Labor unions, however, are increasingly ineffective in protecting workers' fundamental rights against corporate forces set on destroying the labor movement, and labor law has done little to help in recent years. Union membership has plummeted from 26.2 percent of the nonagricultural workforce in 1977 to 15.8 percent in 1993; if only private-sector workers are counted, the figure is 11 percent.[3] The poverty of labor law itself is among the chief causes of the decline.[4] Since the early 1980s, management's aggressive and often illegal antiunion tactics, plus government's spotty enforcement of federal labor law, have eroded labor's rights.[5] Among the rights hardest hit are those that lie at the heart of the National Labor Relations Act and other protective federal legislation: workers' expression rights, including the right to strike, picket, distribute union literature, conduct boycotts, and bargain collectively.[6] These rights, while protected by statute, involve constitutional values and protect the substantive individual interests and goals that allow workers to develop to their full potential and participate in the decisions that affect their lives.[7]

This chapter advances two interrelated arguments: (1) courts and lawmakers should restore and strengthen organized labor's expression rights by adopting a more expansive concept of labor expression, and (2) constitutional protection for labor's expression rights could come through recognition of a link between expression and certain workplace property rights. These property rights could embody protection of workers' basic welfare interests in their jobs and quality of life. They might also afford protection against the employer's abuse of its own sovereign property rights. To that end, this chapter proposes a broader reading of the Thirteenth Amendment, one that acknowledges the essential, substantive nature of workers' expression and other rights.

The expanded concept of labor expression suggested in the first argument might be called *effective voice*. Effective voice as used here includes the traditional definition of freedom of expression as the right to voice ideas and opinions without fear of prior restraint or subsequent punishment by the state, but it means something more as well. Effective voice is expression driven by power; expression that articulates a set of interests and, through that articulation, has a chance to realize those interests. Expression can be effective and powerful if, for example, it is able to set the framework for debate, define and redefine the roles of the participants, give new meaning to old concepts, invent new concepts, or exert pressure to materially change some arrangement, practice, institution, or idea.

In the workplace, effective voice could mean workers' control, individually and collectively, over the conditions that affect their work lives and destinies. Thus, in addition to the more traditional forms of worker expression rights, such as the right to strike, picket, distribute literature, engage in boycotts, and bargain over a range of topics, effective voice rights could be seen as including full worker participation in corporate governance and operation. This could include worker control over investment of pension funds, full access to financial and other vital corporate information and, most important, broad-spectrum codetermination. Codetermination, already widely practiced in some Western European countries, can be defined as labor-management power sharing at all levels of corporate activity through formal mechanisms of participation and voice. As long as workers have substantial control over the direction of the codetermination project (to prevent management from using cooperation to circumvent an existing or potential union), codetermination can meaningfully involve workers in nearly every dimension of corporate governance, from control over the smallest detail of daily work life to major decisions about capital investment (or disinvestment), transfer of labor or capital, product development and promotion, environmental issues, and so on. This essay contends that codetermination, which can give workers direct control over the major issues affecting their economic futures, should be protected and perhaps be required by law, particularly in large firms.[8]

The second argument mentioned above is that constitutional protection for worker expression could be restored and enhanced by recognizing a link between effective voice and property rights, and the constitutional value of certain kinds of property rights. The suggestion is that workers should be seen as having a vital property interest in their jobs and workplaces, an interest that might be called a welfare right. This fundamental property right protects not only workers' welfare interests but the larger society's as well. Furthermore, the welfare right has constitutional value and deserves constitutional protection. Expanding effective voice rights is a powerful way to strengthen workers' welfare property rights. And, in a spiral of rights, these increasingly secure welfare rights can in turn help expand workers' effective voice rights even more, by providing a sound material base on which to understand and exercise those rights.

The chapter contrasts property as a welfare right with property merely as a person's power to exclude others from access to whatever he owns. This idea of property—property as sovereignty[9]—reflects the employer's rights in the workplace. The chapter argues that property as sovereignty, unlike property as a welfare right, does not merit constitutional protection. Rather, workers' expression rights, as well as their welfare property rights, might be protected *against* employer sovereignty through a revised interpretation of the Thirteenth Amendment.

THE LAW OF LABOR EXPRESSION IN CRITICAL HISTORICAL PERSPECTIVE

Through the nineteenth and into the early twentieth centuries, American workers had no rights, expressive or otherwise. Workers tried to practice free speech as a natural right, but they did not enjoy it as a legal right, and federal judges went to great lengths to prevent them from engaging in labor-related expressive activities. Labor law in the 1800s and early 1900s was a state of judicial anarchy in which federal judges unrestrainedly used their injunctive powers to protect employers' sovereign property interests and contract rights against worker incursion.[10]

Judges enjoined not only worker conduct prohibited by statute, but strikes, picketing, parading, boycotts, and all manner of speech, including "abusive language," "annoying language," "indecent language," "bad language," "opprobrious language," and words such as "scab," "traitor," and "unfair."[11] The injunction was often accompanied by sweeping language, such as "from doing any and all other acts in furtherance of any conspiracy to prevent the free and unhindered control of the business of the complainants."[12] As Felix Frankfurter and Nathan Greene charged in their treatise on the labor injunction, the injunction had grown from a "simple, judicial device to an enveloping code of prohibited conduct," through which courts could employ "the most powerful resources of the law on one side of a bitter social struggle."[13]

At the doctrinal level, judicial interpretation of labor relations in this era was governed by the doctrines of legal formalism, liberty of contract, and the at-will rule. Formalism is a legal reasoning style that assumes judges decide cases on the basis of established rules thought to be applicable, more or less directly, in every case.[14] The presumption is that words have plain meaning, and judges must take at face value the language of whatever body of law is at issue. Liberty of contract assumes that both parties to an agreement stand on equal footing and enter into contractual arrangements voluntarily and uncoerced.[15] The at-will rule holds that, in an employment relationship, either party is free to end the relationship without notice, at any time, for any reason or for no reason.[16]

All these seemingly just and equitable concepts in fact put the worker at an enormous disadvantage because they obscured and thus reproduced the actual imbalance of social and economic power between employer and employee. Under capitalism, workers and owner/managers are generally far from equal, and treating them as formal equals can hurt the weaker party in the relationship. The irony is forcefully expressed in Anatole France's famous tribute to "the majestic equality of the laws, which forbid rich and poor alike to sleep under the bridges, to beg in the streets, and to steal their bread."[17]

The classic labor case that best illustrates full-blown formalism and its related doctrines is the U.S. Supreme Court's decision in *Lochner v. New York*.[18] While *Lochner* involved state minimum-hours laws rather than worker expression rights, the Court's majority reasoning here articulates the formalist framework as applied to labor decisions. In *Lochner*, the Court struck down a New York state law restricting bakers (a notoriously overworked group) to no more than a sixty-hour work week, on the ground the law violated freedom of contract between workers and employers, as supposedly guaranteed by the Fourteenth Amendment's due process clause. The Court suggested that such a law constituted "an unreasonable, unnecessary, and arbitrary interference with the right of the individual to his personal liberty [and] to enter into those contracts which may seem appropriate or necessary."[19]

In reality, however, New York bakers, like most workers, were compelled by economic need to enter into labor contracts, under conditions akin to duress; for them, "liberty of contract" had to be a meaningless abstraction. Moreover, the *Lochner* decision masked a transparent instance of judicial social policy-making, a fact not lost on Justice Oliver Wendell Holmes. In stinging dissent, Holmes wrote that "the Fourteenth Amendment does not enact Mr. Herbert Spencer's Social Statics . . . [and] a Constitution is not intended to embody a particular economic theory."[20] Holmes's point is that formalism and related judicial constructs can be used to hide the underlying textual meaning of decisions that are actually substantive policy judgments rooted in certain unquestioned beliefs and assumptions.

It is often thought that legal formalism and its companion dogmas have been discredited and abandoned in the mid-to-late twentieth century, especially after passage of major federal welfare legislation, such as the National Labor Relations (Wagner) Act. Nevertheless, the old dogmas, rules, and reasoning styles and the hidden values and beliefs on which they are based continue to inform modern labor law.[21]

These hidden values and beliefs, as critical labor scholar James Atleson observes, take the form of "unarticulated notions about the inherent rights of employers."[22] Atleson contends that these notions have guided federal labor law and policy since the 1930s, particularly regarding labor's fundamental bargaining and protest rights, but that they originated in earlier doctrine and practice. They include the assumptions that (1) continuity of production must be maintained against employee disruption, (2) workers are basically irresponsible and, unless controlled, will bring anarchy to the enterprise, (3) workers are necessarily subordinate in status in the employment relationship, and (4) employers have a fundamental property right to run the enterprise as they see fit. Even if labor and management were social and economic equals in American society, these hidden assumptions would make a mockery of labor's presumed equality before the law.

Important court decisions since the late 1930s illustrate the point. In 1935, Congress revolutionized labor law by passing the National Labor Relations Act (originally called the Wagner Act), and the Supreme Court upheld its constitutionality in *NLRB v. Jones & Laughlin Steel*.[23] At the Act's core is Section 7, the free-speech clause, which provides that:

> Employees shall have the right to self-organization, to form, join, or assist labor organizations, to bargain collectively through representatives of their own choosing, and to engage in other concerted activities for the purpose of collective bargaining or other mutual aid or protection.[24]

The expression rights enumerated are the right of workers to organize (associational rights), to bargain collectively (a voice in corporate governance), and to engage in concerted activities (expressive protest rights). Less than a year after it declared the Wagner Act constitutional, the

Supreme Court began to limit and redefine the Act's broad protections for labor expression and protest. For example, in *NLRB v. Mackay Radio and Tel. Co.*,[25] the Court ruled that workers engaging in purely "economic" strikes (as opposed to strikes dealing with representational issues) could be permanently replaced, even when the employer is engaging in blatantly unfair labor practices. The strike has long been one of labor's most potent weapons and is potentially a source of effective worker voice. A more expansive judicial interpretation of Section 7 protections would have given workers a real voice in labor disputes, but the Court chose to restrict this right.[26] Over the years, the courts and later the National Labor Relations Board itself have decided that illegal or unprotected strikes include sit-down strikes, slowdowns and related worker efforts to control the work process, wildcat strikes, and mid-contract sympathy strikes when the contract contains a no-strike clause.[27] An illegal strike can either be enjoined, or workers can be fired, permanently replaced, or locked out.[28]

The Court has also restricted labor picketing and boycotting as forms of worker protest and expression. The Court initially found a measure of First Amendment value in labor picketing, in *Thornhill v. Alabama*.[29] Later decisions, however, eroded that protection, as the Court applied fine distinctions between speech and conduct.[30]

Interestingly, while the Court has typically regarded labor picketing and boycotting as conduct and thus subject to regulation, it has tended to view certain instances of nonlabor picketing and boycotting as protected expression. A comparison of two 1982 cases involving picketing and organized boycotts illustrates the contrast. In *NAACP v. Claiborne Hardware*,[31] the Court held that an NAACP boycott and picketing of white-owned businesses in a Mississippi town merited First Amendment protection. The protesters did not lose First Amendment protection "simply because [the picketing and boycott activity] may embarrass others and coerce them into action," the Court wrote.[32] Only three months earlier, however, the Court reached a different conclusion in a similar case involving a labor dispute. In *International Longshoreman's Assn. v. Allied International Inc. (ILA)*,[33] the Court declined to give First Amendment protection to a boycott of Soviet goods by a longshoreman's union, despite the explicitly political nature of the protest. The Court reasoned that the union's "conduct [seemed] designed not to communicate but to coerce," and thus merited no protection.[34] As constitutional scholar Laurence Tribe notes, the contrast between the cases shows "the utter manipulability of the [speech-conduct] distinction and the Court's hostility—perhaps unconscious but quite unmistakable—to the First Amendment rights of labor unions."[35]

Collective bargaining is another area in which labor's expression rights have been restrained. Here, the hidden values and assumptions Atleson identifies are perhaps most clearly evident. Although heavily regulated, collective bargaining is labor's main channel of expression in corporate governance. The last several decades, however, have seen the development of a set of issues the courts have defined as nonmandatory or permissive subjects of collective bargaining. While both labor and management have a duty to bargain in good faith over issues affecting wages, hours, and other conditions of employment, this duty does not extend to subjects identified as "permissive."[36]

The mandatory/permissive distinction is largely a matter of judicial gloss. In principle, labor should benefit from the distinction, because unions can avoid subjects over which they would prefer not to bargain. In practice, however, and particularly in recent years, the distinction generally works against unions, because the kinds of subjects management tends to refuse to discuss are major strategic investment and policy decisions—for instance, whether to shut down all or part of a factory, lay off workers, buy or sell major assets, or relocate. While such actions can drastically affect the terms and conditions of employment, courts have repeatedly ruled that such decisions "lie at the core of entrepreneurial control"[37] and are the realm of management prerogative.

The courts and the National Labor Relations Board have yet to offer a clear reason for excluding some subjects from the duty to bargain. In fact, there really *is* no reason except, perhaps, a set of veiled assumptions about power, property, and innate managerial rights in capitalist society, assumptions that, in Atleson's words, "assume a timeless historical imperative."[38]

In sum, then, the expression and participation rights Americans enjoy as citizens have been and continue to be virtually nonexistent in the workplace context, even though work is one of Americans' most important activities. Equal participation in the workplace and broad rights of worker expression had been the bright promises of federal labor law in the 1930s, but those promises have been repeatedly broken almost from the outset. In recent years, organized labor has been battered by economic turmoil and demographic shifts, but the federal government (labor's supposed ally since the 1930s) has been unwilling or unable to come to the rescue.

The rest of this chapter argues that courts and lawmakers could in fact help labor gain effective voice rights and the power to influence the decisions that affect their work lives. This can be achieved by recognizing a broader set of expression rights and their links to labor's property interests.

The Inadequacy of First Amendment Protection for Effective Voice

The property component is crucial. First Amendment guarantees alone would provide inadequate protection for the effective voice rights proposed here. In general, traditional Western theories of freedom of expression, such as the notion that unfettered discourse is necessary for the pursuit of truth, only obliquely recognize the element of material empowerment central to effective voice. Even a radical individual-rights theory, such as C. Edwin Baker's liberty theory of the First Amendment, provides only partial support for effective voice rights.[39] As long as it is noncoercive, Baker argues, any expression, even expression that takes the form of conduct, should be constitutionally protected if it advances substantive individual rights and goals. Thus, in Baker's view, commercial and corporate expression should not receive First Amendment protection, because such expression does not reflect individual substantive interests but, rather, the exogenous forces of the profit motive. In his argument against First Amendment protection for commercial speech, however, Baker cites as an important exception labor-union speech: "The conditions of employment clearly relate to substantive, although often self-interested, values of the worker," Baker writes, adding that arguments for regulation of commercial speech should not be used "to justify governmental power to regulate labor-organizing or speech activities."[40]

Baker's arguments notwithstanding, there exist at least two potent counterarguments to protecting effective worker voice through the First Amendment alone. The first involves the state action problem, that the First Amendment protects against actions by government, not private parties, such as private-sector employers. Some thoughtful scholars have sought to address this issue, especially as it concerns citizen speech and public access to private mass media.[41] They argue that the state's involvement in writing property and contract laws necessarily extends to expression because of the corporate nature of most mass media organizations. In addition, much of the threat to First Amendment values in recent years has come not from government but from giant media corporations and their wealthy supporters. Owen Fiss, for example, contends that First Amendment values of open discourse not only justify state intervention into the marketplace of ideas but actually require it.[42] Nevertheless, this essay seeks to avoid the doctrinal problems presented by state action question, problems that seem particularly awkward in the private workplace context.

The second counterargument goes to the issue of rights in conflict, specifically workers' substantive expression rights versus employers' sovereign property rights. This view holds that there is no principled basis for granting preferred constitutional status to the former. In fact, strong arguments may exist for granting superior protection to the employer's property rights, either directly or indirectly, by *reducing* the effectiveness of workers' voices, particularly in crucial corporate decisions. (Of course, this view reflects the general posture of American labor law to date). The employer-property argument comes from the natural-law tradition or utilitarian welfare-maximization claims, or both. Property rights are said to be more or less sacred in Western democracies and, in law and practice, have generally superseded minority expression rights. From the utilitarian viewpoint, the claim is that an unregulated business environment will improve material conditions for all.

Given the widespread popularity of the second counterargument, and the doctrinal problems presented by the first, it makes sense to examine in greater detail the property right itself. If it proves true that constitutionally based property rights necessarily protect employers' over workers' interests, then the case for a principled, doctrinally sound right of effective worker voice will be seriously weakened. The case will be much stronger, however, if little evidence can be found to support a largely employer-centered property right. Moreover, if it can be shown that protection for worker expression depends on protection of workers' property rights, then, perhaps, the state action question will be irrelevant.

Property and Expression Rights

Property rights and expression rights are distinct but intimately related in American law. Both reflect constitutional values and enjoy strong constitutional protection.[43] Property rights, however, may be said to be prior to freedom of expression rights, especially in the history of Western liberal societies, where some form of property right has tended to precede freedom of expression and other civil liberties. This arrangement makes some sense politically, practically, and even ethically. No matter how potent the legal protection for expression rights, ordinary citizens may find it hard to exercise those rights unless they are secure in their person and property, however those concepts are defined. Material security is as basic a condition for effective freedom of expression as is a strong charter of rights. Although American law has sought to give a "preferred (constitutional) position" to fundamental civil liberties,[44] the Supreme Court's efforts here have not always been consistent, as the history of American labor law suggests. The rights of freedom of expression, assembly, association, privacy, and due process, for instance, are not as stable as one might hope, and their meaning and application change with the times, the political climate, and the composition of the judiciary. Property rights, however, can both foster and enforce freedom of expression rights, and people can generally be more confident in their speech and expressive conduct if they have decisional power over their economic destiny. Thus, property rights in the workplace can be seen as a necessary condition for effective voice and freedom of expression.

This essay begins to explore the concept of property rights as something more than legal title to tangible goods or the sovereign power to exclude others from what one owns. The claim is that, in principle, expression rights and property rights are closely linked, because, in the workplace context, both promote the ability to pursue and achieve substantive individual goals. Furthermore, workers' effective voice rights and property interests serve different purposes than those of employers. These rights and interests should be protected, because they advance, with little or no coercion or domination, the substantively held values of individuals.

In an important work on property and liberty,[45] Baker argues that while property and expression are closely linked rights, understanding the distinctions and similarities requires an understanding of the nature of property. First, Baker defines the generic term property as "decision authority," with authority signifying "a claim that other people ought to accede to the will of the owner," whether the owner is an individual, a group, or something else.[46] (This definition goes beyond the narrow idea of property as legal ownership of some object or resource, and reveals the expressive element in property, an element that enhances its constitutional worth).

Then, Baker suggests, property is not a unitary concept. Property rights depend on socially created and socially sanctioned rules, and the idea of a natural, absolute property right is incoherent. There is no single property right nor one set of property rules but, in effect, many types of property, each serving different purposes, reflecting different values, and rightly governed by different rules. Baker further argues for a "disaggregation" of the notion of property into its various social purposes and functions, to see what values each function seems to embody or promote. Each property function has its own dynamic and requires different legal treatment. Some functions of property—those that aim to fulfill substantive values and goals—deserve constitutional protection. Others do not. They may have only instrumental value, providing means to certain ends but lacking intrinsic worth. Or they may be driven by externally imposed demands, such as the profit motive, rather than individual values. Or they may involve coercion and domination.

Baker identifies several property functions that seem to involve constitutional issues. Of particular interest in this essay are those of welfare and sovereignty.[47] The claim here is that the welfare function of property reflects labor voice and interests, and, in fact, constitutes a powerful property right for workers. Moreover, this function deserves strong constitutional protection. The sovereignty function, however, is most closely identified with employers' rights and, because this function does not reflect substantive individual rights, it does not merit constitutional protection.

Workers' Rights and Property As Welfare

The welfare function of property is to ensure an individual's access to the basic resources needed for material survival and a quality of life consistent with the standards of her community.[48] Material survival could mean a guaranteed minimum income, shelter, food, clothing and medical care, a job, or, more generally, what has been called "access to the means of life and the means of labour."[49] The quality of life feature could be seen as meaning other property interests beyond survival, such as a chance to determine one's economic destiny through worker self-management and effective voice, or it could mean ready access to schooling, including higher education. Thus, the welfare function of property deserves strong constitutional protection, for many of the reasons freedom of expression is protected. Property for welfare involves a broad right of access to material and intangible resources necessary for survival and, equally important, for individual development and self-realization. A person who lacks the ability to secure the means of survival as well as the tangible and intangible goods necessary for a satisfactory quality of life cannot be considered free, in any credible social sense of the word. Unless chosen voluntarily, poverty is bondage, not liberty.

While welfare rights might be secured through the community's outright grant of money or materials to an individual,[50] they can perhaps better be realized through what is here called enablement. Enablement refers to laws, programs, or policies that give individuals the means of achieving their material and intangible goals, whatever these may be.

The empowered expression rights proposed here represent a straightforward example of the enablement approach to property for welfare. By protecting worker expression, particularly expression directly implicating decision authority, the law provides workers with a way to control their economic destinies and achieve their individual and collective goals. The nature of those goals and the workers' success in obtaining them are not settled issues, nor are they guaranteed by enabling rights. Assuming that the rights under consideration include not only traditional forms of worker expression but broad-spectrum codetermination as well, the enabling rights of effective voice place a tremendous responsibility for self-definition and self-creation on those exercising them. Moreover, because the notion of effective voice advanced in this essay includes joint labor-management control over the decisional *structure,* day-to-day issues, such as the pace of work, are subject to worker control. Thus, in achieving his welfare goals, the worker is unlikely to be forced to work beyond a reasonable speed or rhythm, which could undermine welfare. In short, then, enabling rights of effective worker voice help fulfill the welfare functions of property, by providing the means—empowered expression and decision authority—to secure the chosen goals of the individuals exercising the rights.

To be sure, the affirmative obligation to protect property as welfare has not been an uncontested feature of American legal and social culture. Even in times of economic crisis, when welfare needs are most acute, doubts often arise about the acceptability of extensive public protection of individual welfare in American society.[51] An undisputed tension exists between what might be called the welfare theory and the free-market theory of liberal democracy. Any plausible argument for affirmative protection of welfare rights must confront that tension, and one of the most articulate welfare advocates to have done so is the political philosopher C. B. Macpherson. Examination of Macpherson's "political theory of property"[52] is useful here because the theory is based almost entirely on the welfare function (or its equivalent), and it stresses the decision-authority, or expressive, dimension of property rights. Macpherson's arguments give greater support to the claim that the state has an affirmative duty to protect welfare-property rights, specifically labor's enabling rights of effective voice.

1. The Promise of Liberal-Democratic Society

Macpherson conceives of most Western societies as "liberal-democratic societies," at least in principle, and believes such societies can strive to fulfill both the promise of liberalism (individual freedom, self-development, and autonomy) and of democracy (social equality and popular participation). A major obstacle to the realization of the liberal-democratic potential, Macpherson argues, is capitalism. The capitalist market, in addition to its many inegalitarian and productivity-driven features, requires a "continual net transfer of powers" from some parties to others, thus reducing each person's ability to develop and maximize her human potential.[53] Under capitalism, where resources are normally held and controlled by a minority, people must sell their labor power to the holders of capital to survive and make a living. Thus, most of the society's members actually pay, with their labor power, the resource holders for access to the means of labor. This process and the net transfer of human powers it entails belie any claim by liberal-democratic society to maximize the self-realization capacities of its individual members. If a person is compelled by economic need to spend her time, energy, and abilities in the service of others, in exchange for access to the means of labor and, hence, of life, then her ability to cultivate the authentic human self is seriously compromised.

Macpherson argues that liberal-democratic societies need to revise the dominant theory of property rights and rules, from an outdated *laissez-faire* conception to a practical, political theory of property. Such a theory would grow in part from changing material conditions in Western industrial nations and the world, and in part from a complex, open-ended reordering of thinking about human rights, individual freedom and, most important, the meaning of power.

2. Extractive and Ethical Concepts of Power

Macpherson distinguishes between what he calls the extractive and ethical concepts of power. Extractive power is measured in terms of the degree and kind of command an individual exerts over others' powers and capacities.[54] This is power as domination (or, in its negative form, as subordination). Macpherson calls this conception "extractive" because it involves power over others and the ability to use others' capacities to one's own ends.

The ethical conception of human powers encompasses the individual's potential for achieving any or all of many, possibly unlimited, human ends, and, thus, involves not only the natural capacities (energy, skills, etc.) one *has* but the ability to develop and deploy them as well.[55] Anything that obstructs this ability must be seen as diminishing human powers: The need to sell one's energies and skills at the market is an impediment to and reduction of a person's developmental powers.

Macpherson's political theory of property stresses the ethical view of power and puts access to the means of life and the abililty to achieve self-realization at the heart of the new property right. He contends that social consciousness about property, as well as the social institutions imbricated with that consciousness, has already begun to shift toward greater respect for human developmental capacities. It remains to be seen whether the shift will produce a system of participatory power relations through which the individual can live a "fully human life."[56] But, Macpherson argues, the historical development of the property right in the West points in that direction.

3. The New Property

From the seventeenth through the early twentieth centuries, the old notion of property as extractive power dominated. This notion defined property as the exclusive right (individual or corporate) to material things and to exclude others from those things. The extractive view was consistent with the prevailing Western socioeconomic structure of the era: an autonomous capitalist market society, in which the drive toward accelerated technological and economic development required a powerful incentive for productive labor.[57] The twentieth century brought the transformation of Western labor markets, developing consciousness about the needs of workers (as well as the unemployed and unemployable), the growth of government bureaucracy and the welfare state, new instruments of regulation and social control, and redistribution, however modest, of some of society's resources. Accordingly, property came to be seen more and more as a *right to a revenue,* whether in the form of the right of access to a job (the means of labor) or to social entitlements and welfare benefits.[58]

Macpherson argues that property as a right of access to the means of labor must itself give way to an even broader conception of property as *access to the means of life.* This means nothing less than "a right to share in political power to control the uses of the amassed capital and the natural resources of the society, and ... beyond that, a right to a kind of society, a set of power relations throughout the society, essential to a fully human life."[59] The logical (and ethical) direction for property is toward an individual right of access to "the use and benefit of the accumulated productive resources of the whole society."[60] Macpherson argues that the impetus could come from popular, democratic pressures on governments to ensure fairer and more secure access to the means of labor and of life. While some governing bodies may respond more readily than others to such pressures, sustained popular pressure for increased economic democracy certainly has the potential to alter the collective understanding of property rights.[61]

The idea of property as an exclusive right backed by extractive power makes increasingly less moral and practical sense in the late twentieth century. Property must become a right *not* to be excluded, either from having a portion of society's accumulated material production, or from access to the accumulated means of labor, both of which are still largely held by corporations, government, and quasi-governmental agencies.[62]

The new property of nonexclusion, however, will have to go beyond mere access to society's wealth, if property is to conform to the demands of democracy, Macpherson argues. Property must also be a right to effective political participation and decision authority over the shape of one's own life and that of society. Freedom and the ability to pursue a fully human life would thus become a concrete and practical individual right to share in the accumulated productive resources of society, a right Macpherson assumes would have to be exercised politically—that is, through equal participation in decision-making.

Property, in this view, is an extraordinarily broad right, not to dominate, but to participate in a continuing moral and political dialogue about the distribution of social wealth, the structure of power relations, and determination of where the society should be going and how it will get there. Property is decision authority (Baker's definition), but it is decision authority exercised by individuals joining together to influence broad-scale social policy and welfare, as well to handle matters of everyday life. Macpherson's political theory of property, then, can be seen as an expansion and elaboration of the welfare function of property.

4. The New Property Right and Workers' Expression Rights

The welfare function is closely intertwined with the system of worker expression rights proposed in this essay. If there is any validity to Macpherson's suggestion that American thought and practice is moving toward a view of property as individual decision authority, substantive political participation, and a right to share in society's accumulated wealth, then effective worker voice could be a logical medium for the "new property," and the workplace an important venue for its exercise.

In fact, effective voice in the workplace could perhaps be the principal vehicle for the development and realization of welfare property rights through enablement, which rights, in turn, could reinforce and strengthen effective voice. This is particularly true if effective voice is extended to include broad-spectrum codetermination. Consider, for instance, the possibilities of workers' decision authority, individually and through union representation, over pension-fund investment, corporate strategy within their own firms, and the day-to-day routines of the workplace. Some critics might fear such circumstances would bring economic and social chaos, rather than advancement of welfare. But these fears miss the point and lack cogent grounding in theory and fact. If one sees property for welfare in Macpherson's terms, as an individual right of nonexclusion from society's accumulated wealth and as a political process of popular decision making, then broad-spectrum codetermination (and the more traditional worker expression rights) could fit the concept admirably. A system of participatory welfare rights should not end at the workplace. But the workplace might be a reasonable place to begin.

THE SOVEREIGNTY FUNCTION AND WORKERS' RIGHTS

The sovereignty function of property is characterized by the absolute power to exclude others from access to whatever one owns, including the means of life and of labor. For some, sovereignty is property's defining characteristic. For instance, William Blackstone, the eighteenth-century English jurist, called property "that sole and despotic dominion which one man claims and exercises over the external things of the world in total exclusion of the right of any other individual in the universe."[63]

Sovereign power often has an invasive dimension and can have a greater and possibly more adverse impact on the person subject to this power than on the person exercising it. As Baker puts it, "[t]he owner exercises power by making use of another person's needs or desires. The person influenced engages in a performance that she would prefer to avoid but for the fact that the performance is necessary to secure the exchange."[64] The property at issue may be of little or no value to the owner, but it will be worth a great deal to the person who needs or wants it, Baker notes. Thus, the property-as-sovereignty relationship tends to be one of domination and dependence.[65]

If we can agree that the Constitution protects substantive individual freedoms, it is difficult to claim that it protects one person's freedom to dominate another. On the contrary, constitutional principles should shield individuals from domination, so they can enjoy the benefits of liberty. To the extent the employer is dominant, sovereign power in an employment relationship should not receive constitutional protection. Currently, the employer has the power to hire and fire and to make both long-term and short-term decisions that affect employees' well-being and economic futures. Put another way, the employer exerts sovereign authority over workers by controlling access to their means of life and of labor. This is not altered by a worker's consent to enter into an employment relationship (although it may be modified by an employment contract).

This chapter argues that not only should employers' sovereign property rights be denied constitutional protection, but workers' rights and property interests should be constitutionally protected *against* the employer's exercise of sovereign power as well. Such protection might be accomplished without abandoning the Constitution's state action requirement. As noted earlier, under the state action doctrine, the Constitution protects individuals against domination by others, but, in most current interpretations of that document's provisions, the protection is against government, not private, domination. The main exception is the Thirteenth Amendment, which holds: "Neither slavery nor involuntary servitude . . . shall exist within the United States, or any place subject to their jurisdiction." Enacted and ratified immediately after the American Civil War, the amendment includes the same elastic language characteristic of all the constitutional amendments, language that requires extensive interpretation. (What, for instance, is covered in the expression "involuntary servitude"?) But, unlike some of the other amendments, the Thirteenth has not been read broadly to protect a range of individual rights.[66]

There is no principled reason, however, that the Thirteenth Amendment cannot be interpreted to protect basic labor rights against the employer's sovereign authority, just as the Fourteenth Amendment has been read to protect fundamental individual rights against state abridgement.[67] Expansion of the Thirteenth Amendment to cover basic labor rights, such as free speech, association, participation, and decision authority, could come through an incorporation process such as has occurred with the Fourteenth Amendment.

In a series of cases from 1920 through 1931,[68] the U.S. Supreme Court ruled that the due process clause of the Fourteenth Amendment *incorporated* the freedoms guaranteed in the Bill of Rights, and thus the states, as well as the federal government, were bound by its provisions.[69] As a result, the scope of First Amendment protection in particular was enormously expanded. There was no obvious precedent or doctrinal necessity for incorporating the First Amendment through the Fourteenth. Rather, some Supreme Court justices apparently came to perceive a need to protect free expression from state, as well as federal, abridgment and chose the due process clause of the Fourteenth Amendment as the appropriate legal mechanism.

Likewise, a need arguably exists to protect workers' expression and due process rights against the sovereign power of employers, protection beyond that afforded by state and federal labor laws and the common law. One way to provide constitutional protection for workers' fundamental rights as workers (rather than as citizens) might be to incorporate those rights through the Thirteenth Amendment, just as the rights of free speech and press were incorporated through the Fourteenth Amendment. The Thirteenth Amendment lacks a state action requirement, so there is in principle no textual problem with protecting workers' rights from employer abridgment.

Moreover, the Thirteenth Amendment's "involuntary servitude" clause is no more and no less ambiguous and flexible than the Fourteenth

Amendment's due process clause. Involuntary servitude could mean anything from actual slavery (the narrow definition) to conditions that make work excessively hazardous, insecure, abusive, or otherwise interfere with the dignity and self-determination of the worker (the broad definition). Similarly, the Fourteenth Amendment's provision that no state "shall ... deprive any person of life, liberty, or property, without due process of law" can be read to refer to a formal, procedural right (the narrow definition) or a right to private, sovereign property (an ideological definition) or a range of individual rights from freedom of expression to bodily privacy (the broad definition). While courts in the past have often interpreted the Fourteenth Amendment narrowly, or ideologically, or both, contemporary courts have tended to apply a broader reading. It would perhaps not be too great a doctrinal reach for the Supreme Court to incorporate a broad range of workers' rights against employer sovereignty under the Thirteenth Amendment.

A judicial determination that workers' rights merit constitutional protection would not mean that courts would be in the business of writing labor law. Rather, it would serve as a reminder that fundamental rights do in fact apply in the workplace and would give Congress and other legislative bodies clearer direction in writing and revising labor law.

Some might object that such an expansive reading of the Thirteenth Amendment would be inconsistent with Congressional intent to abolish African-American slavery only. Indeed, there is no evidence that labor-rights issues arose in the course of Congressional debates over the enactment and ratification of the Thirteenth Amendment. Nevertheless, evidence does exist that at least some backers of the amendment believed in workers' rights to organize and protest, as part of the free-labor system the amendment contemplated.[70]

If we understand the current social world as one in which workers are generally disenfranchised and powerless, then it is perhaps not unreasonable nor a violation of constitutional integrity to find a remedy in Thirteenth Amendment protection against the sovereign power of private authorities.

CONCLUSION

The central purpose of this chapter has been to set forth a principled basis for protection of workers' effective voice rights and to do so by establishing a connection to workers' property rights. Such protection requires support beyond that afforded by traditional interpretations of the First Amendment. The chapter argues that property rights and expression rights are closely linked because they both reflect important constitutional values. Indeed, property rights should be a necessary condition for the effective exercise of expression rights. By stressing one of the chief functions of property—the welfare function—and linking that function to workers' effective voice rights and interests, an argument has been advanced for a new kind of property right in the workplace, one that emphasizes the welfare rights of workers rather than the more traditional property rights of employers. This property right might serve as the basis for protecting the effective voice rights of American workers. Workers' expression and property rights might also receive protection through a liberal interpretation of the sovereignty function of property. The sovereignty function, which involves domination of one party by another, merits little if any constitutional protection, and sovereignty is far more closely identified with employers than with workers in the typical American workplace. But the Thirteenth Amendment, which lacks a state action requirement, could be the doctrinal vehicle for protecting workers against employers' exercise of sovereign power.

Notes

1. David W. Ewing, *Freedom Inside the Organization* (New York: E. P. Dutton, 1977), 3.

2. Clyde Summers, "The Privatization of Personal Freedoms and Enrichment of Democracy: Some Lessons from Labor Law," *University of Illinois Law Review* (1986): 697.

3. Aaron Bernstein, "Why America Needs Unions," *Business Week,* May 23, 1994, 70–82, citing Leo Troy, Rutgers University, Bureau of Labor Statistics.

4. Paul C. Weiler, "Promises to Keep: Securing Workers' Rights to Self-Organization Under the National Labor Relations Act," *Harvard Law Review* 96 (1983): 1773. Other causes of the drop in union membership include economic decline in heavy industry, manufacturing, and other areas of traditional union strength; the geographic shift of industry and finance capital from heavily unionized areas to the largely nonunion South and Southwest; the exporting of jobs and outsourcing of work to foreign countries where labor is cheaper; deregulation pressures; the popularity of debt financing in the 1980s; the ambiguous trade policies of the 1970s and onward; employers' eagerness to provoke strikes and replace the strikers with nonunion workers, and growing employer

resistance to traditional collective bargaining protocols and issues. Patricia Cayo Sexton, *The War on Labor and the Left* (Boulder, Colo.: Westview Press, 1991); Paul C. Weiler, *Governing the Workplace: The Future of Labor and Employment Law* (Cambridge: Harvard University Press, 1990).

5. See Richard Freeman and James Medoff, *What Do Unions Do?* (New York: Basic Books, 1984).

6. The main source of statutory protection is the National Labor Relations (Wagner) Act, which was enacted in 1935 (current version at 29 U.S.C., sections 151–168 (1988)). The NLRA has since been amended by the Labor Management Relations (Taft-Hartley) Act (current version at 19 U.S.C., sections 141–187 (1988)). The constitutionality of the NLRA was upheld by the U.S. Supreme Court in *NLRB v. Jones & Laughlin Steel Corp.*, 301 U.S. 1 (1937). Critics have argued that the ideal of industrial democracy contemplated by the NLRA has been undercut by later legislation and court decisions. See Karl Klare, "Judicial Deradicalization of the Wagner Act and the Origins of Modern Legal Consciousness, 1937–1941," *Minnesota Law Review* 62 (1978): 265; Katherine Stone, "The Post-War Paradigm in American Labor Law," *Yale Law Journal* 90 (1981): 1509.

7. The idea that freedom of expression and other fundamental constitutional rights embody substantive individual values and permit self-realization and democratic participation is based on C. Edwin Baker's "liberty theory." See Baker, "Scope of the First Amendment Freedom of Speech," *UCLA Law Review* 25 (1978): 965, and *Human Liberty and Freedom of Speech* (New York: Oxford University Press, 1989). Baker has also argued that labor expression, unlike that of corporations, reflects individual, rather that collective, values. See Baker, "Commercial Speech: A Problem in the Theory of Freedom," *Iowa Law Review* 62 (1976): 1, and "Advertising and a Democratic Press," *University of Pennsylvania Law Review* 140 (June 1992): 2097.

8. In June 1994, the U.S. Labor and Commerce departments issued a joint report on the American workplace that recommended, among other things, movement toward a more cooperative, participatory workplace to improve American competitiveness and preserve living standards. See Catherine S. Manegold, "Study Warns of Growing Underclass of the Unskilled," *New York Times*, June 3, 1994, A9. The European "works council" model, in which workers elect representatives to voice their interests in management decisions, has gained some support in the administration of President Bill Clinton. Bernstein, "Why America Needs Unions," 71, 74.

9. C. Edwin Baker, "Property and Its Relation to Constitutionally Protected Liberty," *University of Pennsylvania Law Review* 134 (April 1986): 751.

10. See Felix Frankfurter and Nathan Greene, *The Labor Injunction* (New York: Macmillan, 1930). Two years after publication of this work, Congress

passed the Norris-LaGuardia Act, 47 Stat. 70 (1932); 29 U.S.C. sections 101–15 (1982), prohibiting federal courts from issuing injunctions in labor disputes except under certain highly restricted circumstances.

11. Frankfurter and Greene, *The Labor Injunction*, 98.

12. *The Labor Injunction*, 99, citing *Houston & Texas Central R. Co. v. Machinists* (S.D. Texas, 1911), unreported; *American Steel Foundries v. Tri-City Trades Council, et al.* (D.C. Ill., June 9, 1914, but quoted in an appeal, 238 Fed. 728 (C.C.A. 7th, 1916).

13. Frankfurter and Greene, *The Labor Injunction*, 200, 81.

14. See Roberto Unger, *Knowledge and Politics* (New York: Free Press, 1975), 92–94; Steven J. Burton, *An Introduction to Law and Legal Reasoning* (Boston: Little, Brown & Co., 1985), 169–170.

15. See Alan Fox, *Beyond Contract: Work, Power, and Trust Relations* (London: Faber & Faber, 1974), 248–296; P. S. Atiyah, *The Rise and Fall of Freedom of Contract* (Oxford: Clarendon Press, 1979), 602–626, 681–715; Phillip Selznick, *Law, Society, and Industrial Justice* (New York: Russell Sage Foundation, 1969), 213–240.

16. See Lawrence Blades, "Employment at Will vs. Individual Freedom," *Columbia Law Review* 67 (1967): 1404; Jay Feinman, "The Development of the Employment at Will Rule," *American Journal of Legal History* 20 (1976): 118.

17. France, "The Red Lily," in *The Six Greatest Novels of Anatole France* (New York: Literary Guild, 1914), 837.

18. 198 U.S. 45 (1905).

19. *Lochner*, 53.

20. *Lochner*, 75.

21. See Harry Wellington, *Labor and the Legal Process* (New Haven: Yale University Press, 1966), 11 ("The rhetoric of the courts [in certain nineteenth-century labor cases] is intriguing because the problems rehearsed are so plainly the ancestors of our own.").

22. James B. Atleson, *Values and Assumptions in American Labor Law* (Amherst: University of Massachusetts Press, 1983), 6.

23. 301 U.S. 1 (1937).

24. 49 Stat. 449 (1935), as amended; 29 U.S.C. sections 151–69 (1982), section 7 ("Rights of Employees").

25. 304 U.S. 333 (1938).

26. See Klare, "Judicial Deradicalization of the Wagner Act and the Origins of Modern Legal Consciousness," 265.

27. See *NLRB v. Fansteel Metallurgical Corp.*, 306 U.S. 240 (1939); *NLRB v. Montgomery Ward & Co.*, 157 F. 2d 486 (8th Cir. 1946); *NLRB v. Elk Lumber*, 91 NLRB 333 (1950); *NLRB v. Draper Corp.*, 145 F. 2d 199 (4th Cir. 1944); and *Indianapolis Power & Light Co.*, 273 NLRB 1715 (1985).

28. See *NLRB v. Mackay Radio and Tel. Co.,* 304 U.S. 333 (1938); *Darling & Co.,* 171 NLRB 801 (1968); and *Harter Equip. Inc.,* 280 NLRB 71 (1986).
29. 310 U.S. 88 (1940).
30. See *Teamsters Local 695 v. Vogt,* 354 U.S. 384 (1957) (summarizing a long line of picketing cases and upholding a Texas court's injunction against union picketing publicizing the nonunion status of the employer's workers).
31. 458 U.S. 886 (1982).
32. *Claiborne Hardware,* 910.
33. 456 U.S. 212 (1982).
34. *ILA,* 226–227 (footnotes omitted).
35. "Speech As Power," in *Constitutional Choices* (Cambridge: Harvard University Press, 1985).
36. See Donna Sockell and J. Delaney, "The Scope of Bargaining: Who Wins When Fewer Issues Are Mandatory Bargaining Subjects," *Labor Studies Journal* (1986): 101.
37. See *First National Maintenance Corp. v. NLRB,* 452 U.S. 666 (1981); *Darlington Mfg. Co. v. NLRB,* 397 F. 2d 760 (4th Cir.), cert. denied, 393 U.S. 1023 (1968); *Air Line Pilots Assn., et al. v. Eastern Air Lines,* 863 F. 2d 891 (D.C. Cir. 1988); *Air Line Pilots Assn., et al. v. Eastern Air Lines,* 701 F. Supp. 865 (D.D.C. 1988); and *Otis Elevator Co.,* 469 NLRB 891 (1984).
38. Atleson, *Values and Assumptions,* 122.
39. See Baker, *Human Liberty and Freedom of Speech,* and "Scope of the First Amendment Freedom of Speech."
40. Baker, "Commercial Speech," 40.
41. See J. M. Balkin, "Some Realism about Pluralism: Legal Realist Approaches to the First Amendment," *Duke Law Journal* (June 1990): 375; Jerome Barron, "Access to the Press: A New First Amendment Right?" *Harvard Law Review* 80 (1967): 1641; Owen Fiss, "Why the State?" *Harvard Law Review* 100 (1987): 781; Cass Sunstein, "Free Speech Now," *University of Chicago Law Review* 59 (1992): 255.
42. Fiss, "Why the State?" 787.
43. See, *e.g.,* Clyde Summers, "The Privatization of Personal Freedoms and Enrichment of Democracy," 689, 693 ("The right to property, . . . like freedom of speech and right of assembly, is also a constitutionally protected value.")
44. See *U.S. v. Carolene Products,* 304 U.S. 144, 152 (n. 4) (1938).
45. Baker, "Property," 741.
46. Baker, "Property," 743.
47. Baker also identifies the functions of use, personhood, allocation, and protection. See Baker, "Property," 745.
48. Baker, "Property," 745.

49. C. B. Macpherson, *Democratic Theory: Essays in Retrieval* (Oxford: Oxford University Press, 1973), 120.

50. The grant could take the form of a guaranteed annual income (regardless of factors such as the individual's merit, his social or family status, or his productivity level), or it might be targeted at a specific set of needs—for instance, free education as far as the individual cares to pursue it, or free food, transportation, health care, housing, and so on. Or it could be some combination of these. This method supplies individuals with certain ready-made ends, ends the community deems necessary for a decent standard of living.

51. During the Great Depression, even socially minded groups such as the American Civil Liberties Union and the American Federation of Labor questioned the wisdom of enabling welfare legislation such as the National Labor Relations Act. See Jerold S. Auerbach, *Labor and Liberty: The LaFollette Committee and the New Deal* (New York: Bobbs-Merrill Co., 1966).

52. See Macpherson, *Democratic Theory*, 120–156.

53. Macpherson, 10–11.

54. Macpherson, 8–9.

55. Macpherson, 40–42.

56. Macpherson, 140.

57. Macpherson, 129–31.

58. Macpherson, 129–31.

59. Macpherson, 123.

60. Macpherson, 133.

61. For a discussion of the effects of mass movements on economic policy, see Francis Fox Piven and Richard Cloward, *Poor People's Movements: Why They Succeed, How They Fail* (New York: Vintage, 1979).

62. See *Democratic Theory*, 136.

63. Blackstone, *Commentaries on the Laws of England*, 2.

64. Baker, "Property," 752.

65. In this account, sovereignty seems almost an unjustified function of property for those who value social and economic equality. Sometimes, however, the exercise of sovereign power involves reciprocal, voluntary, socially useful exchanges. For instance, the sovereignty function of property may exist, to a greater or lesser degree, in the allocation of labor and capital and may help provide incentives for productivity.

66. The Fourteenth Amendment has been interpreted to justify everything from protecting the rights of employers to run their businesses without state interference (such as protective labor laws), to marital and bodily privacy, to the right of non-white children to attend white public schools. See *Lochner v. New York*, 198 U.S. 45 (1905) (striking down a state law limiting the hours bakers could be made to work); *Griswold v. Connecticut*, 381 U.S. 479 (1965) (invalidating a state law that criminalized the use of contraceptives, even by married

couples); *Roe v. Wade,* 410 U.S. 113 (1973) (protecting the right of individuals to choose whether to have an abortion through the second trimester of pregnancy); and *Brown v. Board of Education,* 347 U.S. 483 (1954) (ordering the racial desegregation of public schools).

67. James Gray Pope also suggests using the Thirteenth Amendment to circumvent the state action problem with respect to workers' protest rights. Unlike the argument advanced here, however, he does not see doing so through an incorporation process similar to the Fourteenth Amendment's. See Pope, "Labor and the Constitution: From Abolition to Deindustrialization," *Texas Law Review* 65 (1987): 1071.

68. See *Gilbert v. Minnesota,* 254 U.S. 325 (1920); *Gitlow v. New York,* 168 U.S. 652 (1925); and *Near v. Minnesota,* 283 U.S. 697 (1931).

69. See Donald M. Gillmor, Jerome A. Barron, Todd F. Simon, and Herbert A. Terry, *Mass Communication Law: Cases and Comments,* 5th ed. (St. Paul: West Publishing, 1990).

70. See Pope, "Labor and the Constitution," 1071, 1100–1104.

PART IV
A POSTMODERN TURN

EIGHT

The "Popular First Amendment" and Classical Hollywood, 1930–1960: *Film Noir* and "Speech Theory for the Millions"

NORMAN ROSENBERG

Between about 1930 and the early 1960s, the First Amendment underwent significant reconstruction. To pare down a much broader story, the principle of "more speech" became an increasingly prominent theme in First Amendment discussions.[1] The appropriate remedy for "bad" speech, according to this more-speech doctrine, was not legal restrictions but carefully crafted constitutional protections that discouraged censorship and encouraged additional speech to enter public discourse.[2]

Freedom of speech, secured by concepts such as the more speech ideal, became celebrated during the 1940s as the "First Freedom."[3] Cold war libertarians repositioned free speech as the core liberty upon which the nation's "democratic" polity rested. A strong First Amendment would not only produce additional and "better" speech but, ultimately, social justice.[4] The postwar wave of political repression, popularly known as McCarthyism, confirmed the need, at least in the discourses that came to dominate the elite law schools and the liberal bar, to translate First Freedom ideals into First Amendment law.[5]

Textual markers from this period of First Amendment reconstruction abound. Recent "progressive" challenges to the First Freedom ideal—which have (from various different perspectives) tended to center on its allegedly abstract, ideological, and even anti-"realist" features—have ironically helped to refurbish these historically contingent texts.[6] Guardians of the First Freedom tradition still appeal to Zechariah Chafee, Jr.'s *Free Speech in the United States* (1940), Alexander Meiklejohn's *Free*

Speech and Its Relationship to Democratic Government (1948), Thomas I. Emerson's "Toward a General Theory of the First Amendment" (1963), *New York Times v. Sullivan* (1964), and scores of other treatises, articles, and judicial opinions from this era.[7]

In addition to these legal writings, the era of First Amendment reconstruction generated an even larger body of mass-cultural products. Although Norman Rockwell's 1943 painting "Freedom of Speech" (which lovingly depicts "the common man" speaking at a New England town meeting) is undoubtedly the most familiar of these texts,[8] the graphic arts, popular theater, network radio, mass-circulation literature, and the film and television industries all contributed to what might be called the "popular First Amendment" or "speech theory for the millions." The reconstruction of First Amendment theory between 1940 and 1964, this essay argues, appears in a different light when these mass-cultural discourses are brought directly into view.

Hollywood Speaks about Speech: An Overview

In an effort to remap the familiar terrain of legal studies, students of law are beginning to see motion pictures as legal texts.[9] This kind of "legal reelism" joins broader cultural projects that cross-examine popular and elite legal texts and ask what is distinctively legal about the forms of legal argument. Highlighting the rhetorical and iconographic features of all texts and drawing upon post-structuralist cultural theories, this recent scholarly intervention also looks "beyond conventionally defined legal forums" at how discourses about "law" are "reproduced, legitimized, and possibly reconfigured in behaviors and interpretations not typically considered legal practices."[10]

This type of post-structuralist scholarship also recognizes that, over the course of the twentieth century, "the mode of legal information" has been changing.[11] People who are not connected to the legal professorate or the bar—and who, therefore, are unlikely to read law reviews, court opinions, or even *Gilbert's Outlines*—can turn to *Court TV*, *Divorce Court*, or reruns of *LA Law* to make sense of legal discourses and practices. More broadly, as some media theorists suggest, social relationships, including legal ones, that cannot be represented in mass-mediated forms have become very difficult to represent in public discourse at all.[12] When talking to Spanish law students, for example, Robin Lakoff discovered that they could say very little about legal procedures in their own country but were eager to discuss those in the United States, which they had seen so often in North American motion pictures and television programs.[13]

Even before the mode of legal information included *Court TV*, in other words, the mass media were already representing "things legal," including legally protected speech.[14] Hollywood never produced a commercial film entitled "The First Amendment" or "Freedom of Speech."[15] Beginning in the mid-1930s, however, there were a number of motion pictures that depicted the problems of public communication in the mid-century United States.

Mr. Smith Goes to Washington (1939) and *Meet John Doe* (1940), for example, recount how a mass, bureaucratized system of communication frustrates older ideals of free speech. Frank Capra's small-town heroes discover that powerful media and political bosses dominate the means of communication. Anti-democratic elites both set broad agendas and control the flow of information on specific issues. As a result, even Capra's charismatic protagonists—Jefferson Smith (James Stewart) and John Willoughby (Gary Cooper)—find it difficult to make their voices, and those of their political constituents, heard. In Capra's films, the broader "politics of communication," particularly in the ways that private power restricts opportunities for public debate, work to frustrate and to alienate individual citizens.[16]

In a sense, *Mr. Smith* and *John Doe* simply join a wider cultural conversation.[17] While a succession of technologies—telephones, radios, motion pictures, and television—were erasing barriers of time and distance, works of popular culture were arguing that social and economic changes were eroding the possibilities for genuine communication. Surveying the mass culture, for example, the historian Warren Susman finds a wide range of works that argued, "[I]n an age of easy and mass communications . . . when it appear[ed] that everyone can know what everyone else knows and everyone can know what everyone else thinks . . . no real, private, human communication is possible."[18] Thus, Susman's study of the cultural conflicts associated with the changing mode of information parallels those legal histories that recount the bitterly contested battles over the different constitutional meanings of the term "freedom of speech."[19]

Hoping to position itself above these cultural and legal struggles, Hollywood portrayed itself as the special guardian of liberal, free speech values. Shortly after the outbreak of the European phase of World War II, a member of the Hollywood community hailed the nation's movie palaces as "places of public assembly, meeting halls of democracy," in which "the trend of national thought was discernable." The motion picture theater offered a new American "town hall."[20] And during World War II, Hollywood joined Norman Rockwell in portraying the basic American freedoms, including freedom of speech.[21]

Despite claims of rising above the battle, however, Hollywood was deeply implicated in the politics of speech. On one level, interest in free-speech discourses grew out of the Roosevelt administration's legal attack, for allegedly monopolistic production and distribution practices, against the Hollywood studios.[22] Moreover, despite their claim to represent First Amendment values, the studios themselves, as a consequence of the *Mutual* decision of 1915, lacked the constitutional protection that covered newspapers, magazines, and the publishing industry.[23] Most important, people who worked in Hollywood continually confronted an elaborate system that regulated what could be represented cinematically. Instituted in the 1920s and revised several times during the 1930s, Hollywood's "Code of Production" required every motion picture to pass the critical scrutiny of the Production Code Administration (PCA), headed from 1934 to 1954 by Joseph Breen.

Although Hollywood's Code was a private rather than a public system of regulation, from First Freedom assumptions it personified restrictionist, anti-free speech impulses. The Code appeared to limit Hollywood's ability to portray critical issues of the day. More subtly, to invoke legal phrases that would become prominent in First Freedom discourses, the PCA encouraged studios to exercise rigorous "self-censorship." The mere existence of the PCA, in other words, had a "chilling effect" on cinematic expression.

This position is not wrong, but, by counterpoising an abstract concept called "free speech" to another called "censorship," this heroic interpretation ignores other dimensions of Hollywood's politics of communication.[24] As recent revisionist studies argue, the Code and the PCA operated against the backdrop of a complex representational politics in which the boundaries of what could be said and seen became matters for continual negotiation and renegotiation.

Lea Jacobs's careful reconstruction of the interaction between the PCA and producers suggests that the Code "did not operate as a set of hard-and-fast rules" that mechanically inhibited cinematic expression and frustrated filmmakers. Industry regulators "never simply blocked the representation of offensive material," and "film producers did not give rise to what might be considered 'free speech' in the legal sense of the term."[25] In fact, the day-to-day operation of the Code, in some ways at least, aided, as well as restricted, filmic expression. Discussions between the Code office and studio producers actually "facilitated the task of anticipating public reaction to a film and established guidelines within which producers and industry censors would *discuss* specific problems."[26] The Code, as only one element in a multidimensional politics of communication, *simultaneously* served to inhibit "some speech" *and,* as the PCA and Hollywood filmmakers constantly debated alternative ways of approaching certain issues, to encourage "more" or at least "different" speech.[27]

Fury (1937), for example, illustrates the subtle ways in which Hollywood films negotiated directives from the PCA and from studio heads. Intended as a social-problem picture about lynching, *Fury*'s representational politics involved the fact that neither the PCA nor officials at MGM wanted any direct references to African-Americans, the main target of lynch law in the 1930s. The studio even insisted that a brief scene, in which an African-American man nodded approvingly at a crusading DA's condemnation of lynching, be excised from the release print. Nevertheless, *Fury* still manages to suggest, in several other places, the racial dimensions of lynching. Moreover, the film even contains a brief, but highly intrusive sequence in which patrons of a barber shop discuss legally protected speech. Significantly, it is a foreign-born barber—perhaps a stand-in for the film's Austrian-born director Fritz Lang—who reminds a customer that the Constitution protects certain kinds of speech.[28]

Because of Hollywood's own complex politics of communication, in short, it provided an interesting site from which to produce texts about "speech."[29] Indeed, between the mid-1930s and about 1960, an important group of motion pictures, which has come to be called *film noir,* explore the politics of communication. In contrast to Frank Capra's *Mr. Smith* and *Meet John Doe,* these films do not construct vast political and media conspiracies to explain the difficulties of communication. Even the simplest speech acts, *noirs* suggest, could involve the most complicated of communicative politics.[30]

Film Noir: Talking about Talking in the 1940s

The *noir* cycle, as it gradually gained a solid audience segment after World War II, became intertwined with the politics of communication in Hollywood itself. Generally shot on no-frills budgets with second-line crews and actors, the earliest *noirs* attracted relatively little attention from Hollywood's moguls or even from the PCA. The writer-director Abraham Polonsky recalls that *noir,* which was "a dark, criminal type of picture anyhow," allowed filmmakers considerable latitude for representing political themes.[31] As *noirs* became more popular and tackled more controversial subjects, they helped to bring about changes in the Production Code. Although it took Warner Brothers more than a decade to produce a film version of James M. Cain's hard-boiled novel *The Postman Rings Twice,* this 1946 motion picture—which seems to violate several Code mandates, especially the injunction that "[l]aw, natural or human, shall not be ridiculed"—signaled the beginnings of a new, less restrictive era in Hollywood's regulative politics. A wider range of filmic properties, it seemed, were open to negotiation with the PCA during the immediate postwar years.[32]

The popularity of *noir,* with its harsh view of social realities, also encouraged both the Hollywood studios and independent distributors to seek other motion pictures with representations traditionally discouraged by the PCA. This search for new filmic products, especially European productions geared to the growing "art-house" market, prompted new constitutional challenges to the *Mutual* ruling of 1915. In 1952, in a case involving an Italian film, *The Miracle,* the Supreme Court repudiated the *Mutual* decision of 1915 and held motion pictures to be "a form of expression whose liberty is safeguarded by the First Amendment." Although this decision did not mean the immediate demise of local licensing systems, nor of Hollywood's private Code system, it did add a new element into the politics of film production and distribution.[33]

Noir also mounted subtle, but significant, challenges to the politics of cinematic representation in classical Hollywood. Although *noirs* did not entirely overturn Hollywood's dominant representational politics, they tended, as the film scholar J. P. Telotte suggests, to display "a fascination with the mechanics and *possibilities* of storytelling."[34] On one level, this meant self-critical stances toward Hollywood's own cinematic discourses, especially the emphasis on strong, goal-oriented characters and on narratives that featured clearly delineated cause-and-effect relationships and moved toward relatively assured endings. These older filmic discourses, which constructed Hollywood's dominant notion of "realism," *noir* seemed to be saying, were no longer adequate for representing a rapidly changing social formation and an increasingly complex cultural milieu.[35] *Noir*, for example, often featured protagonists who were so impotent or confused that they could hardly articulate, let alone pursue, clear goals. Similarly, they often featured nonlinear narratives that came to abrupt, jarring endings. And, stylistically, *noir* changed film "grammar" by employing unusual camera angles, lighting patterns, and set constructions.

This concern about the politics of storytelling within the Hollywood production system extended to what *film noir* took to be the broader politics of communication in the mid-century United States itself. In this sense, *noir* added its own dark shadings and bizarre twists to the general theme highlighted in other mass cultural texts: the concern that the channels of everyday communication were becoming structured in ways that frustrated and distorted, rather than facilitated, meaningful communication.

Elaborating on the critical representations found in Capra's *Mr. Smith* and *Meet John Doe*, *noir* looked at both interpersonal and mass communication. In *The Maltese Falcon* (1941), one of the earliest *noirs*, Sam Spade (Humphrey Bogart) easily subdues a young punk, who is brandishing a set of pistols, but he cannot so easily disarm those who want to wound him with words. Verbally sparring with the menacing Casper Gutman (Sidney Greenstreet), Spade must avoid being entrapped by the tangled web of lies within Gutman's elegantly structured monologues. Speech becomes even more dangerous when the hard-boiled private eye must talk to women, especially the enigmatic Brigid O'Shaughessey (Mary Astor), or to legal officials who are scrutinizing Spade's every word in hopes that he will incriminate himself.

In the world of *noir,* the dangers of talking are heightened when the technologies of mass communication are involved. In *Sorry Wrong Number* (1948), the telephone symbolizes not only "the unseen link between a million lives" but betrayal, "horror ... and loneliness ... and death."[36] Indeed, *noir* examines, invariably with a critical eye, nearly every mode of communication and system of cultural production: photography, painting, newspapers, magazines, comic books, motion pictures, the legitimate theater, and television.

Finally, and perhaps most important in light of recent challenges to First Freedom orthodoxy, *noir* oftentimes repositions conversations about communication by linking speech acts with questions of *power*.[37] *Noir* emphasizes that speech does not simply contribute ideas or information to an abstract "marketplace of ideas" or a mythical "public dialogue," phrases common in legal analyses of the First Amendment. Rather, by inscribing a view of communication that derives from Hollywood's own communicative politics, *noir* represents speech acts against a rich backdrop of personal desires and social-economic power.[38]

Finally, *noir* suggests the difficulties of imagining that, by itself, more talking will bring "better" speech. Because speech acts are always rooted in complex networks of discourse and social practices, more speech can just as well "serve as instruments of positive harm."[39] Relationships between speech and power become particularly interesting in those *noirs* that I have elsewhere called *law noirs*,[40] motion pictures whose narratives are located in the legal and judicial systems. To suggest how *law noir* represents speech acts, I want to concentrate on two examples of *law noir*—*The File on Thelma Jordan* (1949) and *Force of Evil* (1948).

The File on Thelma Jordan

As a number of literary theorists have argued, legal dramas can generate special narrative power. Legal stories, especially when set within the halls of justice, can serve to legitimate people and processes by connecting them to the supposed neutrality of the rule of law. They also help, as in the case of freedom of speech, to link legal and broader cultural ideologies.[41]

Consider, for example, *Twelve Angry Men* (1957), a filmic text that uses a legal drama to argue the case for cold-war pluralist ideology. Here, personal and group prejudices threaten a young defendant who has been charged with killing his father. But a single juror, played by Henry Fonda, speaks up and stops the others from rushing to judgment. Significantly, this juror denies harboring any preconceptions about the defendant's guilt or innocence. "All I want to do is talk," he quietly explains. No hidden agenda lies behind this desire, he claims; he simply wants to "talk about" the case. As talk continues, Fonda's character gradually recedes into the background of a group dialogue that eventually results in a verdict of not guilty.

Twelve Angry Men, then, employs a legal narrative to imagine a communicative process in which reason becomes separated from prejudice and socioeconomic power. It endorses the value—and even more broadly, the social possibility—of undistorted communication, of truly free speech. Much like Norman Rockwell's painting of "Freedom of Speech," using jury deliberations rather than a town meeting this film seeks to represent the liberal ideal of freedom of speech. Because of a shared commitment to more speech, good ideas ultimately triumph over bad ones, truth ultimately vanquishes falsehood and prejudice, and reason trumps power.[42]

Film noir, and particularly its *law noir* sub-cycle, takes a very different approach. In contrast to a text such as *Twelve Angry Men,* with its pluralistic faith in the process of reasoned discussion, *The File on Thelma Jordan* highlights the problematics of speech, even in a court of law.

The File on Thelma Jordan features a small-town assistant district attorney who gets trapped by the discursive tools of his own trade.[43] While Barbara Stanwyck's Thelma Jordan receives title billing, Wendell Corey's lawyer centers the narrative. Although his name recalls both a former President and a former Chief Justice, Cleveland Marshall finds both his professional and personal lives in tatters. Patronized by a headline-hungry superior, who calls Marshall his fair-haired "boy," he is also systematically demeaned by his castrating father-in-law, a former judge. "Cleve" shuffles through the film's opening—and dark-lit—sequences in a drunken stupor. A legal career, it seems, has infantilized Cleveland Marshall. He sobers up enough to begin an extramarital affair with the alluring Thelma Jordan, but his supposed skills as a legal communicator remain well-hidden during the adolescentlike romance between Cleve and Thelma.

A telephone call changes all this. Thelma phones to tell Cleve that her wealthy aunt has been murdered. Rushing to the aunt's mansion, Cleveland Marshall becomes an energetic professional—but his legal skills are used to arrange evidence at the crime scene so that his lover, who has apparently stumbled upon her aunt's body, will not become a suspect. Cleve considers Thelma an innocent bystander, and the camera frames the evidence-tampering sequence so as to encourage viewers to cheer Cleve's efforts to save Thelma from the uncaring prosecutorial system for which he works. *Thelma Jordan,* from this angle, challenges the gender boundaries of *noir* and offers a narrative that resembles the popular "women's film" genre.[44]

Cleve cannot cover Thelma's trail, especially when she emerges as her aunt's sole heir, but he promises to "do anything possible, anything," to save her from the law, represented by his ambitious boss. Cleve first plunders his family's bank account to hire "the best defense lawyer in the country," Kingsley Willis (Stanley Ridges). "The world is full of innocent lambs, and I'm their lawyer," Willis assures Thelma. Cleve then anonymously suggests that Willis employ the DA's younger brother as his co-counsel. His brother's involvement forces the DA to disqualify himself and to assign Cleve as Thelma's prosecutor.

As the murder trial unfolds, Cleveland Marshall, in effect, is speaking for *both* the prosecution and the defense, all in the interest of securing Thelma's acquittal. While secretly directing evidence toward Thelma's attorney, Cleve shapes his own discourse so that it will highlight Kingsley Willis's defense strategy and undermine the state's case against Thelma. Cleve's seemingly incoherent, but perfectly performed, opening statement so alienates one juror that Willis advises Thelma that she "ought to thank Mr. Marshall in your prayers." After his dedicated associate, Miles Scott (Paul Kelly), develops a damning "file on Thelma Jordan"—a detailed accounting of her sordid past for use in cross-examination—Cleve secretly advises Willis to keep Thelma off the stand. As a result, Thelma's "file" becomes useless, and the jury acquits her.

The File on Thelma Jordan highlights the dangers of speech as Cleveland Marshall corruptly uses his command of legal discourse to satisfy private desires rather than to advance the public interest.[45] In contrast to the earlier sequences, the trial sequences are brightly lit; it is Cleve's verbal machinations that provide the darkness in these portions of the film. In addition, *Thelma Jordan* portrays the trial as a theatrical performance that seems akin to a professional wrestling match—i.e., a complex mix of legitimate combat and pre-choreographed fakery.[46] A series of different audiences—Cleve's wife and father-in-law, the jurors, his fellow prosecutors, and, finally, the film's viewers—all serve as drama critics, scrutinizing Cleve's performance. Meanwhile, Cleve uses his insider's knowledge and power to manipulate the courtroom discourse. By throwing his legal voice to the side of the defense, he is also able to throw the case. He helps Kingsley Willis persuade the jury to find Thelma innocent, while making his own prosecutorial fumbles seem miscalculations rather than deliberate mistakes.[47]

In *Thelma Jordan,* none of the usual functions of courtroom discourse—serving the cause of justice, unraveling a mystery, or securing a confession from a guilty party—seem to pertain. Pre-trial investigations uncover Thelma's checkered past, but all of the film's legal talk fails to reveal whether or not she actually murdered her aunt. Instead, the film suggests that someone with access to insider knowledge and power can easily construct a convincing legal spectacle. The ambiguity of Cleve's motives—and the ease with which he can use "law talk" to satisfy private passions—are heightened when Thelma finally confesses that she had murdered her aunt after having been surprised while pilfering a valuable necklace. "I guess I knew it all the time," a newly impotent Cleve blankly replies. Thus, Cleveland Marshall is "taken in" by all of Thelma's talk, just as he successfully "takes in" the jury with his own legal rhetoric.

The film's ending highlights the problematics of legal discourse. Although the guilty are punished—as the letter of the Production Code requires—legal officials remain bystanders. A guilt-ridden Thelma, suddenly overcome with remorse (for what she has done to both her aunt and Cleve), forces a car, driven by her lover-accomplice, off the road; Thelma's suicidal act leads to her own deathbed confession and seals Cleve's fate. His subsequent contrition redeems neither the legal profession nor Cleve himself. In the best *noir* tradition, his acceptance of personal responsibility seems merely a gesture, and Cleveland Marshall slinks into the shadows, a person whose skills with legal language neither advance the cause of public justice nor gain him personal happiness.

Force of Evil

The politics and problematics of speech loom even larger in *Force of Evil*.[48] The film's protagonist, Joe Morse (John Garfield), is a successful young lawyer who has talked his way out of a low-income, ethnic neighborhood and into a Wall-Street partnership. Like Cleveland Marshall, however, Joe himself becomes spoken by his legal discourse. More broadly, the boundaries between "legal" and "illegal" enterprises in *Force of Evil* are drawn by means of legal discourses that ultimately rest on the power of the state rather than on any bright-line moral distinctions. In this sense, the film underscores the view that "law" does not passively reflect "society." Rather, legal discourses actively help to construct everyday relationships.

Joe Morse's own partnership—with Hobe Wheelock (Paul McVey), a socially prominent graduate of Harvard Law School—relies on Morse's fancy fees from Ben Tucker (Roy Roberts), a former bootlegger who wants to become king of the numbers racket in postwar New York City. Having lost his family fortune by betting wrong on the stock market, Hobe Wheelock tries to talk himself into believing that Morse's lucrative representation of Tucker carries no moral or legal stigma. "It's the business of lawyers to protect a lot of people," Wheelock muses. "They even teach that at Harvard."

Although Joe Morse remains sanguine about his professional life, he is deeply troubled about his personal relationship with his older brother, Leo (Thomas Gomez). Having abandoned his own dreams of becoming an attorney so that he could finance Joe's legal education, Leo endures ill-health, bribe-seeking police officers, and pressure from Ben Tucker to sustain his own small numbers "bank." Although his numbers operation is illegal, *Force of Evil* represents Leo Morse as the more honest of the two brothers. Much of the film, in fact, depends upon the ways in which it contrasts Joe, the legally licensed corporate attorney, with Leo, the numbers-running small businessperson. "I could have been the lawyer," Leo angrily tells Joe. "You're a crook, a cheat, a gangster." Yet Leo harbors few illusions about his own business; he admits that people call the numbers game "policy" because low-income people divert money from their life insurance and health policies in hopes of striking it big.

Joe, however, lacks even this degree of moral insight. He blindly trusts in his command of legal language to generate millions for himself and a comfortable living for Leo. Practicing almost all of his law outside the courtroom, Joe Morse specializes in talking to people, successfully communicating his, and Ben Tucker's, view of how public life should be legally constructed.

The politics of crisscrossing conversations dominate this film. Morse talks to Hobe Wheelock about the legitimacy of representing Tucker and tries to talk his partner into speaking to Lincoln Hall, a racket-busting district attorney. The son of one of Wheelock's society friends, Hall has been telling the public he will shut down New York City's numbers parlors. Joe claims that he only needs to stall the DA because he has talked Ben Tucker out of crudely muscling his way into the city's illegal numbers racket. Instead, Joe will talk New York's politicians into legalizing the numbers game by force of law. When Joe presses Wheelock about his conversations with the DA, he is assured, "We're talking. . . . Just talking." Simultaneously, Joe is attempting to talk his older brother Leo into merging his own small numbers "bank" into Tucker's corporate-style organization. And, finally, Joe is talking to Doris Lowry (Beatrice Pearson), a young woman who works for Leo, trying to convince her that he is not blindly tempting fate but fully appreciates the risks of talking for Ben Tucker.

In foregrounding these interwoven public and private conversations, *Force of Evil* uses the telephone as a recurrent symbol of the promise and perils of speech.[49] Joe relies on phones as his primary means of legal communication. When his brother refuses to listen to his schemes, Joe uses a pay phone to initiate a police raid, a form of tattling, which he hopes will convince Leo to join Tucker's operation and accept Joe's assistance. And in one of the film's most powerful symbols, Joe keeps a special telephone in a locked desk drawer.

In the film's pivotal sequence, Ben Tucker's wife Edna (Marie Windsor) confronts Joe. "I couldn't telephone," she mysteriously tells him.

JOE: "Telephone about what?"
EDNA: "Telephone about the telephone."
JOE: "What about the telephone?"
EDNA: "Your prosecutor friend Hall has tapped Ben's telephone."

Though shaken, Joe tries to convince Edna, and himself, that there is nothing to worry about.

JOE: "I'm an attorney. Legally, I'm in a fiduciary relationship with your husband."
EDNA: "Is your telephone with Hall?"
JOE: ". . . Wiretapping evidence isn't always admissible. I'll look it up [for Ben]."
EDNA: Look it up for yourself, too, while you're at it. . . . Have you ever used that telephone of yours for anything that [the DA] shouldn't hear? . . . You might spend the rest of your life remembering what you shouldn't have said."

Force of Evil was in production well after the beginning of the Red-baiting that crippled Polonsky's career and contributed to Garfield's early death. This sequence might be read as an exploration of new threats, from both public and private surveillance institutions, to progressive voices in the film industry.[50] Even legally-protected conversations, Joe recognizes, can help "a smart lawyer" build a case against him. "People can be made to talk," he muses to himself. "Was my phone talking, too? A man could spend the rest of his life trying to remember what he shouldn't have said."

Thus, this sequence, with its voice-over narration, epitomizes *noir*'s haunting vision of the politics of communication in the postwar United States. Previously, the camera has privileged Joe's telephone as the key to his law practice: He quickly unlocks his lower desk drawer, spins out numbers, and confidently talks about legal business. But following his conversation with Edna, an extreme low-angle shot positions the desk, and its telephone drawer, so that they loom menacingly over Joe. Inching toward the desk as if it contained a ticking bomb, Joe slowly unlocks the drawer; he carefully removes the phone; and, upon lifting the receiver, he hears the dreaded "click" Edna warned him means that the phone line is tapped. A sudden and extreme closeup catches Joe holding the receiver to his ear, the soundtrack provides the "click," and another extreme closeup captures the fear in Joe's eyes. He cranks out a number, and a mechanical voice replies: "At the tone, the time will be seven-twenty-three and one-quarter."

The exchange with Edna about the dangers of speech signals Joe Morse's demise. The law practice he expected to be worth millions depends upon his ability to speak freely over the phone. Deprived of his telephone, Joe watches his career spiral downward.

Although the film is barely half over, Joe becomes powerless to shape events. More speech only leads to his professional and personal collapse. Hobe Wheelock, it seems, has been *"talking"* to the DA, *informing* him about the details of Joe's connection with Tucker. Instead of garnering political support by talking about the benefits of a legalized numbers game, Joe's lobbying attracts the attention of Ben Tucker's old rival, a murderous mobster named Ficco (Paul Fix), who decides to move into the numbers racket himself. Most tragically, Joe's efforts to talk his brother into joining Tucker's operation result in Leo's death at the hands of Ficco's thugs. Joe's conversations with Doris also lead nowhere. In the film's final sequence, when Joe hits "the bottom of the world," going underneath the Brooklyn Bridge to retrieve Leo's body, he and Doris have nothing to say to one another. Joe's haunting voice-over comes from no identifiable place and talks to no one in the film story itself; it speaks only to the film's audience, all of the anonymous people watching, in silence—and in "the dark."[51]

Force of Evil and *The File on Thelma Jordan,* in short, highlight the degree to which speech acts, even within law's own majestic empire, are located in complex networks of power. Speech seems more often a *force* for evil than for good.

NOIR AND THE POLITICS OF SPEAKING

In *The File on Thelma Jordan* and *Force of Evil* at least, speech theory for the millions lacks the forward-looking, quasi-religious, even millenarian tone of the First Freedom/more-speech tradition, which was being simultaneously invented during the 1940s.[52] Although *Force of Evil* ends with Joe Morse saying that he will cooperate with Lincoln Hall, the enigmatic, never-seen DA, nothing in the film's text even hints that talking to legal authorities will have any impact on the political corruption, the moral decay, or the maldistribution of power the film so hauntingly portrays.[53] The final sequence, with Joe Morse's strange voice-over, seems primarily a gesture to Hollywood's Production Code rather than anything that flows from—or connects to—the film's own narrative. Similarly, though *Thelma Jordan* does visually represent the public legal system, in the person of Cleveland Marshall's incorruptible (but largely ineffectual) deputy Miles, it offers little to suggest that legal discourse would have corrected Cleve's corrupt speech acts. Only Thelma's private intervention redresses public wrongs and closes the film's narrative.

In addition, both films refuse to romanticize "speech" or to separate it from "action."[54] By making Joe Morse, rather than one of Kingsley Willis's "innocent lambs," the target of surveillance,[55] *Force of Evil,* like *Thelma Jordan,* highlights the extent to which speech acts, even within law's own empire, remain enmeshed within complex networks of power. Unlike some of the most prominent texts in the First Freedom canon,[56] then, these *noirs* do not imagine legally protected speech as a kind of "luxury liberty" that can be tolerated because it seems entirely unlikely to disturb familiar routines or entrenched concentrations of power.[57]

Both *The File on Thelma Jordan,* a film in which the male-oriented discourses of *noir* confront those of the "women's film," and *Force of Evil,* with its crisscrossing of public and private stories, also foreground conflict among different narrators for control over the telling of their own filmic stories. As with so many other *noirs,* they offer many different "points of view and a struggle within the text for one viewpoint to gain hegemony."[58] And they offer no guarantees that these intratextual speech battles will produce clearer, more "truthful" cinematic narratives.

Force of Evil deals with the politics of speech in more imaginative cinematic ways than *Thelma Jordan.*[59] Undermining liberal theory's notion of a unified (speaking) subject,[60] for example, the film uses the technique of the voice-over to fragment Joe Morse's own voice: Joe speaks, from some unknown place, as *Force of Evil*'s narrator; and, from a Wall Street law office, another Joe Morse tries to communicate within a world in which communication seems increasingly difficult.[61] In addition, *Force of Evil* constantly seeks to juxtapose the vibrancy of individual speech, especially that of Joe Morse, with the deadness of the socioeconomic and cultural contexts in which it must circulate and try to produce meanings. In this type of setting, in contrast to the "democratic" society imagined by celebrants of the First Freedom ideal, liberty of speech could hardly be seen as a foundational freedom. In this sense, both *Thelma Jordan* and *Force of Evil* suggest the contingent nature of all conversations, including ones about the meaning of "free" speech. Moreover, these films parallel contemporary dissents from the First Freedom/more-speech tradition, dissents that seek to unpack the politics of talking about the First Amendment itself.

Conclusion: Talking about the First Amendment

Although critical First Amendment texts tell their stories in many different ways, they all argue for "freeing" contemporary discourses from their own semiotic chains. Does not much of the discussion about legally protected speech, they ask, display a narrow, ideological quality?[62] Does not much of the normative talk about the First Amendment assume a self-referential tone as writers inject, oftentimes uncritically, "their own" politics into "our" First Amendment?[63] And might not much of the conversation about the First Amendment, like the broader legal-constitutional discourse of which it is a part, exemplify the flat bureaucratic rhetoric produced by the contemporary judicial bureaucracy itself?[64]

Law professor Paul Campos links these types of critiques to the familiar trope of decline. Back in the 1940s, when the First Amendment was undergoing renovation, even Supreme Court opinions contained a "warm" and "living" voice that contrasts with the "weary, mechanistic rhetoric" of recent judicial discussions of legally protected speech. During the immediate postwar era, the First Amendment opinion was a "still-fresh genre."[65]

Perhaps a careful cross-examination of Supreme Court opinions past and present will support such a judgment. More subversively, though, this brief trip to the movies of the 1940s offers another possibility: that during the era in which "our" contemporary First Amendment was being reshaped by legal elites, there was also a "popular First Amendment" that talked about speech in ways that went beyond and undermined a legalistic formalism, that, from the very beginning, sought to dominate discourse about legally protected speech. At least as articulated in Hollywood's *noirs,* this popular First Amendment jettisoned the pieties of pluralism and looked "realistically" at the politics of speech in the mid-twentieth-century United States.[66]

Even more subversively, filmic images from *noirs* of the 1940s might be viewed against the many current critiques that question the hegemonic place of legal-constitutional discourses in "public" debate about the politics of speech. "It seems to me," suggests law professor Steven Smith, "that the lay public is probably better able to appreciate the flexible, nonessentialist character of free speech protection than lawyers and legal scholars are."[67] Similarly, I would suggest, Hollywood films of the 1930s and 1940s, and their "speech theory for the millions," imagined the politics of speech in ways that were more complex and interesting than those found in the contemporary legal-constitutional texts, which are now enshrined in the First Freedom/more-speech tradition.

Finally, and most subversively, it even seems possible to position the celebratory discourses in the First Freedom tradition as the legal-constitutional responses to noirish images that suggested the possibility, as Stanley Fish recently put it, that there was "no such thing as free speech," only the historically contingent politics of speech in the postwar United States. In this sense, the First Freedom/more-speech discourse, for all of its noble, normative promises in the face of "McCarthyism," might be seen, from the beginning, as a form of constitutional solace, a legalistic reassurance that the fate of Frank Capra's frustrated "everyman" or of *film noir*'s haunted protagonists will not be "our" own.

Notes

I have presented different versions of this essay at the University of Minnesota, at a conference in honor of Paul Murphy entitled "Two Hundred Years of Liberty and the Bill of Rights"; at Central Michigan University; at Whittier College; and at Macalester College. For helpful comments, I want to thank, among others, Paul Murphy, Kermit Hall, Richard Archer, Richard Cheatham, Emily Rosenberg, Avlam Soifer, and Clayton Steinman.

1. At the outset, I freely concede that my focus on the "more speech" principle serves to construct a "very thin" First Amendment. My First Amendment lacks the intricate "tests" and doctrinal "principles" that were being used to build, between about 1930 and 1964, a new, much "thicker" First Amendment; this First Amendment makes its full-blown appearance in, say, Thomas I. Emerson's *The System of Freedom of Expression* (New York: Random House, 1970). On "thin" (and presumably "thick") First Amendments, see Pierre Schlag, "How to Do Things with the First Amendment," *University of Colorado Law Review* 64 (1993): 1095–1107, at 1099–1100.

2. The "more speech principle" had been elegantly articulated by Louis D. Brandeis in *Whitney v. California,* 274 U.S. (1927) 357, 374–77 (Justice Brandeis concurring). See Vincent Blasi, "The First Amendment and the Ideal of Civic Courage: The Brandeis Opinion in *Whitney v. California*," *William & Mary Law Review* 29 (1988): 653. The more-speech principle remains an important theme in First Amendment discourse and has been updated in Paul Chevigny, *More Speech: Dialogue Rights and Modern Liberty* (Philadelphia: Temple University Press, 1988).

3. See, for example, Nat Hentoff, *The First Freedom: The Tumultuous History of Free Speech in America* (New York: Delacorte, 1980). The term "First Freedom" was popularized during the 1940s by the indefatigable Morris Ernst. See, for example, Ernst's *The First Freedom* (New York: Macmillan, 1946).

4. Stories about this era of First Amendment reconstruction have been told many times and in many ways. See, for example, Paul Murphy, *The Meaning of Freedom of Speech* (Westport, Conn.: Greenwood, 1972); Harry Kalven, *A Worthy Tradition,* Jamie Kalven, ed. (New York: Harper & Row, 1988); and David Kairys, "Freedom of Speech," in Kairys, ed., *The Politics of Law: A Progressive Critique* (New York: Pantheon, 1982), 140–171.

In addition, Robert Post elegantly maps some of the theoretical issues, especially ones related to how "our constitutional tradition has so far understood democracy," in "Managing Deliberation: The Quandary of Democratic Dialogue," *Ethics* 28 (1993): 654–78. And in "Some Realism about Pluralism: Legal Realist Approaches to the First Amendment," *Duke Law Journal* (1990): 375–430, J. M. Balkin reemphasizes the extent to which the more-speech ideal was an important part of the identity of the political "left."

5. See, for example, Henry Steele Commager, et al., *Civil Liberties Under Attack* (Philadelphia: University of Pennsylvania Press, 1951). For a shrewd appraisal of the role of First Amendment guarantees during this period, see Vincent Blasi, "The Pathological Perspective and the First Amendment," *Columbia Law Review* 85 (1985): 449–514.

6. Given the contemporary nature of scholarly and law review publishing, the revisionist canon is growing at exponential rates. See, for example, Mari Matsuda *et al.*, *Words that Wound: Critical Race Theory, Assaultive Speech, and the First Amendment* (Boulder, Colo.: Westport, 1993); Owen Fiss, "Free Speech and Social Structure," *Iowa Law Review* 71 (1986): 1405–25; Martha Minow, "Listening the Right Way," *New York University Law Review* 64 (1989): 946–962, and "Speaking of Silence," *University of Miami Law Review* 43 (1988): 493–511; Balkin, "Some Realism about Pluralism," *Duke Law Journal* (1990): 375–430; Richard Delgado, "First Amendment Formalism Is Giving Way to First Amendment Legal Realism," *Harvard Civil Rights–Civil Liberties Law Review* 29 (1994): 169–74.

7. For recent examples of studies that still celebrate the First Freedoms texts of the 1940–1964 era, see Samuel Walker, *Hate Speech: The History of an American Controversy* (New York: Oxford University Press, 1994), and Anthony Lewis, *Make No Law: The Sullivan Case and the First Amendment* (New York: Random House, 1991).

8. See Stuart Murray and James McCabe, *Norman Rockwell's Four Freedoms: Images That Inspire a Nation* (Stockbridge, Mass.: Berkshire House, 1993).

9. See, for example, the special issue of *Legal Studies Forum* 15 (1991), and John Denvir, ed., *Legalism Unreeled: The Hollywood Film as Legal Text* (Champaign, Ill.: University of Illinois Press, forthcoming).

10. Rosemary J. Coombe, "Room for Manoeuver: Toward a Theory of Practice in Critical Legal Studies," *Law and Social Inquiry* 14 (1989): 69, 115–16.

11. See generally, Mark Poster, *The Mode of Information: Poststructuralism and Social Context* (Chicago: University of Chicago Press, 1990).

12. See, for example, J. M. Balkin, "What Is a Postmodern Constitutionalism?" *Michigan Law Review* 90 (1992): 1966–1990; and David James, "Rock and Roll in Representations of the Invasion of Vietnam," *Representations* 29 (1990): 77. For the difficulties of representing the process of free speech in visual form, see Norman Rosenberg, "Freedom of Speech," in Kermit Hall, ed., *By and For the People* (Chicago: Harlan Davidson, 1991), 39–40.

13. Robin Tolmach Lakoff, *Talking Power: The Politics of Language* (New York: Basic Books, 1990), 85–86.

14. The marvelous phrase "things legal" comes from Karl Llewellyn, "Some Realism about Realism—Responding to Dean Pound," *Harvard Law Review* 44 (1931): 1222.

15. In the late 1930s, however, several screenwriters closely associated with leftist politics did develop a "treatment" entitled "Freedom of the Press." Brian Neve, *Film and Politics in America: A Social Tradition* (London and New York: Routledge, 1992), 241.

16. Although elite critics of the early 1940s generally dismissed *Meet John Doe* and *Mr. Smith* as "Capracorn," these films arguably offer more complex and challenging perspectives about the context of disputes over legally protected speech than those found in many elite legal texts of the 1930s and 1940s. See Rosenberg, "Another History of Free Speech: The 1920s and the 1940s," *Law and Inequality* 7 (1989): 333, 345–48 (and sources cited therein), and John Denvir, "Frank Capra's First Amendment," *Legal Studies Forum* 15 (1991): 255–63. On *Meet John Doe*, see the shooting script and critical essays in Charles Wolfe, ed., *Meet John Doe* (New Brunswick, N.J.: Rutgers University Press, 1989).

17. When, for example, a writer sued Warner Brothers studio, the distributor of *Meet John Doe*, for copyright infringement, one legal consultant advised the studio to claim that critical stories about media politics were so common that the theme could no longer be copyrighted. Charles Wolfe, "Meet John Doe: Authors, Audiences, and Endings," in *Meet John Doe*, 8, fn. 9.

18. Warren Susman, *Culture as History* (New York: Pantheon, 1984), 261.

19. See, for example, Murphy, *The Meaning of Freedom of Speech*, still the best study of legal-constitutional discourses.

20. Quoted in Charles Wolfe, "Mr. Smith Goes to Washington: Democratic Forums and Representational Forms," in Peter Lehman, ed., *Close Viewings: An Anthology of New Film Criticism* (Tallahassee: Florida State University Press, 1990), 300, 302–303.

21. See, for example, the final sequence of *Star Spangled Rhythm* (1943), in which Bing Crosby and a cast of (literally) thousands stage an impromptu town meeting that resembles, at least on the surface, a larger version of the one depicted in Norman Rockwell's "Freedom of Speech."

22. See, for example, Ernest Borneman, "United States versus Hollywood: The Case Study of an Antitrust Suit," in Tino Balio, ed., *The American Film Industry*, rev. ed. (Madison: University of Wisconsin Press, 1985), 449–62.

23. The *Mutual* decision held that motion pictures were not protected by the First Amendment. They were *not* part of the "press" or "organs of public opinion." Although perhaps "vivid and entertaining," motion pictures were "mere representations of events, of ideas and sentiment published and known." *Mutual Film Corporation v. Ohio Industrial Commission*, 236 U.S. 230 (1915). See also Garth S. Jowett, " 'A Capacity for Evil': The 1915 Supreme Court *Mutual* Decision," in Ray B. Browne and Glenn J. Browne, eds., *Laws of Our Fathers: Popular Culture and the U.S. Constitution* (Bowling Green, Ohio: Bowling Green State University Popular Press, 1986), 42–65. More broadly, see

Daniel Czitrom, "The Politics of Performance: From Theater Licensing to Movie Censorship in Turn-of-the-Century New York," *American Quarterly* 44 (1992): 525–53.

24. The notion of a "heroic interpretation" is developed by Clayton Koopes in his review essay, "Film Censorship: Beyond the Heroic Interpretation," *American Quarterly* 44 (1992): 643–49. One of the important books in this tradition, which Koopes reviews, is Leonard J. Leff and Jerold L. Simmons, *The Dame in the Kimono: Hollywood, Censorship, and the Production Code from the 1920s to the 1960s* (New York: Grove Weidenfeld, 1990). A special symposium entitled "Hollywood, Censorship, and American Culture," appears in *American Quarterly* 44 (1992).

25. Lea Jacobs, *The Wages of Sin: Censorship and the Fallen Woman Film, 1928–1942* (Madison: University of Wisconsin Press, 1991), 150.

26. Jacobs, *The Wages of Sin*, 35 (emphasis added).

27. Seen from the First Freedom ideal and from a liberal-constitutional perspective, of course, such a system is fatally flawed simply because "politics" is involved.

28. For an analysis of *Fury*, see Rosenberg, "Hollywood on Trials," *Law and History Review* 12 (1994): 341–67.

29. I am not contending that classical Hollywood provided the "best" perspective from which to imagine speech issues; but, on the other hand, what evidence is there to suggest that the legal system provides the "best" perspective either? For the claim that the "actual training and experience" of appellate court judges, to whom the First Freedom/more-speech tradition assigns a crucial role in framing legal protections for speech, are of dubious value for preparing them to understand or protect speech acts, see Robert F. Nagel, "How Useful Is Judicial Review in Free Speech Cases?" *Cornell Law Review* 69 (1984): 302–40, 334. See also Mary Becker, "Conservative Free Speech and the Uneasy Case for Judicial Review," *University of Colorado Law Review* 64 (1993): 975–1050.

30. My cross-examination of *film noir* in terms of speech issues is greatly indebted to J. P. Telotte, *Voices in the Dark: The Narrative Patterns of Film Noir* (Urbana: University of Illinois Press, 1984). See also Ann Lawrence, *Echo and Narcissus: Women's Voices in Classical Hollywood Cinema* (Berkeley and Los Angeles: University of California Press, 1991), 109–45.

31. Quoted in Neve, *Film and Politics*, 150.

32. Leff and Simmons, *Dame in the Kimono*, 128–35.

33. *Burstyn v. Wilson*, 243 U.S. 495 (1952). The Hollywood background to this decision is sketched in Leff and Simmons, *Dame in the Kimono*, 141–61, 180–81, 186–87.

34. Telotte, *Voices in the Dark*, 3. See also Christine Gledhill, "Klute 1: A Contemporary Film Noir and Feminist Criticism," in E. Ann Kaplan, ed., *Women in Film Noir* (London: British Film Institute, 1981), 6–21; and Pam

Cook, "Duplicity in *Mildred Pierce*," in Kaplan, ed., *Women in Film Noir*, 68–82.

35. Telotte, *Voices in the Dark*, 3–14.

36. These lines crawl across the screen as a prologue to the filmic narrative. On this important *noir*, see Telotte, *Voices in the Dark*, 77–87.

37. The most important and suggestive work in this vein begins with Michel Foucault. See, for example, *Power/Knowledge: Selected Interviews and Other Writings, 1972–1977*, Colin Gordon, ed. (New York: Pantheon, 1980). Some of the implications of Foucauldian theories are worked out in Sue Curry Jansen, *Censorship: The Knot that Binds Power and Knowledge* (New York: Oxford University Press, 1991).

38. In hailing *noir*'s attention to issues of socioeconomic power, it should not be forgotten that *noirs* of the 1940s and 1950s still contained significant cultural blinders, especially on issues of gender and race. See, for example, Kaplan, ed., *Women in Film Noir*; Elizabeth Cowie, "*Film Noir* and Women," in Joan Copjec, ed., *Shades of Noir* (London: Verso, 1993), 121–65; and Manthia Diawara, "*Noir* by *Noirs:* Toward a New Realism in Black Cinema," in *Shades of Noir*, 261–78.

39. The quoted words, as well as much of legal background for my approach to *film noir*, comes from Delgado, "First Amendment Legal Realism," 171, and the sources cited therein.

U.S. v. Josephson, 105 F. 2d 82 (1947), for example, directly raised the issue of whether or not the House Un-American Activities Committee violated the rights of those who claimed a First Amendment right to refuse to answer questions of the Committee. A majority of the Court, implicitly invoking the principle of "more speech," rejected the First Amendment claim of a person who refused to respond to questions about his political affiliations. The Supreme Court refused to hear an appeal. *U.S. v. Josephson*, 333 U.S. 838 (1947); 333 U.S. 899 (1947). For a broad overview of controversies over the First Amendment rights of persons brought before the Committee, see Victor S. Navasky, *Naming Names* (New York: Viking, 1980), especially 47–51.

40. See Rosenberg, "*Law Noir*," in Denvir, ed., *Law Unreeled: The Hollywood Film as Legal Text*.

41. See Dana Polan, *Power & Paranoia: History, Narrative, and the American Cinema, 1940–1950* (New York: Columbia University Press, 1986), 21–22; and Rosenberg, "Hollywood on Trials," *passim*.

42. This is not to say, however, that *Twelve Angry Men* is completely successful in its representations. See, for example, the critique in Peter Biskind, *Seeing Is Believing: How Hollywood Taught Us to Stop Worrying and Love the Fifties* (New York: Pantheon, 1983), 10–20. And for a broader critique of the repressive elements within the pluralist vision of the 1950s, see Ellen Rooney, *Seduc-*

tive Reasoning: Pluralism as the Problematic of Contemporary Literary Theory (Ithaca, N.Y.: Cornell University Press, 1989), 24–33.

43. For a brief overview of *Thelma Jordan* and its relationship to other *noirs* by its director, see Michael Walker, "Robert Siodmak," in Ian Cameron, ed., *The Book of Film Noir* (New York: Continuum, 1993), 145–51.

44. Walker, "Siodmak," 150–51.

45. Given the critical ways in which the narrative has represented the law, and Cleve's efforts to save Thelma, who is fairly benign as *noir* villainesses go, *Thelma Jordan* encourages viewers to root Cleve on. And since the narrative also conceals who killed Thelma's aunt, one is encouraged to see Cleve's performance as a well-meaning attempt to prevent a fallible legal system, headed by a publicity-seeking DA, from convicting an innocent woman. Thus, the broader context of Cleve's use of speech to commit a criminal act is not entirely evident until the end of the film. The most complete legal analysis of speech and crime is Kent Greenawalt, *Speech, Crime, and the Uses of Language* (New York: Oxford University Press, 1989).

46. See, for example, Roland Barthes, *Mythologies* (New York: Hill & Wang, 1972), 15–25, and Abraham Blumberg, "The Practice of Law as a Confidence Game: Organization Cooption as a Profession," *Law and Society Review,* 1 (1967): 15–39.

47. Some of this is done in secret, but many of Cleve's ploys are casually performed in open court. In this sense, *Thelma Jordan* parallels one of the most famous of all *films noir*, *Double Indemnity* (1944), in having an insider manipulate professional discourse in order to satisfy private desires. In both films, those charged with policing the profession cannot see through the discursive flim-flam.

48. From the standpoint of liberal (and not-so-liberal) anticommunists, this film brought together some of the most suspicious characters in cold-war Hollywood. Both writer-director Abraham Polonsky and star John Garfield would later run afoul of postwar red-hunters, and *Force of Evil*'s bleak portrayal of American culture even surpasses that offered in an earlier Polonsky-Garfield effort, *Body and Soul* (1947). On *Force of Evil*, see Jack Shadoian, *Dreams and Dead Ends* (Cambridge: MIT Press, 1977), 116–19, 134–48; Biskind, *Seeing Is Believing,* 194–96; Christine Noll Brinckman, "The Politics of *Force of Evil*: Analysis of Abraham Polonsky's Preblacklist Film," *Prospects* 6 (1981): 357–86; and Clayton Steinman, "Hollywood Dialectic: *Force of Evil* and the Frankfurt School's Critique of the Culture Industry," (Unpublished Ph.D. dissertation, New York University, 1979).

49. On the importance of telephone imagery in *film noir*, see Telotte, *Voices in the Dark,* 74–87, and Lawrence, *Echo,* 130–45.

50. See, generally, Bernard F. Dick, *Radical Innocence: A Critical Study of*

the Hollywood Ten (Lexington: University of Kentucky Press, 1989); Stephen Englund and Larry Ceplair, *The Inquisition in Hollywood: Politics in the Film Community, 1930–1960* (Garden City, N.Y.: Anchor/Doubleday, 1983); Navasky, *Naming Names;* Michael Wilson, *Salt of the Earth: Screenplay* (Old Westbury, N.Y.: Feminist Press, 1978); John Cogley, *Report on Blacklisting,* vol. 1, *Movies* (New York: Fund for the Republic, 1956); and Jeffrey Tancil, "Through a Lens Darkly: The Blacklist in Hollywood" (Senior Honors Thesis, Macalester College, 1993).

51. At least in my reading, *Force of Evil* lacks any heroic—or even affirmative—images of law officers or the legal process. The police are portrayed as tough, uncaring goons who can be bought by both Leo Morse and Ben Tucker. The crusading DA, Lincoln Hall, is a mysterious figure, unseen in the film, who taps phones and pressures pathetic informers like Hobe Wheelock. Joe Morse is brought down less by the force of law than by the force of evil that is, ironically, set in motion by his own legal discourses. For a very different cinematic view, which celebrates the more speech ideal and the politics of informing, see *On the Waterfront* (1954).

This phrase echoes the final sequence of another classic *noir*, Billy Wilder's *Sunset Boulevard* (1950), in which a demented former silent film star tries to speak to her lost audience—all of "you lovely people out there in the dark."

52. On the religious, millenarian tones in free-speech discourse, see Stanley Fish, *There's No Such Thing As Free Speech, and It's a Good Thing, Too* (New York: Oxford University Press, 1994), 109–10.

Although *Thelma Jordan* and *Force of Evil* certainly reject millenarianism, they do not, at the other extreme, simply posit the "futility" of speaking out. Instead, they represent, more "realistically" than traditional legal texts in the First Freedom/more-speech tradition, the complex politics of speaking out. On First Amendment "realism," see Balkin, "Some Realism about Pluralism," and Delgado, "First Amendment Formalism." On *noir*'s "realistic" appraisal of communicative politics, see generally Telotte, *Voices in the Dark, passim.*

53. For recent legal essays that question the First Freedom's "naive" faith in the efficacy of more speech, see Richard Delgado & Jean Stefancic, "Images of the Outsider in American Law and Culture: Can Free Expression Remedy Systemic Social Ills?" *Cornell Law Review* 77 (1992): 1258–84; Nagel, "How Useful Is Judicial Review in Free Speech Case?" *passim;* and Martha Minow, "Speaking of Silence," *passim.*

54. On the "romantic" origins of discourses about legally protected speech, see Steven H. Shiffrin, *The First Amendment: Democracy and Romance* (Ithaca, N.Y.: Cornell University Press, 1990); for a brief critique of the speech/action distinction, see Schlag, "How to Do Things with the First Amendment," 1099–1101.

55. One might usefully compare *Force of Evil* with *Guilty By Suspicion*

(1991). Abraham Polonsky wrote a screenplay for this later film but ended up only as an "informal adviser" after the film's producers insisted upon making the target of surveillance and blacklisting, played by Robert DeNiro, an "innocent lamb"—an apolitical film director rather than a member of the Communist Party.

56. See, for example, the classic dissent of Justice Holmes in *Abrams v. United States,* 250 U.S. 616 (1920), which finds no danger flowing from a "silly leaflet" written by an "unknown man." See also the similarly constructed dissent of Justice William O. Douglas in *Dennis v. United States,* 341 U.S. 494 (1951).

57. The concept of a "luxury liberty" is developed in Kalven, *A Worthy Tradition,* 139–46. It is possible, of course, to recognize that speech is "not merely a matter of ideas" and that people employ speech "to do things" and still articulate a broad view of what counts as legally protected "speech." See, for example, C. Edwin Baker, "Of Course, More Than Words," *University of Chicago Law Review* 61 (1994): 1181–1211.

58. Gledhill, "Klute 1," 17; see also Cook, "Duplicity in *Mildred Pierce,*" *passim,* and Walker, "Siodmak," 150.

59. This paragraph relies on the excellent analysis of *Force of Evil* by my colleague Clay Steinman in his unpublished dissertation, "Hollywood Dialectic," chapter 3.

60. For some implications of recent literature on "the subject," from the standpoint of legal studies, see Pierre Schlag, "The Problem of the Subject," *University of Texas Law Review* 69 (1991): 1627–1743, and James Boyle, "Is Subjectivity Possible? The Postmodern Subject in Legal Theory," *University of Colorado Law Review* 62 (1992): 489–62.

61. On the use of voice-overs in *noir,* see Telotte, *Voices in the Dark,* 24–26, *passim.*

62. See, for example, Frederick Schauer, "The First Amendment As Ideology," chapter 2 in this volume.

63. See, for example, Schlag, "How to Do Things with the First Amendment," 1096; Martha Minow, "Speaking and Writing against Hate," *Cardozo Law Review* 11 (1990): 1393–1480; and Stanley Fish, "Fraught with Death: Skepticism, Progressivism, and the First Amendment," *Colorado Law Review* 64 (1993): 1061–1090. For a broad critique that looks at the politics of contemporary speech, see William Greider, *Who Will Tell the People: The Betrayal of American Democracy* (New York: Simon & Schuster, 1992), 35–78.

64. See, for example, Paul Campos, "Advocacy and Scholarship," *California Law Review* 81 (1993): 817–861, at 855–57. More broadly, see Mark Tushnet, "Style and the Supreme Court's Educational Role in Government," *Constitutional Commentary* 11 (1994): 215–25, and Pierre Schlag, "Normative and Nowhere to Go," *Stanford Law Review* 43 (1990): 167–91.

65. Campos, "Advocacy and Scholarship," 859.

66. Pitting an abstraction called "formalism" against another called "realism" has contradictions of its own, of course. Again, I imagine these terms as suggested in Rosenberg, "Another Story"; Balkin, "Some Realism about Pluralism"; and Delgado, "First Amendment Formalism."

67. Steven D. Smith, "The Politics of Free Speech: A Comment on Schauer," *Colorado Law Review* 64 (1993): 959–964, at 961. See also Toni M. Massaro, "Post, Fiss, and the Logic of Democracy," *Colorado Law Review* 64 (1993): 1145–69; Becker, "Conservative Free Speech," 1045. More broadly, see Robin West, "The Authoritarian Impulse in Constitutional Law," *University of Miami Law Review* 42 (1988): 491–555.

NINE

Trigger: Law, Labeling, and the Hyperreal

SANDRA BRAMAN

Technological change is forcing us to reconsider the First Amendment, since as Pool effectively noted, our different communication regulatory systems (including broadcast and common carriage, or telecommunications, as well as the First Amendment) each evolved in response to the development of different types of communication technologies, and those technologies have now converged.[1] While the First Amendment developed in a communications environment dominated by print, it has long been clear that there are problems translating application of its principles to other media.

In addition to shifts in the communications infrastructure, other fundamental assumptions underlying the First Amendment and its interpretation are being challenged: The existing interpretation assumes the nation-state is the legitimate and important focus of journalistic practice, while today the subject matter, institutional forms, working procedures, and constituency (audience) of journalism have become globalized. The interpretation of the First Amendment is built on a relatively simple conception of communications processes, while our understanding of the nature of these processes has grown far more sophisticated, and sees them as much more complex than we did two centuries ago. The interpretation of the First Amendment assumes linear causal relations underlie our social processes, while both experience and theories of self-organizing systems are teaching us to recognize the importance of nonlinear causal relations. While we have assumed that journalism fulfills specific social functions, in today's communications environment, those functions are also being fulfilled by other types of information creation, processing, flows, and use.

It is also an underlying assumption of the First Amendment that language use, whether oral or in print, is intended to be referential. The First Amendment was written at the height of modern narrative fixation on facticity, at a time when fact and fiction, journalism and novels, had become clearly distinguished from each other out of the previously undifferentiated matrix of narrative form.[2] From Locke until the postmodern turn, all narrative was absorbed in the question of the referentiality of text to the "real" world outside of the text, whether it claimed referentiality or denied it. This absorption in facticity is, indeed, a hallmark characteristic of modernity. Debates over the nature of journalism, such as that generated by the practice of "new journalism" in the 1960s and 1970s, revolved around issues of the procedures by which validly referential text is generated.[3]

This, too, is an assumption that no longer holds today. The hallmark characteristic of postmodernity is that referentiality has declined in relative importance; there is now slippage in the relationship between text and the material world. This is the condition Baudrillard refers to as the hyperreal, a communications environment in which symbols and text refer not to any world outside of themselves, the real, but only to other symbols and texts.[4] The significance of this slippage for our interpretation and application of the First Amendment has not yet been explored. Yet it is as important to do so as it is to look at the implications of new media for our regulation of the communications environment, for the postmodern condition and the information society are two ends of the same elephant. Postmodern theories discuss the cultural experience of this period, while those who look at the information society are starting from the technological developments that have stimulated today's qualitative shifts in the cultural, political, economic, social, and ecological environments.

Here, a study of United States Supreme Court cases dealing with labeling offers a first pass at examining the significance of hyperreality for First Amendment interpretation. Labeling cases are a tempting place to start because they explicitly deal with the relationship between text and symbols (information) and the material objects to which they refer. Because we put labels on everything from the most common items (milk, butter, sausage) to the most exotic (hazardous waste materials), the study of labels also drags our attention insistently across the empirical environment.

Labeling cases have not received much attention outside of the offices of trademark lawyers, but this does not diminish their importance from the perspective of theories of self-organizing systems. These theories, which are useful in understanding the democratic potential[5] and relationships between the law and social systems,[6] emphasize the potential significance of seemingly trivial events or differences in conditions for generating large-scale qualitative change in a system. This is known as the "butterfly effect," referring to the possibility that the flap of a butterfly's wings in Africa could ultimately generate a hurricane in North America.

Thus "Trigger" as a title. It is argued here that the development of constitutional thinking about labeling—seemingly insignificant in our communications environment—has actually triggered the emergence of hyperreality. Since facticity, the claim to a directly referential relationship between communications content and a world outside of text and symbols, is a fundamental assumption of the First Amendment and its interpretation, beginning to understand the ways in which constitutional law itself has undermined the effort and desire to sustain that referentiality seems critical. This in turn should be useful as we begin to think about what the First Amendment should mean or do in a hyperreal environment.

Labeling cases are not the only areas of constitutional law concerned with matters of facticity. Other major streams of cases include those dealing with libel, fraud, identity questions that arise for citizenship purposes, creation of property rights through definition of fact, and lying in both public (perjury) and private (falsehood or misrepresentation). Other cases that deal with the relationship of text to material object include those that explore the nature of advertising, and those that discuss regulatory and accounting categories of various kinds. Fact *qua* fact is very much the stuff of the law. Thus, changes in the nature of facticity are central to the law in both theory and praxis. In Geertz's words, "Explosion of fact, fear of fact, and, in response to these, sterilization of fact confound increasingly both the practice of law and reflection upon it."[7]

It is beyond the scope of one chapter, however, to cover all this territory. Here, we begin with an exploration of Baudrillard's understanding of hyperreality and other pertinent features of the postmodern environment; review the development of labeling law, including its justifications, media considered to be labels, and details of required relationships between labels and the objects to which they refer; and analyze these cases as manifestations of the emergence of postmodernity and as they themselves trigger the hyperreal. As Marshall and Eric McLuhan noted, the ultimate effect of any communications process or technology is the opposite of the effects that dominate the bulk of our experience or that we most commonly see.[8]

BAUDRILLARD ON THE HYPERREAL

Among those thinkers identified as "postmodernists," Baudrillard stands out in his originality, clarity, and level of impact. Kroker, writing about a number of theorists of technology, claims that Baudrillard offers us "the most intimate, the most intensely historical, and the most radically ideological of all theories of technology."[9]

Baudrillard's term, "the hyperreal," introduced in the 1983 book *Simulations,* refers to the condition in which symbols, images, and language no longer have any intention or pretension to referentiality to a world—material or otherwise—outside of themselves, instead referring only to other symbols, images, and language. Baudrillard distinguishes four stages in the history of the image, each of which is related to a particular way of determining an image's value:

1. The image reflects basic reality. This is what Baudrillard refers to as the "natural" stage. Images have a natural referent, meaning they intend to refer to the "natural" world. The value of the image is its use value simply construed as being generated through the natural use of the natural world.

2. The image masks and perverts basic reality. This is the "commodity" stage. Images refer not to the natural world, but to the general equivalence mechanism of capital. The linkage, that is, is no longer between the image and the material world, but between the image and its capital equivalent. The value of the image is its exchange value, generated through the commodity logic.

3. The image masks and perverts the absence of basic reality. This is the "structural" stage. Images refer neither to the natural world nor to capital, but to the structural codes that shape capital accumulation and flows. The value of the image is its sign-value, generated by reference to a set of models.

4. The image bears no relation to reality whatsoever, being its own pure simulacrum. This is the "fractal" stage, also described by Baudrillard as radiant or viral. There is what he calls an epidemic of value because there is no longer any point of reference or mode of equivalence at all.

Baudrillard describes the radicalness of the shift marked by the last stage:

> Speculation is not surplus-value, it is a sort of ecstasy of value, utterly detached from production and its real conditions: a pure, empty form, the purged *form* of value operating on nothing but its own revolving motion, its own orbital circulation.... What possible riposte could there be to such an extravagance, which effectively co-opts the energy of poker, of potlatch, of the "accursed share," and in a way opens the door to Political Economy's aesthetic and delusional stage?... [T]his ... phase transition is fundamentally more original than all our old political utopias.[10]

Baudrillard does attribute transitions from phase to phase to technological development. With industrialization, he argues, signs are detached from unique and caste-specific origins—and therefore the desire or need for counterfeiting—because of mass production. Origin, he argues, lies no longer with the maker, but with technique, and the real is "that of which it is possible to give an equivalent reproduction."[11] Events in the world, too, have changed their form: "In earlier times an event was something that happened—now it is something that is designed to happen. It occurs, therefore, as a virtual artifact, as a reflection of pre-existing media-defined forms."[12]

Baudrillard goes on to argue, however, that it is still important to distinguish between forms of falsity in this environment. Dissimulation, he notes, is to feign not to have what one has (implying a presence), while simulation is to feign to have what one hasn't (implying an absence). The two kinds of falsity relate to the reality principle quite differently. Dissimulation leaves the reality principle intact—the difference between the real and the fake is clear, only masked. Simulation, however, threatens the distinction between the "true" and the "false," the "real" and the "imaginary" altogether.

Finally, Baudrillard describes the role of law in the hyperreal environment:

[T]he law is a second-order simulacrum whereas simulation is third order, beyond true and false, beyond equivalence, beyond the rational distinctions upon which function all power and the entire social.[13]

These ideas of Baudrillard resonate with the development of U.S. constitutional thought about labeling. These cases are introduced in the next section.

REGULATION OF LABELING

Beginning in 1871, the U.S. Supreme Court has looked at the right of the government to regulate labeling, justifications for regulating specific types of labels, and different media considered to be labels.

The Right of the Government to Regulate

The right of the government to regulate labels has four bases: protection of labels via trademark legislation is held to derive from British common law; it is held to be a subset of the general area of intellectual property rights, with its constitutional status; it is held to be a concomitant of the mandate to regulate interstate commerce; and it is held to be based in other statutory law.

Common Law. It was in *Trade-mark Cases*, 100 U.S. 82 (1879) that the common law argument was first made, an argument further supported by later cases such as *Hanover Star Milling Co. v. Metcalf*, 240 U.S. 403 (1916). A history of trademark and intellectual property rights that reached far back into British common law was identified, supporting the right to regulate in this area on the grounds that such intervention existed long before either legislative or constitutional activity.

Intellectual Property Law. The first discussion of the government's right to exert power in the area of labeling came in 1871, when trademark litigation was identified as a distinct subdomain of the law in *Canal Co. v. Lark*, 80 U.S. 311. The impetus behind the protection of trademarks paralleled the argument in other areas of intellectual property rights: The purpose of the trademark was to assert a relationship between the producer of an object and the object itself, and one earned the right to use a trademark by the labor involved. Thus, in *Manufacturing Co. v. Trainer*, 101 U.S. 51 (1879), the Court held that one can attach a trademark only to things one has produced oneself. The importance of a labor investment in asserting the right to use a trademark is now held to apply to the mark itself, as well as to the object to which it is applied.[14] The importance of labor relative to procedural assertions of rights in a mark was articulated in *Trade Commission v. APW Paper Co.*, 328 U.S. 193 (1946), in which the Court held that a mark in use before intellectual property rights were asserted in it by someone else can't be deemed illegal in use, though the original user may be required to use additional language or symbols as a qualifier (under discussion was the use of a red cross on toilet paper and paper towels before the Red Cross was formed in 1905).

Trademark is distinguished from other areas of intellectual property rights in the level of creativity required, however, either in the object labeled or in the label itself. One need not have invented the object labeled, nor exercised any particular creativity in the shaping of particular products, in order to have the right to label those objects as the result of one's own labor. Similarly, the creation of trademarks themselves is understood to be the result of a process less creative and distinctive than that required for the assertion of copyright or patent. What was the dissent in 1871's *Canal Co. v. Clark*—which argued that trademarks denote not originality, but origin, producer, ownership, or place of manufacture of sale of the article to which it is affixed—became the majority view by 1879. In *Trade-mark Cases*, the Court described the process of development of a trademark as an essentially historic and organic process, rather than a creative one:

> The ordinary trade-mark has no necessary relation to invention or discovery. The trade-mark recognized by the common law is generally the growth of a considerable period of use, rather than a sudden invention. It is often the result of accident rather than design. (100 U.S. 82, 94 [1879])

The issue of how much processing of a material constitutes sufficient labor to assert labeling rights has also been problematic at times. In *U.S. v. Sullivan*, 332 U.S. 689 (1948), the Court called it misbranding to remove pills from a large, correctly labeled package and put them into a small, incompletely labeled package for retail resale, noting that labeling must be correct at every stage of the transaction. In *Champion Spark Plug Co. v. Sanders,* 331 U.S. 125 (1947), on the other hand, there was such a large investment of labor on the part of spark plug reconditioner's and such significant alteration to the materials involved that the Court supported Champion in insisting that reconditioned plugs be clearly marked with the reconditioner's label, both on the product and on the packaging.

Trademarks, then, are implicitly understood to emerge out of communities of meaning to which the producer of the goods labeled themselves belong. Thus, *Trade-mark Cases* also distinguished trademark from other areas of intellectual property law by stating that words in common use can be taken for a trademark if at the time of adoption those words are not employed to designate the same or like articles of production. Still, a trademark doesn't permit the owner to claim monopoly in the sale of any goods other than those produced or made by him- or herself, the mark can't be used to deceive, and the owner can't claim property rights in all the uses of a generic term.

Interstate Commerce Law. The argument that the interstate nature of commerce justified extension of government regulatory efforts in this area across space was first presented by the prosecuting attorney in 1879's *Trade-mark Cases,* in which he claimed that the effects of wrongdoing in trademark cases can't be confined to a state, but "extends to all places where there is a market for the goods which are simulated by the false device."[15] By 1913, the Court specifically asserted federal control over states in this area, locating its mission in the mandate to keep interstate commerce free from transportation of illicit or harmful articles.[16] In 1946, the Court emphasized that Food and Drug Administration (FDA) rules about misbranded materials applied as much to commerce within a state as to that which is interstate, as long as it involves someone who regularly engages in interstate commerce.[17] In 1958, in the related area of false advertising, the Court did, however, decide that mass-produced materials distributed to local distributors for distribution should be governed by local, not federal, law.[18]

Other Statutory Law. More than once the Court has pointed out that there is no legal way of addressing misleading or false labeling unless there is specific law addressing the matter. The point is explicitly made in *U.S. v. Mersky,* 361 U.S. 431 (1960). There, the Court said that an importer can't be prosecuted for removal of labels identifying violins as manufactured in the Soviet Union and the General Democratic Republic (GDR, the former East Germany) after importing but prior to sale because the concern of the pertinent law was collection of duties, not protection of consumers; labeling is not important to those assessing duties. Again, in *Compco Corp. v. Day-Brite Lightday*, 376 U.S. 234 (1964), the Court held there can be no suit over the quality of a copy of something if the entity being copied was not protected by intellectual property rights in the first place.

Justifications for Regulation

All of the cases involve issues of facticity, examining distortions either of the label or of the product being labeled that generate a disjuncture between the two. Falsity alone, however, has not been sufficient to justify legal intervention; rather, the Court has looked at the consequences of falsity or distortion of either kind.

Three types of arguments have been used by the Supreme Court to justify the regulation of labeling in specific cases, all aimed at impact on the consumer or purchaser of a product. The original, though not often expressed, concern was simply with the right of producers to mark their own goods and did not therefore require those objects to be transferred to other hands through commerce. Commercial concerns soon dominated, however, focused on the possibility that one might be misled about the producer or origin of a particular product. As the development of labeling law blossomed through the period of development of antitrust and other bodies of law concerned with consumer protection, so it too turned more toward possible effects (primarily health) for the consumer or user of a product. These three types of arguments might be called the justification from labor, the justification from perception, and the justification from consequence.

The Justification from Labor. In *Trade-mark Cases* (1879), the Court took the position that one did not have to be in business to have a trademark—only to be the producer of the articles marked. The potentially damaging consequence associated with this argument is to the producer of the good, whose personal right to take credit for what has been produced might be contravened. Even though the Court in the same year moved beyond this position, stressing effects on consumers in

Mfg. Co. v. Trainer, this same case continued to state that one can attach a trademark only to things one has produced oneself. This argument continues to hold sway. For example, in 1987, when a San Francisco arts organization was permitted to use the generic term "Olympics," the Court explained that the exertion of investment and energy into even a generic term is sufficient to generate intellectual property rights.[19] Conversely, lack of use is sufficient to lose rights, as the Court noted in *United Drug Co. v. Theodore Rectanus Co.,* 248 U.S. 90 (1918). The strength of investment as an argument has grown over time; in *Kellogg v. National Biscuit Co.,* 305 U.S. 111 (1938), the Court held that no rights could be held in the term "shredded wheat" because it is generic.

In today's environment, however, the relationship between producer and good has become problematic. A pair of cases, *K Mart v. Cartier,* 485 U.S. 176 (1988) and *K Mart v. Cartier,* 486 U.S. 281 (1988), dealt with the complexity of the relationships between various parts of a transnational corporation, of concern because of labeling issues that arise when a product crosses a border. At issue was the importation of gray-market goods—goods that are manufactured outside of the United States but bear a valid U.S. trademark and are imported without the consent of the U.S. trademark owner. The Tariff Act of 1930 prohibits importation of certain gray-market goods, while the Customs Service regulations allow importation where the foreign manufacturer is affiliated with the U.S. trademark owner or has received the owner's authorization to use its trademark. The Coalition to Preserve the Integrity of American Trademarks and two of its members filed suit against the government, claiming the regulations in conflict. K Mart and 47th Street Photo intervened as defendants, arguing that appropriate jurisdiction of the dispute lies with the Court of International Trade because the issue revolved around the construction of a significant trade embargo that had large-scale economic consequences. The Court took the position that the Customs Service's actions legitimately lay within the jurisdiction of U.S. courts because it dealt not with an embargo but with a question of labeling requirements before importation.

Having decided this was a labeling case, not a trade embargo case, the parties in the second suit then went on to distinguish between three types of possible relationships: that in which the right to use a registered U.S. trademark is purchased, that in which there is an identity relation between the United States and foreign firm (the latter a subsidiary or parent or the same as the U.S. firm), and that in which the use of a registered U.S. trademark is licensed for a particular foreign location. It became obvious, through the course of discussion, that there is great confusion over what "ownership" of a trademark means when a corporate entity crosses national boundaries. The case in which a domestic firm establishes a manufacturing division abroad, for example, was found to be quite problematic. While the Court here held that importation of gray-market goods can't be prohibited in cases in which the foreign manufacturer is authorized to use the trademark, Justice Brennan and others, concurring in part and dissenting in part, point out that the Tariff Act in effect gives a virtual monopoly, free from intrabrand competition, on domestic distribution of any merchandise bearing the trademark. Brennan noted that such action would deny access to the very firm that manufactured the graymark merchandise abroad, to affiliates of foreign manufacturers, or to firms that authorize the use of their trademarks abroad. Justice Scalia, in a dissent, also emphasized the economic impact of legal confusion over the status of graymark goods. Since intellectual property rights are now understood to lie at the root of international tensions over trade, this issue is likely to rise again.

A related issue is the role of labels as a structural economic force subject to the rules of antitrust law. In *U.S. v. Topco Associates*, 405 U.S. 596 (1972), the operation of a cooperative association of small- to middle-sized grocery store chains, in which members had exclusive territories for sale of the goods, was held in violation of the Sherman Act as a horizontal restraint of trade. Chief Justice Burger dissented here, noting that there was no price-fixing collusion, only labeling agreements; the effect of the activity was to increase competition of these smaller grocery store chains with larger chains, not to decrease it.

The Justification from Perception. In 1879's *Mfg. Co. v. Trainer* the Court began to build its argument that the purpose of protecting trademarks is to prevent customer mystification, an economic argument concerned with quality assurance. In the 1879 case, it was made clear that infringement need not require the copying of an entire label, though context is important to determining whether there has been infringement; here, the infringement claim was denied because it was not really possible to mistake one product for another.

Even once arguments about consequences for the consumer had emerged, the importance of perception remained. In 1942, the Court in

Trade Co. v. Raladam, 316 U.S. 149, ruled that if health reasons for challenging a trademark can't be found, the commercial arguments will do. A second 1942 case, *Mishakawa Manufacturing Co. v. Kresge,* 316 U.S. 203, made the point that value in a trademark is generated through successful conveyance to the minds of potential customers of the desirability of the commodity upon which it appears. In 1946, the Court explicitly held that a word can't be used as a trademark if it is misleading about constituent materials (in this case, *Siegel Company v. Trade Commission,* 327 U.S. 608, the term "Alpacuna" applied to a material that included no alpaca).

Misperception is important, even when it is clear that no danger to health can be shown, as in two cases involving ultimately the correct labeling of imitation milk in a situation in which no damage to health had ever been either claimed or demonstrated.[20]

The Justification from Consequence. In 1913, the justification for regulation of labeling because of potential damaging consequences for consumers emerged. In *U.S. v. Lexington Mills,* 232 U.S. 399 (1914), which involved the adulteration of flour, the Court was concerned not about falsity, but about the potential health-damaging effects of the food product's adulteration. Intention was seen by the Court here as key. In *CIBA Corporation v. Caspar W. Weinberger, Sec. of HEW,* 412 U.S. 640 (1973), the Court upheld the Food and Drug Administration's insistence that approval of a drug be withdrawn if there is not substantial evidence of the level of effectiveness of the drug claimed on its label. Health consequences of misleading labels were seen as so significant that they justified multiple seizures of misbranded articles in *Ewing v. Mytinger & Casselberry,* 339 U.S. 594 (1950).

It was concern about consequence that lead the Court in 1964 to distinguish two different ways of altering the relationship between text and the object to which it ostensibly refers: the label can be changed, or the product can be changed (adulterated). In *U.S. v. Wiesenfeld Warehouses,* 376 U.S. 86 (1964), the Court decided that adulteration of contents of a product even by storage in a warehouse under conditions that may lead to potential damage to public health is illegal.

It took until 1976, however, to recognize that sometimes there is change in a labeled product that is natural, not adulteration. In *Jones v. The Rath Packing Co.,* 430 U.S. 519 (1976), the Court dealt with a clash between California labeling laws and federal law. California laws did not deal with moisture loss in products like meat and flour, so that labels constructed under their provisions were ultimately misleading to consumers. Federal law, however, does take natural moisture loss over time into account so as not to mislead consumers in this way. Federal law was held here to preempt state law.

Because of the culpability associated with altering either products or labels, and in recognition of the lengthening of production chains so that more than one person is often involved in the production and delivery of a product, in *Moskal v. U.S.*, 498 U.S. 103 (1990), the Court addressed the question of the difference between falsity and the making of falsity. *Moskal* dealt with automobile titles with falsified odometer readings that were carried across state lines for reissuance, and then carried back again for car sale. The question was whether, once the titles had been issued in good faith by one state government, carrying them across state lines constituted carrying "false" titles. While the Court here went with a broad construction of the relationship between falsity and making false, Scalia's dissent argues for an important difference between the two.

Media Considered to Be Labels

While the popular notion generally considers labels to be those printed materials affixed to or embedded within material objects, the Court has held a far wider range of media to be labels. Seven media that *are* considered to be labels are discussed below, as well as one that is *not*.

Design Characteristics. In *Plumley v. Massachusetts*, 155 U.S. 461 (1894), it was deemed by the Court that food coloring is to be considered part of the label of the product oleomargarine and subject therefore to accusations of misleading the public about whether the product is oleo or butter. Despite the fact that the product was correctly labeled oleomargarine, the Court decided that manufacturers were not permitted to use yellow food coloring in their product, as this would mislead the public. A dissent pursued the legitimacy of this ruling, given that butter itself is made yellow through the use of food coloring. The manufacture of generic pills in such a way as to make them resemble patented pills as much as possible, however, was not held sufficient to hold the manufacturer liable for the ultimate mislabeling of those pills by pharmacists at the point of sale (*Inwood Laboratories, Inc. v. Ives*

Laboratories, Inc., 456 U.S. 844 [1982]). Once a mark has been claimed incontestably, it cannot be challenged on the grounds that it is generic (*Park 'N Fly v. Dollar Park and Fly,* 469 U.S. 189 [1985]).

More recently, in *Two Pesos v. Taco Cabana,* 112 S.Ct. 2753 (1992), "trade dress" was held to serve the purposes of a label. By trade dress the Court means the "total image and appearance of a business," which is protected if it either is distinctive or has acquired a secondary meaning. (In this case, involving two chains of Mexican restaurants with similar decor, the Court held that distinctiveness is sufficient.)

Advertising. In *Kordel v. U.S.,* 335 U.S. 345 (1948), the Court held that all labeling is in a sense advertising, and that all advertising is in a sense labeling. In this the Court contradicts itself, however, when in *Thomas Cipollone v. Liggett Group Inc.,* 112 S.Ct. 2608 (1992), it suggested, while remanding proceedings, that further investigations look into the question of whether advertising may have neutralized the effects of potentially misleading labeling on cigarette packages. While cases dealing on their surface with advertising, not labeling issues, were not as a category included in this study, this would be an exploration worth undertaking.

Pamphlets. Leaflets sent separately from a machine explaining the machine's use are labels—despite the fact that the leaflets were sent 18 months after the machine's delivery—because both interstate deliveries were considered to be part of the same transaction.[21] In the Court's holding here, a transactional relationship, not a material one, is held sufficient to link information with a material good. In *Kordel v. U.S.* (1948), descriptive pamphlets distributed separately from the drug that they described were held to be labels, as the Court stressed the textual, rather than the physical relationship between the information and the material.

Invoices. Invoices are considered to be labels because they are media through which deception can be spread. Thus, in *FTC v. Mandel Brothers,* 359 U.S. 384 (1959), a list of specific types of information to be included on labels was also required to be included on invoices in an industry in which customers routinely removed labels from the products themselves—fur coats.

Regulatory Categorization. In 1987's *Meese v. Keene,* 481 U.S. 465, application of a regulatory category to a film was explicitly considered to be a label, though in this case the labeling of a particular film by the U.S. Attorney General as "political propaganda," thus denying entry of the film into the United States, did not infringe the First Amendment rights of a citizen who wished to distribute the film. Here, the Court made the argument that the descriptors "political propaganda" were neutral and accurate, contradicting its earlier position that context is irrelevant in determining the meaning and effect of labels. Aside from *Meese v. Keene,* however, these cases do not explicitly explore the role of the categorization as a label, and so are not included here, though their study from this perspective would be fascinating.

License Plates. The New Hampshire requirement that nonofficial automobile license plates bear the motto "Live Free or Die" was held to be an abridgment of the First Amendment rights of Jehovah's Witnesses in *Wooley v. Maynard,* 430 U.S. 705 (1977). The license plates were here considered to be labels with consequent legitimate requirements regarding their content when it distinguished between facilitating individual vehicle identification, legitimately required, and the motto, which doesn't play the same labeling role.

Use. In *Wisconsin Public Intervenor v. Mortier,* 501 U.S. 597 (1991), it was held that the Federal Pesticide, Fungicide, and Rodenticide Act, originally only a licensing and labeling act, could be used to regulate use of these chemicals.

Information Collection. About the only medium that has been discussed by the Court in a labeling context that was *not* held to be labeling is the process of information collection. The question was explored in *Dole v. United Steel Workers,* 494 U.S. 26 (1990), a case in which the United Steel Workers (USW) challenged the Occupational Safety and Health Administration (OSHA) to require the same labeling of hazardous chemicals and training on all types of work sites, not just the currently regulated manufacturing sites. OSHA developed regulations of this kind and took them to the Office of Management and Budget (OMB) for review. The OMB, which has responsibility for reducing governmental paperwork, including reducing the amount of information collected and processed, rejected three elements of the OSHA plan. The USW took the issue to court, claiming that the OMB has responsibility for information collection procedures, not for labeling and training, and that the agency therefore had no right to review the OSHA plan. After discussing differences between information collection and labeling procedures at length, the Court agreed with the USW.

Labels and the Hyperreal

The history of cases dealing with labeling in constitutional law exhibit the move into a hyperreal condition in the relationships between labels and the material objects to which they refer, between labels and facticity, and between labels and stages of the image.

Labels and the Objects to Which They Refer

While the first labeling cases assumed a direct material relationship between labels and the objects to which they were intended to refer, over time this relationship became detached. Four types of relationships are discussed: material, transactional, textual, and use.

The material cases—based on a commonsense understanding of the relationship between label and object—dominate early history of the labeling cases. Then a transactional relationship was deemed to be sufficient in invoices in *U.S. v. Bruno,* 329 U.S. 207 (1946), a case that dealt with paper invoices, and in *FTC v. Mandel Bros.,* 359 U.S. 384 (1959), the case that dealt with fur coat invoices. In *U.S. v. Urbuteit,* 335 U.S. 355 (1948), leaflets sent separately from a machine but explaining its use were similarly held to be labels. Then a textual relationship was deemed to be sufficient, in *Kordel v. U.S.,* 335 U.S. 345 (1948), the case in which pamphlets informing consumers of use of drugs held that those pamphlets were, for the purposes of the law, labels. Finally, the very use of something was held treatable under labeling laws in *Wisconsin Public Intervenor v. Mortier,* 501 U.S. 597 (1991).

In sum, we see in these cases a drifting away of the label from the object to which it refers. The result is a loss of location of the label itself, almost an ephemeralization of the label as it participates in the growing nonspecificity of globalization processes.

Labels and Facticity

While on the surface it is claimed that the purpose of labeling laws is to ensure facticity, in fact, the kinds of facticity concerns expressed vary widely. There are cases in which:

The Information Is Factual but Misleading. In *Carolene Products v. U.S.* (1944), it was found that correct labels are not enough if the public can misperceive the product (in this case, "filled" milk for whole milk). In *62 Cases of Jam v. U.S.*, 340 U.S. 593 (1951), imitation jam that labels itself as such was determined not to be misbranded in a decision written by Justice Frankfurter, though Justice Douglas's dissent emphasized that had there not been confusion, there would not have been a case.

The Information Is Factual but the Material Good Is Damaging to the Health. In *Reilly v. Pinkus*, 338 U.S. 269 (1949), the Court turned aside from the question of whether a diet plan actually works for the purpose of dieting as claimed, instead basing its decision on the evidence that the plan, which uses iodine, clearly hurts some people's health.

Investment in Information, Not Facticity, Is What Counts. In a striking example of this, the Court supported the legality of bringing a dispute over the Food and Drug Administration's requirement that all drug labels had to include generic as well as trade names on all of its packaging in *Abbott Laboratories v. Gardner*, 387 U.S. 136 (1967). Claiming that this would be an enormous economic expense to the industry, requiring disposing of large amounts of existing packaging and requiring resetting of type on all new packaging to be printed, Abbott Laboratories sought the right to challenge the FDA in court. The Supreme Court supported Abbott in this effort, arguing that doing so would in this case assist timely implementation of the law.

In terms of facticity, this can be understood as a case in which the FDA sought to increase the level of facticity by upgrading the level of referentiality. By asking the drug industry to include generic as well as trade names on its labels and packaging, the FDA was asking that the information provided move from a level of particularity so specific as to be confounding to a categorical level comprehensible by the consumers of the products described. The drug industry resisted this increase in level of facticity, knowing if it failed there would be a potential for economic loss as consumers became more economically savvy in their drug shopping, by arguing that even the change would create a sizable economic loss. The Court's support for judicial review of the FDA's decision can be read as tacit agreement that level of investment is to be considered at least as important as level of facticity.

Thomas Cipollone v. Liggett Group Inc. (1991) provides another example in which the level of investment by large corporations appears to influence the Court's treatment of the facticity of labels. This case explored the relationship between federal and state laws regarding the labeling of cigarette packages, a question that arose as a consequence of a suit by a man who claimed that his wife had died of lung cancer because she was misled by the labels on cigarette packages as to the possible health consequences of smoking. The Court here remanded the case for determination as to the specific ways in which the labels were deemed to be misleading in order to ultimately determine which law applies; the willingness of the Court to tolerate the question demonstrates the relative weightings of facticity and the potential for economic loss.

The Information Is Factual, but Only to a Degree. In *Leech v. Carlisle*, 258 U.S. 138 (1922), Justice Clarke's opinion for the Court argued that it was one thing to call a patent medicine a medicine (a question of identity) and another to call it a panacea (a question of degree). Because the Court left the decision as to which was involved in the case at hand to the Post Office, Justices Holmes and Brandeis here dissented, calling it an unconstitutional exercise of prior restraint.

Cultural and Institutional Conceptions of Factual Referentiality Differ. In the 1919 decision *Houston v. St. Louis Packing Co.*, 249 U.S. 479, it was held that the term "sausage" can't be used if a product has more than 2 percent cereal, though many recipes in use at the time used up to 10 percent. Problematically, many sausage recipes with very long histories within particular cultural communities also used relatively large amounts of cereal. In this case, cultural understandings were forced to give way to institutional definitions. While we are well aware of the health concerns that lay behind such bureaucratic determinations, surely this decision stimulated a sense of hyperreality in those who were told that the sausage they had made for generations was no longer sausage.

Labeling and Stages of the Image

Chronologically, the labeling cases fall into four periods that, in their development, map directly onto Baudrillard's four stages of the image and their correspondent notions of value. These chronological stages are not bright lines, but rather general indicators, for there is overlap among stages and glimmers of "later" kinds of value appear in even the earliest cases. As with all social institutions, new forms do not replace existing forms; instead, they form an overlay on top of earlier forms that continue to exist.

The Natural Stage. The first period, which may be considered to include the period before any labeling cases arose to the Supreme Court in 1879, was marked by ambivalence between the natural stage and the commodity stage of the image. This is not surprising, since these cases emerge deep into the industrialization process. While the right to interfere with labeling practices is defended,[22] there is confusion as to whether a mark or label must be in commerce in order to be protectable. In the same year, 1879, the Court both held that a good does not have to be commerce in order to have a trademark,[23] and used engagement in commerce as a justification for interference.[24]

The Commodification Stage. The second period, from 1890 to 1944, is characterized by cases concerned about the role of labels and trademarks in their impact on commodification and commerce. While during the first period the natural value of labels derived from the information they provided about the producer of a good (and therefore about other characteristics expected of the good), during this second period the value of labels derives from their contribution to commodification. In 1894, for example, the Court held that oleomargarine cannot be dyed yellow to look like butter—even though, as Justice Fuller noted in a dissent, butter itself was dyed.[25] Clearly, this argument is being made to protect certain competitive conditions. In 1937, the Court upheld the Filled Milk Act, which forbade the shipping of skimmed milk compounded with any other fat or milk products so as to resemble milk or cream; of note here is the Court's argument that such "imitation" is particularly dangerous when consumers can neither distinguish the product from that which it imitates, nor note any link between the product and any health problems.[26] And in one more example, in 1941, the Court held that while an earlier examination of Marmola's false claims about its ability to help reduce weight were rejected because harm to health couldn't be proven, arguments that it takes market away from others are acceptable.[27]

The Structural Stage. The third stage involves cases that deal with labels from the perspective of what Baudrillard described as structural value—value derived not from referentiality nor the distortion of referentiality offered by commodification, but by sign-value in which value is derived from relationships to models. Beginning in 1944, there is a shift in the kinds of questions about labeling that were raised. In the second *Carolene Products* case, *Carolene Products v. U.S.* (1944), *correct* labels were held illegal based on perceptions of consumers; in this case, even correct labels were not deemed legally acceptable if the filled milk product they identify can be perceived by the public as the same as whole milk. In 1946, the Court used the case of *Siegel v. Trade Com.*, which dealt with a material called "alpacuna," which did not include alpaca, to determine that a word can't be used as a trademark if it is misleading about constituent materials. Siegel here was not claiming the material in use was alpaca, but the suggestive symbolic reference relative to a "model" of what alpaca is was enough to be disturbing.

In *U.S. v. Bruno,* 329 U.S. 207 (1946), the false grading of paper on invoices, which meant a higher price for consumers, was determined to be unlawful. This was a particularly interesting case, for it was decided during a period in which paper was so scarce that customers often accepted whatever paper arrived, whether it was what had been ordered, and whether it cost more than what had been ordered. Thus, the material model against which the labeling (via invoice description) occurred was itself shifting in nature. In another case involving a shift in the materials to which labels referred, *Champion Spark Plug Co. v. Sanders,* 331 U.S. 125 (1947), reconditioners of spark plugs marked as such but still bearing the trademark of the original manufacturer, Champion, were ordered by the Court to ensure that the mark denoting reconditioning was clear both on packaging and on the plugs, along with the name and address of the reconditioner. (They were *not* ordered to remove the Champion mark altogether, however, which Champion had sought.) In a final striking example, 1972's *U.S. v. Topco Associates*, 405 U.S. 596, treated shared labels as if they held the same effect as explicit structural agreements among firms for the purposes of treatment by antitrust laws.

The Fractal Stage. The 1894 case *Plumley v. Massachusetts*—in which it was held that oleomargarine can't be dyed yellow to look like butter, which is also dyed yellow—may be considered the first example of fractal value in labeling cases. In terms of the history of modernity and postmodernity, the date of this case is not problematic if it is remembered that the first aesthetic experiments with detaching symbols from the need for referentiality occurred in the same period. Indeed, in the long view that places the beginnings of modernity in the 17th century, the turn of the 20th century can be seen as offering the first signs of postmodernity.

It is the most recent cases, however, that more clearly show what Baudrillard referred to as the stage of fractal value. This stage may be said to have begun in the 1980s, with the two *K Mart v. Cartier* cases, which found it essentially impossible to clearly determine ownership of intellectual property rights at all in a global environment of multiple and complex institutional relationships. The notion, in *Two Pesos v. Taco Cabana* (1991), that a general mode of being may be covered by intellectual property rights might appropriately be referred to as an "ecstasy" of value. And the decision that use is, for legal purposes, treatable as labeling under *Wisconsin Public Intervenor v. Mortier*, 501 U.S. 597 (1991), similarly moves the "image" away from referentiality altogether.

CONCLUSION

Though referentiality is a fundamental assumption underlying First Amendment interpretation, this analysis of the history of the treatment of labels in U.S. constitutional law demonstrates that referentiality is no longer assumed in other areas of constitutional adjudication dealing with symbol and language use. Rather, we find labels detaching themselves from material objects and dispersing themselves across space and time as well as into actions and modes of being rather than materials. The question of facticity in labels is placed behind concerns about consumer health and economic issues in terms of relative importance. And the initial question of whether labor was involved in the creation of the labeled good has moved to the question of whether there was labor involved in generating the label itself rather than the good.

Indeed, we find these cases demonstrating many of the characteristics Baudrillard has described as features of the postmodern condition. The history of the cases replays the four stages of value Baudrillard identifies. Contemporary cases find labels and their objects placeless in the globalized context. Only with great difficulty are they attached to particular entities, exhibiting in one more domain the identity problems that plague the postmodern condition. Labels no longer refer, factually, to the material goods with which they are associated, but rather to other symbols, whether cultural or economic. The use of labels increasingly deprives longstanding cultural practices of their content and meaning, stimulating in individuals and communities an increasing sense of the hyperreal.

To say that these cases "trigger" the hyperreal is not to deny that they also reflect and are produced by broader social, cultural, economic, and political trends. The question of whether the Supreme Court makes policy is an old one. Histories of the Court exhibit periods of greater and lesser overt policy-making activity, and individual justices are to varying degrees self-aware about this aspect of their activities. On the spectrum of agency involved in the production and reproduction of culture, constitutional law moves variably somewhere towards the middle. It can't be denied that constitutional law manifests general social conditions and thinking, but at the same time, if it has any import at all, it must also be acknowledged that—again to varying degrees—the decisions of the Supreme Court make things happen, within legal discourse and as that discourse affects other social processes.

In this sense, then, these cases in the history of constitutional law dealing with labels can accurately be said to have played a role in triggering the hyperreal aspects of the postmodern condition. By suggesting that the sausage you have always known is no longer sausage, that an instructional pamphlet received a year after purchasing a product or that restaurant paint jobs are labels, and by placing referentiality behind clearly commercial concerns in determining a label's "facticity," these cases encourage the move away from any expectation of referentiality in language and symbol use for the purposes of the law. While we have tended to understand the law as a conservative force, we can see in this instance at least that the law can also serve as a stimulus to radical social change.

A number of assumptions that no longer hold underlie our interpretation of the First Amendment. Premier among them is the sense that the speech and press activities that are the subject of First Amendment law involve language and symbol use that are referential to a material reality both in intention and in actuality. Clearly this assumption, among others, must be reexamined as we seek to understand the import of the First Amendment under the conditions of our contemporary communicative environment.

Notes

The author thanks Donald Gillmor, who encourages constant enrichment of approaches to understanding the First Amendment in general, and Stuart Ewen, who encouraged "Trigger" in particular.

1. Ithiel de Sola, *Technologies of Freedom* (Cambridge, Mass.: Belknap Press, 1983).

2. Lennard Davis, *Factual Fictions: The Origins of the English Novel* (New York: Columbia University Press, 1983).

3. Sandra Braman, "The 'Facts' of El Salvador According to Objective and New Journalism," *Journal of Communication Inquiry* 4, 2 (1984): 75–96.

4. Jean Baudrillard, *Simulations* (New York: Simeotext(es), 1983).

5. Braman, "The Autopoietic State: Communication and Democratic Potential in the Net," *Journal of the American Society for Information Science* 45, 6 (1994): 358–368.

6. See Niklas Luhman, "Autopoiesis: What Is Communication," *Communication Theory* 2, 3 (1992): 251–259, and *A Sociological Theory of Law* (London: Routledge & Kegal Paul, 1985).

7. Clifford Geertz, *Local Knowledge: Further Essays in Interpretive Anthropology* (New York: Basic Books, 1983), 171.

8. Erik McLuhan and Marshall McLuhan, *Laws of Media: The New Science* (Toronto: University of Toronto Press, 1992).

9. Arthur Kroker, *The Possessed Individual: Technology and the French Postmodern* (New York: St. Martin's Press, 1992).

10. Baudrillard, 35.

11. Baudrillard, 146.

12. Baudrillard, 4.

13. Baudrillard, 40.

14. See, for example, *San Francisco Arts & Athletics v. U.S. Olympic Committee*, 483 U.S. 522 (1987).

15. *Trade-mark Cases*, 100 U.S. 82 (1879).

16. *McDermott v. Wisconsin*, 228 U.S. 115 (1913).

17. *U.S. v. Walsh*, 331 U.S. 432 (1947).

18. *FTC v. National Casualty,* 357 U.S. 560 (1958).
19. *San Francisco Arts & Athletics v. U.S. Olympic Committee.*
20. See *U.S. v. Carolene Products,* 304 U.S. 144 (1938), and *Carolene Products v. U.S.,* 323 U.S. 18 (1944).
21. *U.S. v. Urbuteit,* 335 U.S. 355 (1948).
22. *Canal Co. v. Lark,* 80 U.S. 311 (1871).
23. *Trade-mark Cases.*
24. *Manufacturing Company v. Trainer,* 101 U.S. 51 (1879).
25. *Plumley v. Massachusetts,* 155 U.S. 461 (1894).
26. *U.S. v. Carolene Products Co.*
27. *Trade Com. v. Raladam,* 316 U.S. 149 (1942).

PART V
OUTSIDER VOICES

TEN

Feminism and Free Expression: Silence and Voice

ROBERT JENSEN AND ELVIA R. ARRIOLA

After what happened all those years ago,
I wonder if I'll ever live free again.

Those words, posted on a "survivors' wall"[1] on a university campus by a woman who was raped, raise critical questions about what it means to be free and live free in our society and how well the notion of freedom of expression works for members of oppressed groups. In this essay, we suggest that dominant First Amendment theory regarding free expression is not very good *theory* because in *practice* it does little to promote the expression of the people who most need to find their voices; if an idea is said to be good in theory but not in practice, then it's not really a good theory.[2]

From a feminist perspective, women's lives—and particularly sexual-abuse survivors' lives—highlight this gap between free-expression theory and practice. In theory, the woman who posted those words on the survivors' wall is free: She is a citizen of what we call a free country, with at least some freedom to move and work where she pleases, with certain rights said to guarantee the freedom to express herself in whatever way she chooses. Her posting—telling her story and naming its legacy—might be seen as an exercise of the First Amendment's guarantees of free speech and press, which are intended to contribute to living free lives. But this survivor's speech act is hardly a success story of the American political system's procedures and rules, which grant her specific freedoms by law but do not necessarily operate to foster those freedoms. Her posting takes place within a historical and cultural context in which the vast majority of survivors of sexual violence are ignored, blamed, pathologized, threatened, disbelieved, and otherwise revictimized when they protest the violation and try to hold their offenders accountable.

Current statistics suggest that, in the United States, at least one of four women will be raped in her lifetime,[3] one of three women is a victim of childhood sexual abuse (usually by a family member or trusted adult),[4] and countless millions of women are subjected to sexual harassment at school, in the workplace, in the marketplace, and on the streets.[5] With this level of sexual violence—described by one of the leading rape researchers as "a scourge, if not an epidemic"[6]—questions, made concrete here in the voice of a rape survivor, emerge: What does freedom mean? What sociopolitical, legal, historical, and psychological factors would lead a survivor of sexual violence to fear that her freedom had been permanently compromised? Is her fear of not ever living "free again" a sign of her own pathology or of deeply rooted societal problems? What is there about the experience of sexual violence that calls a woman's freedom into question not only for the discrete time period of the violation but also, seemingly, for the rest of her life? Is there, in fact, something about our sexually violent culture that threatens the freedom of all women, survivors and nonsurvivors alike? Finally, does the general freedom of others to portray a woman as a natural victim of men's natural sexual aggressiveness increase women's chances of being victimized?

These questions about the relationship between freedom, social location, and lived experiences are essential to further questions about the exercise of power and voice in this society. Power, privilege, and oppression play a key role not only in the quality of life of different members of our society but also in the strength, credibility, and resonance of voice. Thus, any analysis of freedom of expression must attend to the power relations of diverse men and women as they manifest themselves in their everyday lives.

In essence, we ask: What if traditional First Amendment law protects the freedoms of some, but constricts society's ability to recognize the common suppression of others' expression? What if First Amendment theory helps create the illusion of "free speech" in a society where so many know or believe that they cannot speak freely?

Feminist Theory, the Law, and Sexual Violence

This article challenges several underpinnings of Anglo-American law and justice. We join, with added commentary, the critiques in other essays in this volume of these philosophical positions—such as the public-private dichotomy, law's assertion of objectivity, the quest for allegedly neutral principles, and individualism.

The traditional liberal view that has influenced law and social policy-making is that justice will emerge through neutral, objective rules and processes that avoid partiality. We reject the notion that law is neutral in any sense. Laws are made and enforced based on assumptions and definitions that are the product of human choices and, hence, are politically charged. The prevailing cultural myth is that people with power shape neither lawmaking nor judicial decision-making; consequently, judicial forums beckon the people to resolve their conflicts before impartial and neutral judges. The problem, of course, is that this notion of principled jurisprudence does nothing to aid those people who are displaced in the existing power structure; such people are invisible to those who build and maintain these "impartial" forums.

The history of Anglo-American law is a history of the privileging of the perspective of white heterosexual men of the upper classes and the corresponding exclusion of outsiders to the power structure, such as women, non-whites, and lesbians and gays. Consequently, in the liberal dichotomy between universal principles and individual preferences, the experiences of the powerful are cast as "universal principles," while experiences of the marginalized citizen are inevitably characterized as individual preference or egregious whim. So, the question is not whether individual experience and perceptions—which are rooted in one's class, race, gender, and sexual identities—will shape the law, but *whose* experiences count and how honest the system will be about that fact.

Because free-expression law is even more explicitly rooted in the myth of objectivity and neutrality, a critical approach is even more crucial. Accepting current free-speech law doctrine, which centers on governmental noninterference, requires denying that the government and legal system are inextricably involved in the structuring of both the public and private worlds. In practice, this obfuscation means that free-expression doctrine is part of a system that helps maintain the status quo; those who have power continue to have the greatest opportunities to speak in an effective manner. From that assertion, which is adequately defended in greater detail both in this volume and in more than 50 years of critical legal scholarship, we turn to the feminist critique supporting this and other critiques of how traditional free-expression law silences the disempowered.

Feminist theorizing challenges any definition of freedom which holds that an agent acts freely if her actions are perceived as voluntary and if she can choose between available options. Marilyn Frye argues that women in this culture are oppressed by a "systematic network of forces and barriers that tend to the reduction, immobilization and molding of the oppressed."[7] Such forces are neither accidental nor occasional, and women can't simply avoid them; rather, women's lives are caged in.[8] Like Frye's metaphor of a bird caught in a bird cage, oppressed people can mistakenly focus on the one wire that seems to entrap them—the wire they need only fly around to be free—rather than to step back and grasp the larger systemic and structural forces that shape, restrict, and confine their lives. On this view, freedom is not sufficiently understood by merely referring to discrete moments in time or even to specific situations, but must be both contextualized and historicized. Returning to the example of a rape survivor, the question nags: If a rape survivor truly had expressive freedom, why would she have to resort to posting an anonymous statement on a wall? What forces in legal and social systems restrict a survivor to a bulletin board to protest her violation and express her despair, pain, and outrage? The answer to this question lies in a feminist conception of a patriarchal system that *legitimates* sexual violence against women by its own legal practices.

The common wisdom is that rape, incest, and other forms of sexual abuse are difficult for the legal system to control because of inherent difficulties in proving that an unwanted attack took place. Because of that, and the companion phenomenon of victim-blaming, in the United States only 2 percent of intrafamilial child sexual abuse, 6 percent of extrafamilial sexual abuse, and 5 to 8 percent of adult sex assault cases are reported to police.[9] This state of affairs is the predictable result of a legal system that is patriarchal both in the means and ends toward which it works. The "problems" in prosecuting rape are rooted not in unavoidable difficulties of proving a case but in the systematic devaluation of women and children in the culture. That status has usually rendered them either unreliable witnesses to their own violation or even contributors to the injuries inflicted upon them.[10] When it operates most efficiently, a patriarchal system suppresses the victim's ability even to name the violation and allows the mostly male perpetrators to avoid sanctions in most cases. Sexual assault—and society's typical response to it—makes it clear that a patriarchal culture can see itself as fair, just, and well-meaning in the face of systematic brutality and institutionalized disregard for women and children. This may appear as a strong statement, but in response we must ask: How could a society allow the documented levels of sexual abuse of women and children if it did not, at some level, have contempt for the victims?

A Feminist Approach to Women's Oppression by Silencing

Part of what it means to be oppressed is to be silenced. Anyone can be silenced as a result of trying to protest injustices, correct distortions, name injuries, tell her own story, and participate fully in the construction of knowledge. Silencing members of oppressed groups, however, can work in subtle and insidious ways; oppressed people are discouraged, mocked, shamed, and simply ignored, as well as explicitly punished for speaking out when their voices do not support the status quo. And they are silenced when theorists, researchers, thinkers, lawmakers, and citizens generalize about human "truths" from a position that logically and psychologically excludes them.

Feminist theorizing helps us define and explore how various systems of oppression interact and support one another so as to continually recreate hegemonic power relations among different groups, in particular between women and men. Although there are different theories within feminism, some central tenets emerge. Jane Flax, for example, identifies three assumptions common to feminist theory: (1) that women's experiences are different from men's experiences; (2) that women's oppression is a unique set of social problems that is not to be understood as merely a subset of some other social structure; and (3) that women's oppression is not just a matter of "bad attitudes" but of the way the world is organized.[11]

Ruth Ginzberg suggests that *survival* is the issue and that

> theory-making must place the survival of women at the center: Women must constantly concern ourselves with how to survive batterings, rapes, wars and other violence, racism, homophobia, depression, mother-blaming, poverty, hatred, isolation, silencing,

rupturing of our communities, exhaustion, spiritual co-optation, conceptions of health that view us as diseased in ways that we are not and that do not address or even acknowledge our actual suffering, indoctrination in patriarchal thinking in the place of genuine education, demands on us to do more than our share of the work of the world, trivialization of our knowledge, and destruction of those things that are beautiful and that nourish our souls. None of these things is of our own doing. They are the results, and evidence, of our oppression. In one way or another, we often find ourselves not knowing whether, or how, we will survive. When we do survive, we often suffer survivors' guilt.[12]

Broadly construing Ginzberg's argument, we might say that good feminist theory affirms women's lives and experiences, in particular their critical need to survive. "The nature of oppression," Ginzberg writes, "is such that no form of survival is assured to those who are oppressed."[13] Feminist theory, then, places the survival of women at its center.

History abounds with examples of the silencing of specific women and ways in which that silencing contributes to the oppression of women as a class. However, while the oppression of women is not merely a subset of other social relationships, issues of oppression cannot simply be reduced to an analysis of the ways in which men oppress women. Gender does not arise naturally as the most salient and essential feature of the self or of oppression, but is one aspect among many that comprise identity. In its broadest sense, "gender" is an analytic category that serves to organize relations of power among people, just as is, for example, race. Oppression affects different women in different ways, always inflected by race, class, sexual orientation, ethnicity, and other relevant factors that operate within a complex network of power relations. Gender oppression should not be subsumed under other categories, but neither should it be viewed as the most important, or most harmful kind of oppression. It is best to think of these sites of oppression as constituting a web; when a woman is oppressed as a woman, for example, those actions pull on race, class, and other relevant categories, which affect the gender oppression. Furthermore, women's oppression is directly affected by the fact that masculinity is also marked with hierarchies. Men oppress other men along the axes of class, race, and other factors. For men or women, any thorough discussion of "who oppresses whom" cannot ignore each person's race, class, sexual orientation, ethnicity, bodily abilities, etc.[14]

Diversity among women presents both theoretical and practical political difficulties within feminism. Much feminist work has been criticized for being dominated by white middle-class women, thus perpetuating hegemonic power structures. One manifestation of this domination—as bell hooks, Elizabeth Spelman, and others have argued—takes the form of feminist theorizing that is done from a perspective of universalizing *white* feminists' voice.[15] Such universalizing erases important differences among women and distorts theories of alleged liberation. By erasing differences and falsifying or distorting some women's experiences, feminist theorists effectively silence less powerful voices. The goal of shaping a liberating system of freedom of expression thus requires ways in which citizens and free moral agents can use and experience the power of their voices.

The concept of free expression is incomplete without a recognition that oppressive silencing is distributed in this society unequally and unjustly. Oppression—the act of reducing another's will to one's own and usurping another's autonomy and agency based on one's perceived differences or group membership—calls for both resistance and change. Given the legal, social, and political power structure of our society, one can assume *in theory* that those who need or want liberation can and should express their outrage at the harms inflicted by an unjust system. *In practice,* however, many do not share the power, privilege, or right of the mostly white men in this society, who have traditionally used the law to protect their own interests. Our concern, then, is to see whether current methods of ensuring "free speech" actually create the needed space for the members of oppressed groups to articulate their experiences and have them addressed.

As noted earlier, the continued domination of powerful voices is a problem within feminism as well as in society overall. In working to become more inclusive in feminist circles, both thinkers and activists have raised critical questions about voice and experience. As Maria Lugones states:

> Feminism is, among other things, a response to the fact that women either have been left out of, or included in demeaning and disfiguring ways in what has been an almost exclusively male account of the world. And so while part of what feminists want and demand for women is the right to move and to act in accordance with our own wills and not against them, another part is the desire and insistence that we give our own accounts of these movements and

actions. For it matters to us what is said about us, who says it, and to whom it is said: having the opportunity to talk about one's life, to give an account of it, to interpret it, is integral to leading that life rather than being led through it.... We can't separate lives from the accounts given of them; the articulation of our experience is part of our experience.[16]

As variously positioned in relation to power, privilege, and oppression, then, we must learn how to attend to the lived experiences of one another. Consciousness-raising is one way people "can emerge from the unthinkable (silence) to an alternative conception of the world (voice)."[17] Consciousness-raising, understood as "collective critical reconstitution of the meaning of women's social experience, as women live through it,"[18] is a distinctive aspect of feminist methodology. But, as we suggested above, the process of "women telling their stories" is not politically neutral: Women do not come together as equals but as situated selves whose power relations play out along various dimensions. It is crucial for an oppressed person's voice and experience to be given play and expression in her own space and context, within her own world, and not to be usurped and colonized by dominant persons and groups. Altering the most subtle of power dynamics can transform inequalities of voice, and ultimately transform the material conditions of marginalized groups.

Attending to the particularities of various diverse women's lives is a complex and destabilizing task for feminist theorists. One of the more critical questions feminists face is the extent to which we can generalize about women-as-a-class at all. Some feminists suggest we avoid oppressive, totalizing generalizations by practicing "pattern perception" in order to open up inquiry and generate new meaning.[19] The goal is to allow the generalizations that theory and politics require, without giving in to reductionism and totalitarianism, which can only come with a commitment to seeing patterns rather than drawing final conclusions. Mari Matsuda has expressed a similar hope:

> Complexity is not the same as chaos. No two snowflakes are alike, but when it is snowing, it is cold outside. There are parallels and intersections in the maze of complex structures that are the human condition. Knowing one structure of subordination makes it easier to know another. We are not the same. But we are not so different

that we are bereft of the chances of knowing anything at all about one another and thereby about ourselves.[20]

Categories need to be "explicitly tentative, relational, and unstable."[21] Furthermore, we need humility in theorizing. This approach is an exercise in negotiating the terrain between a naive foundationalism and a politically debilitating postmodernism. Traditional approaches to the law generally ignore this need for humility, routinely generalizing in ways that wipe out important differences in the distribution of power in this society, equating for example, the free-speech concerns of a corporation with that of the individual.[22] Again, we approach this issue with a focus on the realities of power in society and a sensitivity to the way in which theorizing, including feminist theorizing, can overgeneralize.

The Survivors' Wall

Sexuality is one of the most important sites of men's oppression of women, where the dynamic of male domination and female subordination is eroticized. The eroticization of power most often occurs in the form of male domination over women, but it also emerges as a dynamic in many relationships, heterosexual or same-sex, where one party is vulnerable because of physical or mental disability, relative lack of knowledge, or age. Our focus here is on female survivors of male violence.

The feminist view of rape and sexual violence rejects the myth that sexual abuse is committed only by deviant men. Rape, incest, and battering are, in an important sense, political acts, individual expressions of institutional woman-hating. Far from deviant, they are in fact the norm; sexual violence and harassment occur so frequently that the majority of women experience such abuse at least once in their lives, and such violence is in sync with, not a deviation from, masculinist conceptions of sex and gender relations. As Wendy Stock points out:

> [R]ape is not only the result of uncontrolled lust, exaggerated gender role behavior, miscommunication, or a misguided desire for physical intimacy. These factors do not sufficiently explain why rape occurs when alternative sexual outlets are always available, including masturbation, when aggression could be exhibited by a nonsexual attack, or where direct communication by the woman is

often ignored, not misunderstood by the rapist. Rather, rape and other forms of sexual coercion can be viewed as both the expression and confirmation of male power, dominance, and control of women.[23]

This perspective informs the free-expression issues involved in the survivors' wall. At first blush, it may seem like a somewhat eccentric case study for exploring a new theoretical approach to speech. But the routineness of patriarchal sexual violence and the power of that violence to silence survivors compels us to account for it in a free-expression theory. Also, this focus makes clear the need to place free-expression theorizing in a context of the structure of power in this society and the limits of liberalism. This perspective does not guarantee simple answers to the questions we pose. In fact, we find ourselves struggling to find workable solutions. One of the appealing qualities of conventional 20th-century liberal free-speech theory is its simplicity and apparently seamless quality: Free speech simply is allowing all to speak. A critical reconstruction of free-speech doctrine is far messier and less reassuring, and we see no reason to pretend that the approach we endorse is simple.

On the surface, the survivors' wall seems to bolster the case for liberal free-expression doctrine. In response to requests for space for expression, a government agency (a state-funded university) provides part of a public commons reserved as a free-speech area for a group that seeks a voice. The state does not censor the content of the board, and anyone who chooses to read it may stop and engage the material. Women's accounts of sexual assaults against them have long been suppressed, and the creation of spaces for their expression is an act of resistance to patriarchy. The forum benefits a number of people: The women who post the writings have a channel to speak. Some women who are survivors may stop to read the wall and may find comfort and support in the writings. Men who have little understanding of the effects of rape have the chance to stop, read, and learn.

At that level, the wall is a success. Liberalism works. Free-speech ideology is vindicated. But under those same liberal rules, that board creates some problems and fails to address others.

Content Neutrality

One of the central tenets of the liberal free-speech paradigm is content neutrality, the idea that the government cannot target for suppression particular views.[24] A number of Supreme Court decisions have set forth this doctrine, warning that the government "has no power to restrict expression because of its message, its ideas, its subject matter, or its content."[25] Under that theory, Nazis must be allowed to march in a predominantly Jewish suburb,[26] and misogynist pornography is protected as the expression of a political idea.[27]

But, what if a man who believes feminists have concocted rape stories to punish men for their natural, healthy sexual aggression, presses his right to post a misogynist diatribe against women on the survivors' wall, or demands space next to that board for a "persecuted perpetrators" wall? Should the doctrine of content neutrality in public forums be applied to guarantee his ability to post such a notice? From the liberal view, such a concession is acceptable, even beneficial. As the argument goes, in the "marketplace of ideas," all ideas are allowed in without judgment. But, what if the posting of such writings by men silences even one survivor? Some women might respond by posting critiques of the men; the attacks by men might actually push women who would not have written to write. The more likely result is that such an attack would silence other women who already feel hesitant about writing. It could make some women and men reluctant to read the survivors' wall. It is not difficult to imagine a representative of the men's rights point of view using that bulletin board to exercise *his* First Amendment right to criticize or politely denigrate women who post writings on survivors' walls and people who stop to read them.

The traditional liberal response to this kind of problem is the "more speech" solution. Justice Louis Brandeis's suggestion, that the remedy for harms is "more speech, not enforced silence,"[28] has become a key tenet of liberal free-speech ideology. But when the playing field is decidedly not level—when cultural myths and stereotypes about women reinforce male domination and female victimization—then "free speech" is unlikely to lead to a situation in which all speak freely. Survivors and perpetrators don't enter the conversation with equal power; indeed, if we lived in such an egalitarian world, sexual assault would not be the problem it is. If the goal is government neutrality, or collective impartiality, we need to ask: What does it say about a society that seeks to be impartial in a dispute between rapist and survivor?

This is not an argument for the wholesale silencing of men, perpetrators, or nonfeminists. The point is to highlight how traditional First Amendment doctrine cannot deal with a relatively simple case in which members of an oppressed group seek some sliver of space to name the violence the culture encourages. Given the realities of power in the culture, government noninterference in expression by perpetrators and survivors may in fact bolster the power of perpetrators. There is little damage done to the psychological or political interests of an antifeminist in limiting his "free speech" by restricting his ability to confront survivors face-to-face or message-to-message. But even that small effort would likely be deemed unconstitutional by a Supreme Court that has declared:

> [T]he concept that government may restrict the speech of some elements of our society in order to enhance the relative voice of others is wholly foreign to the First Amendment.[29]

Defamation

Another problem arises when women choose to name their abusers. This has been an issue not so much with survivors' walls, but with campus bathroom walls and fliers, where women have publicized the names of men who have raped them. This guerrilla tactic has been the result of women's frustration with campus and criminal justice procedures, which inadequately respond to the problem of rape, especially date or acquaintance rape. When those names get posted, officials quickly wipe them clean. At Oberlin College, for example, administrators tried to locate the people who put up posters identifying an alleged date-rapist, with the goal of punishing them. The right of free speech is constrained by concerns for defamation, and the survivors are trapped. A legal system that refuses to see rape as a serious crime also cuts off the survivors' chance to express their anger at the system and the perpetrator in the name of protecting the reputation of the accused.[30] Such results are not surprising given libel law's roots in a concern for "protecting the best men."[31] So long as the perpetrator has not been convicted of a crime, the presumption of innocence silences the survivor trying to name the crime.[32]

A case study of how this can work: In the 1980s, the group Women Against Rape (WAR)—a volunteer feminist collective that provided counseling services for rape survivors and engaged in political action in Santa Cruz, California—published fliers in which women could publicly name their rapists, even if the survivor had not reported the rape to police. When Steve Carney's name appeared in a 1984 flier under the heading "Assault/Attempted Rape," he sued the organization and the woman who accused him for libel, invasion of privacy, and intentional infliction of emotional distress. Carney and the woman, who countersued him for assault and battery and emotional distress, settled out of court. The case against WAR proceeded, and the jury awarded Carney $7,500 in compensatory and $25,000 in punitive damages. The appeals court overturned the verdict on procedural grounds and remanded the case for further proceedings.[33]

The case ended with an agreement that Carney would not refile the suit and WAR would not seek the attorneys' fees from Carney that the appeals court awarded. Independent of that settlement, WAR stopped producing the fliers naming assailants. WAR's attorneys advised the group that while it likely could offer a successful First Amendment defense if sued, the women who provided the information would be vulnerable to damage awards. Because the goal of WAR was to give women options, not subject them to further harm, the group decided to stop the flier campaign.[34] The group's intent was to use speech not to punish men but to help women protect themselves, but the simple assertion of "our right to talk about what's going on for us"[35] was undercut by First Amendment doctrine.

We know of no research that has charted how often libel suits and threats are used against survivors, but the WAR case is clearly not unique. For example, in Boulder, Colorado, in the late 1980s, two such suits were filed by men against the women who accused them of rape, with the rape survivors filing counterclaims. In one of those cases, prosecutors did not file criminal charges, and the civil suit resulted in a default judgment against the rape victim, who chose to return to her native Indonesia. In the other, the man was acquitted of the criminal charge, after which the man and woman agreed to a dismissal of the civil case.[36] In a slightly different context, but with the same effect, men accused of sexual harassment have learned that countersuits against women who complain are an effective strategy for silencing.[37] At least one man has successfully used a malpractice lawsuit against his daughter's therapists to counter claims of incest.[38]

All of this takes place, of course, in a culture that has a notoriously difficult time defining rape and other forms of sexual violence and intrusion. Only when the rape fits a culturally acceptable profile—perpetuated by a stranger, on a woman of "good moral character," preferably with a weapon and with bruises or cuts to prove that violence actually took place—is the crime likely to be prosecuted.[39] When women try to name as rape those attacks that don't fit this profile, the system works to shut them down. When aggressive and coercive sexual behavior by men is deemed the norm, the legal system is understandably hesitant to hold individual men accountable for a range of questionable behaviors that seem "normal."

A Mass-Mediated World

Stepping back from those doctrinal questions, we must ask about the impact of a survivors' wall in a culture dominated by mass media, and especially electronic media. Whatever the benefits to the small number of participants and readers, a survivors' wall can do little to counter the very different message about rape that pervades mainstream media. Television, movies, and news accounts of rape that endorse certain rape stereotypes, or at best do little to counter those myths, are prime shapers of public attitudes.[40] Notes on a survivors' wall have little power to counter such messages.

While liberal free-speech doctrine has evolved in the 20th century to protect the rights of the individual speaker in a public space—the speaker on a soapbox in a park—that doctrine has been less successful at coping with changes in technology and in media industries. As newspaper competition dwindles and corporations gain control of more publications, liberal free-speech doctrine has been unable to find a way to guarantee citizen access.[41] In broadcast media, where the government has assumed some regulatory authority, significant citizen input or access is hardly any more meaningful.[42] As other contributors to this book have argued, the underlying issue is the dominance of corporate, commercial media in the United States and the way in which the First Amendment has been used to block public input into decisions about those media.[43]

When feminists argue that entertainment media's portrayals of women as sexualized objects is one factor that heightens the risk of sexual assault, media companies can simply explain that the First Amendment precludes the government from taking any action to hold them accountable.[44] Only when profits are threatened, are media corporations spurred to act.[45]

So, when for every one person who reads a survivors' wall and comes to a new understanding of the oppressive nature of sexual violence, there are 10,000 or 10 million (a specific number isn't crucial to the argument) viewers watching a film that depicts a woman enjoying being raped, it is important to ask whose speech is freer and what the First Amendment is protecting. In that context, the survivors' wall, while a useful channel for some people, is not a serious challenge to patriarchy.

Before Speech Happens

Stepping back again, another question appears: What about the speech of women who have not yet found their voice? How does the First Amendment work for women who have been silenced by the patriarchal violence of cultural attitudes that deny the existence of their harm? Again, when power differentials rule in intimate settings, neutral rules and procedures regarding speech have the effect of favoring the powerful. In this context, the problem isn't even about equal access to major media outlets, since access is of no value without a voice. The concern at this level is for the woman who was raped or sexually abused by a trusted member of the family and could not find, or has not yet found, the words to put on the board; the woman who, no matter what vehicles are available to her, has been silenced, maybe permanently, by patriarchal violence and her own feelings of shame and fear. What of the women who, living in a state of oppression, are left without a voice? Liberal free-speech ideology has no theory, no doctrine, and no rules to reach people for whom powerlessness prevents them not only from being heard, but from having anything to say. Liberalism addresses the issue of silencing, but only when someone is poised to speak and is stopped from speaking by the government. The question of collective action to help people find their voice, however, is almost never a part of legal discourse, especially when the root cause of the silence is deeply embedded in the private sphere, where patriarchal violence so often takes place.

Feminism can be used to redefine the boundaries between traditional notions of free speech and the silencing rooted in the oppression of women. What has long been thought of as outside the purview of the law (e.g., the silent cry of rape or incest) can be defined as a central issue in First Amendment jurisprudence. Recognizing that some women may want to speak but cannot out of fear, or do not because of restraints imposed by existing doctrine (e.g., libel suits), would force society to redefine the meaning of freedom and the meaning of speech. It would require government to work toward a society in which the meaningful exercise of freedom is possible. Are there risks that, in pursuing such collective solutions, individual expression will be squelched? Yes, but perhaps the more important question is why legal liberalism is so unconcerned with those voices that go unheard under traditional First Amendment doctrine.

Sketching a Feminist Theory of Free Expression

Because our goal is something more than an abstract notion of freedom protected by neutral rules and procedures, it is crucial to be clear about our first principles: resisting oppressive systems that maintain unequal distributions of power and resources, and finding ways to give voice to those who are silenced by such systems. Justice—the rectification of past injustice and elimination of present forms of subordination, "the human plea for decent lives"[46]—should be the goal of theory. The goal of feminism is an end to all oppressions, not just gender oppression, and one way toward that goal is theorizing free expression from a feminist point of view.

We begin with an often ignored question, which Frederick Schauer put as "why is speech special"?[47] That is, why give speech more protection than other forms of behavior? Like Schauer, we conclude there is no compelling reason to do so. Schauer admits the "intellectual ache" in his acceptance of the speech-is-special position; we avoid the ache and argue that it is not. That allows us to question the assumption that all speech starts out as protected speech and that we should carve out exceptions only when massive evidence of harm exists. We start with the assumption that any speech that injures can be restricted through collective action. Under traditional libertarian First Amendment doctrine, protecting some dangerous, harmful, offensive, or even oppressive speech is the price we pay for freedom. We ask questions about what counts as speech and who is identified as an affected party in the speech, so that we can be clear who is being asked to pay for what.

Notions of the nature of the individual and the formation of the self are important in understanding freedom of expression. Robin West describes the liberal order as premised on a separation thesis, "[t]he claim that we are physically individuated from every other" and "that what separates us is epistemologically and morally prior to what connects us."[48] Our feminist view of freedom of expression is based on the rejection of that thesis and the assertion that we better understand ourselves as "second persons," people constantly learning the art of personhood.[49] We live in relation, and any conception of the self as standing outside of relationships is unrealistic. Thus, the goal in both epistemology and morality is "an appropriate interplay between autonomy on the one hand, and communal solidarity on the other."[50] We always are partly who others construct us to be, and in contemporary society, various mass media channels have great power to do that.

In traditional freedom of expression law, the focus is primarily on the speaker and his or her right to speak, on rare occasions on consequences of that speech on listeners, and in even rarer cases on a third party who has been affected by the actions of the listeners (when direct causal links between the speaker's inciting speech and the listener's act can be shown). In West's terms, this liberal position views speech as primarily expressive, with a focus on the individual. A more progressive view frames speech as primarily communicative, something that creates community and "a social soul."[51] Here, the value of speech depends on the quality of the relationships and communities the speech engenders.

Lisa Heldke similarly argues that speaking is better understood as a collective activity than the product of an individual, and that the focus on the speaker limits our ability to understand the position of listeners, potential speakers, potential listeners, and other community members whose lives might be indirectly affected. We should view communication as something that is created among people and affects all in the chain. In Heldke's words, this view changes the question from:

> "Is this speaker free to say what he or she will?" to "Is the talk in this situation free—are all members of the group participating at a level that promotes, rather than prohibits, the speech of others?"[52]

If we are in crucial ways always in the process of being constructed by others at the same time as we work to construct ourselves, we must reexamine any rule or doctrine that is justified by an appeal to individual autonomy, especially in regard to issues involving the media and representation. Because the speech of some can perpetuate hierarchies and silence others, subordinated people have an especially important stake in gaining some control over how dominant forces in society construct them.

The difficult question, of course, is whether there can be "individuality without individualism"?[53] Is there a way to acknowledge and attend to those connections between people that are truly constitutive of personal identity without denying particularity? Liberalism's attention to, or obsession with, individualism has not been without its benefits in freeing people from the direct constraints of authoritarian powers; it is important to remember that two centuries ago people in England were tortured for speech critical of government, and that well into this century government officials at all levels in the United States did not hesitate to throw into jail socialists, radicals, union organizers, and others deemed to be stirring up trouble through speech. The point we press, however, is that liberalism also protects the individuality of some at the expense of others, whose subordinated status sometimes negates the possibilities of individual expression. The vague charge that collective action necessarily leads to totalitarianism—so central to liberal attacks on such things as hate-speech codes—not only is hyperbolic but obscures the suppression that is inherent in the workings of a liberal system in an unequal society, where power and oppression go unnamed.

If one accepts that *speech is not special*, then the considerable energy devoted by scholars to identifying the line between speech and action is of questionable value. Both speech and action, used here with common definitions, have tangible effects in the world. The law punishes a number of types of pure speech—blackmail, threats, conspiracy, participation in criminal acts by speaking—without concern for First Amendment implications. In those cases, the harm involved is not considered debatable. From our view, the harm from a variety of other kinds of speech—sexist or racist insults, pornography, and the general category of hate speech—is equally clear and worthy of society's concern. Forms of expression/action that may seem harmless on the surface—such as mainstream images in journalism, advertising, and entertainment that sexualize, trivialize, and marginalize women—are also of great concern. That does not mean that laws must be passed in each case to limit those expression/actions, but that each deserves scrutiny. Following West, we argue the First Amendment should focus on

> the protection and facilitation of communication rather than expression, and the well-functioning community, rather than the soul-baring, expressive individual of conscience, as its inherent ideal.[54]

This theoretical perspective leads to a clear doctrinal commitment: Freedom of expression should not be limited to political speech—seen as speech specifically about politics—a tactic used by the right to try to construct a narrow First Amendment[55] and by the left/center to try to construct a more defensible First Amendment.[56] The idea that speech-about-government is at the heart of the First Amendment makes some intuitive sense in a democracy, if one accepts the public/private split. But if we understand politics to be the play of power in relationships, then the political or nonpolitical (using conventional terms) nature of expression is less relevant to First Amendment law. The more important question is how expression reinforces or challenges oppressive power. Expression that helps maintain patriarchal systems may or may not be political, in that narrow sense of the word. If, as we have argued, a conception of freedom of expression must remain focused on power, then we must accept the political nature of decisions about such a system of free expression and acknowledge that such victories on those decisions will be difficult to secure. Rather than search for neutral principles, the goal should be a political process that gives oppressed people a voice in the shaping of such doctrines. Rather than focus only on state action, the goal should be freedom of expression in the public and private realms.

To sum up: We contend that freedom of expression is about more than just the absence of government restraints on a speaker (a negative freedom concerned only about public power). It also is about oppressed people being free from the communication of others that harms them, both directly and indirectly (a negative freedom, but expanded into the private sphere) and about people being free to communicate to others the reality of their lives (a positive freedom). This involves restraints on both public and private power to prevent harm and the positive use of public power to help people find a voice.

An Application of the Theory

How might a feminist view change the way we adjudicate free expression disputes? We borrow from Martha McCluskey's analysis of the Colby College fraternity case, in which school administrators banned fraternities and later punished members of underground fraternities.[57] The fraternity members unsuccessfully sued, highlighting First Amendment issues of speech and association and the interpretation of the state's hate speech law. From a feminist framework, McCluskey points out that, while the college won, it won for the wrong reasons.

One of the reasons for the college's action was the fraternities' role in promoting sexist behavior and sexual violence toward female students.[58] The Maine Civil Liberties Union took up the cause of the fraternities, arguing that the college violated fraternity members' First Amendment rights. Both trial and appellate courts upheld the punishment of fraternity members, basing their decision on the state action doctrine: Because Colby is a private school, First Amendment concerns were not applicable, and the court should not mediate such a dispute between two private parties.

McCluskey points out a number of lessons from the case: how violence by members of privileged groups (such as mostly white and all-male fraternities) goes not only unpunished but unseen, and how American society exaggerates male suffering that results from a loss of privilege and trivializes the physical violence against marginalized groups. She also hints at how fraternity members' speech and actions restricted the free speech of women and some non-fraternity men on campus.[59] But we would push the point further and highlight the way in which men's violence can be a direct cause of the silencing of some women.[60] If, as McCluskey states, and we have no reason to dispute,[61] the fraternity in question had "a central purpose of fostering misogyny, and an actual practice of harassing and terrorizing women and other students,"[62] then the fraternity members' First Amendment defense can be answered by a more compelling First Amendment argument by women. Sexual violence silences women. The First Amendment is, most importantly, about promoting speech. The activities of those fraternity members were suppressing women's speech, not to mention restricting their ability to move and live free of fear. Here, the words of Andrea Dworkin, written specifically about pornography, are powerful and appropriate:

> If what we want to say is not *hurt me,* we have the real social power only to use silence as eloquent dissent. Silence is what women have instead of speech. Silence is our dissent during rape.... Silence is our moving, persuasive dissent during battery.... Silence is a fine dissent during incest and for all the long years after that. Silence is not speech. We have silence, not speech.[63]

How should a judge approach such a case, framed as competing First Amendment interests? Instead of retreating behind neutral principles and state-action doctrine, we would argue that judges should ask certain basic questions about power, privilege, and their effects on the ability of all involved to speak. If the fraternity members' misogynistic terrorist activities worked to silence women in classrooms, in college dorms, and on campus, then it seems clear that a decision to eliminate fraternities would be not an assault on the constitutional guarantees of free speech and association, but should be seen as First Amendment friendly.

This case reminds us that for the First Amendment to be truly a vehicle for protecting freedom of expression, we must allow it to reach beyond the narrowly defined public arena and hold private power accountable. We must listen not only to privileged voices but to the stories and concerns of oppressed people, with the goal of taking seriously the injuries they suffer at the hands of power. We must also be willing to use the political process to give those people hurt a chance to protect themselves and fight back.

We offer no detailed program for implementing these goals. But despite the liberal contention that the only choice is between authoritarian censorship and laissez-faire approaches to speech, viable solutions to these problems are possible. For example, we look to the antipornography civil rights ordinance as a model for feminist jurisprudence in action.[64] We have not focused on that critique of pornography, in part because it has been the subject of extensive debate and discussion for more than a decade, and also because it tends to polarize the debate. However, the ordinance—either overtly or implicitly—is consistent with most, if not all, of the principles we have outlined, and it would be disingenuous for us not to support it. The ordinance showed how tort law could provide women an avenue to both individual empowerment and societal change.

The radical feminist critique of pornography and sexuality focuses on how pornography sexualizes male dominance and female submission; pornography is understood as a kind of sexist hate literature, the expression and reinforcement of male sexuality rooted in the subordination of women that endorses the sexual objectification of, and can promote sexual violence against, women. This view was written in a proposed ordinance by Andrea Dworkin and Catharine MacKinnon in the mid-1980s. In its statement of policy, the ordinance identifies pornography as "a practice of sex discrimination" and a "systematic practice of exploitation and subordination based on sex that differentially harms and disadvantages women." The definition of porn used is "graphic sexually explicit subordination of women through pictures and/or words" that include one of eight types of images: women presented (1) dehumanized as sexual objects; (2) as sexual objects who enjoy humiliation or pain; (3) experiencing pleasure in sexual assault; (4) as sexual objects tied up or physically hurt; (5) in postures of sexual submission; (6) as body parts; (7) as being penetrated by objects or animals; and (8) in scenarios of degradation, humiliation, injury, torture, shown as filthy or inferior, bleeding, bruised, or hurt in a context that makes those conditions sexual.[65]

The ordinance creates five causes of action: coercion into the production of pornography, forcing pornography on a person, assaults directly related to pornography, defamation in pornography, and trafficking in pornography. Women can bring civil actions for damages from pornographers and for injunctions to remove pornography from distribution, either directly to court or through a government's civil/human rights agency. There are no criminal sanctions in the ordinance, and it does not give governmental agencies any power to initiate complaints.

Through these causes of action, the ordinance considers several different kinds of harm to women in pornography. The first four cases affect individuals, women who are hurt either by how pornography is made or by how it is used by men. The trafficking cause of action aims at the larger harm of pornography, the way in which the existence of misogynistic pornography contributes to the subordination of all women by portraying them not just as sexual objects, but as objects who should be, and always are, sexually available to all men.

The Court's rejection of that approach to pornography suggests we are far from being able to apply the ordinance's reasoning to more mainstream media,[66] but there are no theoretical reasons not to. The ordinance's strengths are in its refusal to accept liberal definitions of the issue, its attack on private forces that threaten women and children, and its strategy of placing the power to initiate legal actions against pornographers in the hands of the women who are hurt by it.

Another proposal that incorporates elements of our argument is Cynthia Grant Bowman's suggestion of a state statute or municipal ordinance to provide both criminal and civil remedies for women harassed on the street by strangers.[67] Bowman argues that street harassment results in an informal ghettoization of women to the private sphere, due in large part to "the thinly concealed violence underlying each of these encounters."[68] In balancing the harms with First Amendment concerns,

Bowman argues that harassing speech (1) is outside commonly accepted boundaries of the First Amendment, (2) falls within established exceptions, and (3) is low-value speech far afield from central concern of the First Amendment that should be subject to minimal scrutiny. Even if subjected to strict scrutiny, such a law passes muster, Bowman argues, because "it is essential to compelling state interests unrelated to the suppression of free expression: the security, liberty, and equality of women."[69]

Like the antipornography ordinance, Bowman's proposed law rejects male definitions of what happens when a woman is harassed on the street,[70] focuses on private forces that produce the injury, and, through the civil remedies, gives the women hurt by men the power to initiate legal actions.

CONCLUSION

To say that patriarchy silences oppressed people or women or survivors of rape and incest is not to say that no one from those groups ever finds their voices. A liberal system of free expression does result in such expression by some. But it also raises often insurmountable barriers that silence others. Often, those who break through remind us that we do not know how many have been silenced forever. Elly Danica's account of her life as an incest victim and survivor is such a work. She concludes her book with these words and this question:

> Survival. Dreaming with a pen in my hand. Writing. Writing. Writing. Who will hear me?[71]

NOTES

The authors would like to thank Nancy Potter for her contributions to early drafts of this chapter and for her continued support of this project.

1. As feminist critiques of sexual violence have made inroads in our culture, an increasing number of survivors of those assaults are finding a voice to speak about the abuse. One of the places this has happened is on "survivors' walls," typically on college campuses. These are simple bulletin boards on which survivors can post written accounts of their attacks and their reactions to them. Those accounts range from detailed descriptions of rape and incest, to analyses of the attacks, to calls for political action.

2. See Catharine A. MacKinnon, "From Practice to Theory, or What Is a White Woman Anyway?" *Yale Journal of Law and Feminism* 4:1 (Fall 1991): 13–22.

3. Diana E. H. Russell, "The Prevalence and Incidence of Forcible Rape and Attempted Rape of Females," *Victimology* 7 (1982): 81–89; and Allan Griswold Johnson, "On the Prevalence of Rape in the United States," *Signs* 6:1 (Autumn 1980): 145. For an overview of the problem, see Mary Koss and Mary R. Harvey, *The Rape Victim: Clinical and Community Interventions*, 2d ed. (Newbury Park, Calif.: Sage, 1991).

4. See, for example, Diana E. H. Russell, *Sexual Exploitation: Rape, Child Sexual Abuse, and Sexual Harassment* (Beverly Hills, Calif.: Sage, 1984) and *The Secret Trauma* (New York: Basic Books, 1986); and Judith L. Herman, *Father-Daughter Incest* (Cambridge: Harvard University Press, 1981) and *Trauma and Recovery* (New York: Basic Books, 1992). For an account of the politics of the response to child sexual abuse, see Louise Armstrong, *Rocking the Cradle of Sexual Politics* (Reading, Mass.: Addison-Wesley, 1994).

5. Amber C. Sumrall and Dena Taylor, eds., *Sexual Harassment: Women Speak Out* (Freedom, Calif.: Crossing Press, 1992); Michele A. Paludi and Richard B. Barickman, *Academic and Workplace Sexual Harassment: A Resource Manual* (Albany: SUNY Press, 1991).

6. Mary Koss, "The Women's Mental Health Research Agenda: Violence against Women," *American Psychologist* 45:3 (March 1990): 375.

7. Marilyn Frye, *The Politics of Reality* (Freedom, Calif.: Crossing Press, 1983), 59.

8. Frye, 4.

9. Koss, "The Women's Mental Health Research Agenda," 375.

10. For a discussion of how this plays out in the courtroom, see Alice Vachss's compelling account of her experience as a rape prosecutor, *Sex Crimes* (New York: Random House, 1993). For a British perspective, see Sue Lees, "Judicial Rape," *Women's Studies International Forum* 16:1 (1993): 11–36, in which she describes the way rape survivors are put on trial during the prosecution of rapists. See also Gregory M. Matoesian, *Reproducing Rape: Domination through Talk in the Courtroom* (Chicago: University of Chicago Press, 1993).

11. Jane Flax, "Women Do Theory," in Marilyn Pearsall, ed., *Women and Values* (Belmont, Calif.: Wadsworth, 1993), 4.

12. Ruth Ginzberg, "Philosophy Is Not a Luxury," in Claudia Card, ed., *Feminist Ethics* (Lawrence: University of Kansas Press, 1991), 130.

13. Ginzberg, 127.

14. Arriola, "Gendered Inequality: Lesbians, Gays, and Feminist Legal Theory," *Berkeley Women's Law Journal* 9 (1994): 103–143.

15. bell hooks, *Feminist Theory: From Margin to Center* (Boston: South End

Press, 1984); and Elizabeth V. Spelman, *Inessential Women* (Boston: Beacon, 1988).

16. Maria Lugones and Elizabeth Spelman, "Have We Got a Theory for You! Feminist Theory, Cultural Imperialism, and the Demand for 'the Woman's Voice,' " in *Women and Values,* 19.

17. Margaret Jane Radin, "The Pragmatist and the Feminist," in Patricia Smith, ed., *Feminist Jurisprudence* (New York: Oxford, 1993), 569.

18. Catharine A. MacKinnon, "Feminism, Marxism, Method, and the State: An Agenda for Theory," *Signs* 7:3 (Spring 1982): 543.

19. Marilyn Frye, "The Possibility of Feminist Theory," in Deborah L. Rhode, ed., *Theoretical Perspectives on Sexual Difference* (New Haven: Yale University Press, 1990), 174–184.

20. Mari Matsuda, "Pragmatism Modified and the False Consciousness Problem," *Southern California Law Review* 63:6 (September 1990): 1776–1777.

21. Angela P. Harris, "Race and Essentialism in Feminist Legal Theory," *Stanford Law Review* 42:3 (February 1990): 586.

22. *First National Bank of Boston v. Bellotti,* 435 U.S. 765 (1978).

23. Wendy Stock, "Feminist Explanations: Male Power, Hostility, and Sexual Coercion," in Elizabeth Grauerholz and Mary A. Koralewski, eds., *Sexual Coercion: A Sourcebook on Its Nature, Causes, and Prevention* (Lexington, Mass.: Lexington Books, 1991), 62.

24. First Amendment doctrine has long allowed, of course, the establishment of *categories* of speech that can be regulated or suppressed, such as obscenity and commercial speech. These regulations are not seen as violations of content neutrality because they do not discriminate on the basis of viewpoint; all obscene speech, for example, can be sanctioned, not just obscene speech that takes a certain point of view. This is not to say that we are supporters of absolute protection for either of those categories, but is meant only to point out the semantic game being played.

25. *Police Department of Chicago v. Mosley,* 408 U.S. 92, 95 (1972). For variations on this, see *Texas v. Johnson,* 109 S. Ct. 2533 (1989); *Frisby v. Schultz,* 108 S. Ct. 2495 (1988); *Boos v. Barry,* 108 S. Ct. 1157 (1988); *Carey v. Brown,* 447 U.S. 455 (1980); *Heffron v. International Society for Krishna Consciousness,* 452 U.S. 640 (1980); and *Cohen v. California,* 403 U.S. 15 (1971).

26. *Collin v. Smith,* 578 F. 2d 1197 (7th Cir. 1978), *cert. denied* 439 U.S. 916 (1978); *Village of Skokie v. National Socialist Party of America,* 373 N.E. 2d 21 (Ill. 1978).

27. *American Booksellers Association v. William H. Hudnut,* 771 F. 2d 323 (7th Cir. 1985); *reh'g denied,* 106 S. Ct. 1664 (1986).

28. *Whitney v. California,* 274 U.S. 357, 377 (1927).

29. *First National Bank of Boston v. Bellotti,* 435 U.S. 765, 790–791 (1978), quoting *Buckley v. Valeo,* 424 U.S. 1, 48–49 (1976).

30. See *Bingham v. Struve,* 184 A.D. 2d 85, 20 Med. L. Rptr. 2266 (N.Y. App. Div. 1992), in which a preliminary injunction was granted against a libel defendant who picketed in front of the plaintiff's apartment. After A. Walker Bingham sued her for calling him a rapist, Catherine Struve picketed outside his apartment, carrying a sign that read, "Attention residents of 19 East 72nd St. A. Walker Bingham raped me and is now suing me for libel." Struve was seeking an apology from Bingham for a date rape committed in the 1950s, which Bingham alleged was consensual sex. When the libel suit failed to silence Struve, Bingham sought the injunction. While the circumstances of this case are unusual, it is hard to justify the court's abandonment of a central principle of modern First Amendment jurisprudence—the doctrine that one cannot enjoin a libel, laid down in *Near v. Minnesota,* 283 U.S. 697 (1931).

31. Norman L. Rosenberg, *Protecting the Best Men: An Interpretive History of the Law of Libel* (Chapel Hill: University of North Carolina Press, 1986).

32. Martha McCluskey describes how this rule barred her from speaking about fraternity violence against women on a public radio station. See McCluskey's "Privileged Violence, Principled Fantasy, and Feminist Method: The Colby Fraternity Case," *Maine Law Review* 44:2 (1992): 310.

33. *Carney v. Santa Cruz Women Against Rape,* 221 Cal. App. 3d 1009, 271 Cal. Rptr. 30, 18 Med. L. Rptr. 1123 (6th Cal. Dist. Ct. App. 1990).

34. Personal communication between Robert Jensen and Jan Shirchild, former member of the WAR collective, January 25, 1994. Shirchild said the disbanding of the group in 1992 was the result not of the lawsuit or financial problems, but because of the dissipating energy of volunteers.

35. "Keeping Ourselves Safe," interview with WAR members, *Matrix* (monthly women's publication in Santa Cruz), July 1987, 3.

36. Mike O'Keeffe, "Running Scared," *Westword* (Boulder alternative weekly), November 29, 1989, 10–19; and personal communication between Jensen and Dan Hale, February 2, 1994. Hale represented the woman in the second case.

37. A query about this problem to a women's studies computer discussion list produced reports on several cases. For details of such a case, see Todd Ackerman, "UH Dismisses Professor Accused of Harassment," *Houston Chronicle,* January 8, 1994, A25; and Ackerman, "UH Sex Harassment Case about to Become a Nightmare," *Houston Chronicle,* March 8, 1993, A6.

38. B. Drummond Ayres, Jr., "Father Who Fought 'Memory Therapy' Wins Damage Suit," *New York Times,* May 14, 1994, A1. Gary Ramona, who claimed a therapist's treatment led to false memories of abuse against him by his daughter, won a $500,000 judgment. His daughter, Holly, continued to state that her father had abused her. Her sexual-abuse lawsuit against her father was dismissed seven months later, with the judge declaring that it had been deter-

mined in the malpractice trial that no abuse took place. Katy Butler, "Holly Ramona Suit Dismissed," *San Francisco Chronicle,* December 13, 1994, A18. For a discussion of the debate over false memories and incest recovery, see Elizabeth F. Loftus, "The Reality of Repressed Memories," *American Psychologist* 48: 5 (1993): 518–537; and the responses in *American Psychologist* 49: 5 (1994): 439–445. Loftus testified for Gary Ramona in the trial.

39. See Vachss, *Sex Crimes;* and Lees, "Judicial Rape."

40. For specific studies of these stereotypes, see Helen Benedict, *Virgin or Vamp: How the Press Covers Sex Crimes* (New York: Oxford University Press, 1992); and Susan L. Brinson, "TV Rape: Television's Communication of Cultural Attitudes towards Rape," *Women's Studies in Communication* 12:2 (Fall 1989): 23–36.

41. *Miami Herald v. Tornillo,* 418 U.S. 241 (1974), invalidating a right-of-reply statute.

42. Much is made of the Reagan-era FCC's decision to scrap the Fairness Doctrine, which the Supreme Court had upheld in *Red Lion v. FCC,* 395 U.S. 367 (1969). In reality, the FCC rules have never been a vehicle for serious citizen access to broadcast media.

43. Some First Amendment scholars have tried to address this issue while remaining true to liberal ideology. The results are tentative calls for some government intervention to mandate that, in very limited circumstancs, citizens have access to mass media. See Jerome A. Barron, *Freedom of the Press for Whom? The Right of Access to Mass Media* (Bloomington: Indiana University Press, 1973); and Thomas I. Emerson, "The Affirmative Side of the First Amendment," *Georgia Law Review* 15 (Summer 1981): 795–849.

An example is cable television, where the solution often has been for local governments to mandate that private cable companies provide a public access channel. But in competition with up to a hundred or more channels showing professionally produced material, the amateur productions on a public access station rarely attract many viewers.

44. There is a certain irony in this argument. Corporations use their private status to block public (government) intervention, also known as censorship. So, when private citizens, acting outside government through private associations, use various forms of pressure (letter-writing campaigns, picketing, threats of boycotts) to make their concerns known and press for action, the media corporations accuse them of trying to impose censorship.

45. As we write this, media corporations are taking half-hearted steps to respond to public disgust with the heightened levels of gratuitous violence, possibly as a way to head off potential government responses to the call of citizens by imposing regulations on broadcasters. This current debate has rarely touched on violence against women.

46. Matsuda, "Pragmatism Modified," 1768.

47. Frederick Schauer, "Must Speech Be Special?" *Northwestern University Law Review* 78:5 (December 1983): 1284–1306.

48. Robin West, "Jurisprudence and Gender," *University of Chicago Law Review* 55:1 (Winter 1988): 2.

49. Lorraine Code, "Second Persons," in Marsha Hanen and Kai Nielsen, eds., *Science, Morality and Feminist Theory* (Calgary: University of Calgary Press, 1987), 357–382. A revised version of this paper appears as chapter 3 in *What Can She Know? Feminist Theory and the Construction of Knowledge* (Ithaca, N.Y.: Cornell University Press, 1991).

50. Code, 382.

51. Robin West, "Toward a First Amendment Jurisprudence of Respect: A Comment on George Fletcher's 'Constitutional Identity,' " *Cardozo Law Review* 14:3–4 (January 1993): 761.

52. Lisa Heldke, "Do You Mind if I Speak Freely? Reconceptualiizing Freedom of Speech," *Social Theory and Practice* 17:3 (Fall 1991): 359.

53. This phrase is from Marilyn Friedman, "Individuality without Individualism: Review of Janice Raymond's *A Passion for Friends*," *Hypatia* 3:2 (Summer 1988): 131–137.

54. West, "Toward a First Amendment Jurisprudence of Respect," 765.

55. The most often-cited example is Robert H. Bork, "Neutral Principles and Some First Amendment Problems," *Indiana Law Journal* 47:1 (Fall 1971): 1–35.

56. The classic text here is Alexander Meiklejohn, *Political Freedom* (New York: Oxford University Press, 1965).

57. McCluskey, "Privileged Violence."

58. For evidence that fraternities tolerate, if not actually encourage, sexual coercion of women, see Stacey Copenhaven and Elizabeth Frauerholz, "Sexual Victimization among Sorority Women: Exploring the Link between Sexual Violence and Institutional Practices," *Sex Roles* 24: 1–2 (1991): 31–41.

59. McCluskey, "Privileged Violence," 310.

60. This also is a contention of the feminist antipornography movement. See Andrea Dworkin, "Against the Male Flood," in her *Letters from a War Zone* (London: Secker & Warburg, 1988), 253–275.

61. For a study of patterns of such behavior, see Peggy Reeves Sanday, *Fraternity Gang Rape: Sex, Brotherhood, and Privilege on Campus* (New York: New York University Press, 1990).

62. McClusky, "Privileged Violence," 296.

63. Dworkin, *Letters from a War Zone*, 269–270.

64. For the clearest articulation and defense of the ordinance, see Andrea Dworkin and Catharine A. MacKinnon, *Pornography and Civil Rights: A New Day for Women's Equality* (Minneapolis: Organizing against Pornography, 1988).

65. Dworkin and MacKinnon, *Pornography and Civil Rights*, 138–142.

66. *American Booksellers Association v. Hudnut*. Ordinance judged invalid, 598 F. Supp. 1316 (S.D. Ind. 1984). Judgment affirmed, 771 F. 2d 323 (7th Cir. 1985). Judgment affirmed, 106 S. Ct. 1172 (1986), and petition for rehearing denied, 106 S. Ct. 1664 (1986).

67. Cynthia Grant Bowman, "Street Harassment and the Informal Ghettoization of Women," *Harvard Law Review* 106:3 (January 1993): 517–580. Bowman describes street harassment as cases in which a male harasser targets a woman he doesn't know in a face-to-face encounter in a public space with speech that isn't intended as public discourse and is "objectively degrading, objectifying, humiliating, and frequently threatening in nature" (p. 524). For a discussion of street harassment and African-American women, see Deirde Davis, "The Harm That Has No Name: Street Harassment, Embodiment, and African American Women," *UCLA Women's Law Journal* 4:2 (Spring 1994): 133–178.

68. Bowman, 526.

69. Bowman, 546.

70. Elizabeth Arveda Kissling discusses how the unwanted "compliments" men say they give to women mark men's space, construct women as being for sex, and create "an environment of sexual terrorism" for women in general. "Street Harassment: The Language of Sexual Terrorism," *Discourse & Society* 2:4 (1991): 456.

71. Elly Danica, *Don't: A Woman's Word* (San Francisco: Cleis Press, 1988), 104.

ELEVEN

Why Lesbians and Gay Men Need Traditional First Amendment Theory

PAUL SIEGEL

The organizing principle of this volume seems to be that traditional perspectives on the First Amendment are inadequate, perhaps elitist, and in any event unresponsive to the needs of a culturally and economically diverse citizenry. This essay may constitute a dissenting voice. In what follows I hope to show that, for lesbians and gay males, traditional theories of the system of freedom of expression work quite well. Indeed, such theories may be the single cause for optimism in an otherwise hostile reception by the legal system.

The legal struggles faced by lesbian and gay litigants almost invariably involve issues of freedom of expression. In one sense, this is a trivial and obvious truth. Gays are, after all, often described as an "invisible minority"; implicit in this characterization is the unlikelihood of suffering antigay discrimination in the absence of some kind of communicative action that ends the invisibility.[1] Whether such an act takes the form of directly "coming out" to a potential employer (or landlord, etc.) or living an "openly gay lifestyle" that might by itself or through media coverage come to the attention of such an employer, issues of free speech and freedom of association are clearly implicated.

Perhaps a more substantive argument in support of the thesis that gay rights are, first and foremost, a First Amendment issue, would center not on the mechanism by which gays are "found out" but instead on the nature of the official reaction to such discovery. As David A. J. Richards cogently points out, antigay prejudice cannot any longer be justified in an intellectually honest way on the basis of the traditionally asserted "harms" (homosexuality as unnatural, or as mental illness, or equated with pederasty, etc.). When such prejudice manifests itself in official sanctions, Richards argues, gays confront "the functional equivalent of a heresy prosecution."[2]

Support for this view can be gleaned from social science findings in the area of antigay prejudice, which clearly indicate that one of the best predictors of such prejudice is an attitudinal rigidity concerning the family and gender roles. Lesbians and gays, according to this view, are devalued because they are perceived as agitators, questioning traditional roles.[3] As Richards puts it:

> Homosexuality is today essentially a form of political, social, and moral dissent on a par with the best American traditions of dissent and even subversive advocacy.... Those that support criminalization find today in homosexuality what they found before in the family planning of Sanger, the atheism of Darwin, the socialism of Debs, or the Marxist advocacy of the American Communist Party.[4]

It is no surprise, then, that on the few occasions when the United States Supreme Court has reviewed a controversy involving gay rights, the First Amendment was implicated in almost every instance.[5]

Lesbians and gay males should be especially cautious about First Amendment revisionism not only because that particular constitutional provision suits us so well (in that we are, at our core, a free speech movement), but also because other plausible legal theories have more often failed us. We are almost universally unsuccessful when we argue for our cause based on the equal protection under law supposedly guaranteed by the Fourteenth Amendment,[6] and even the quaint mythical notion that all Americans should be granted a sphere of privacy, a right "to be let alone," could not persuade five members of the Supreme Court to find Georgia's sodomy statute unconstitutional.[7]

The following pages are intended to convey, through an examination of relevant case law, how and why the lesbian and gay rights movement has been most likely to prevail when its advocates could articulate a clear and plausible argument based on traditionally accepted First Amendment principles. This is not to suggest that the First Amendment necessarily trumps judicial homophobia. Indeed, much of what follows might have been subtitled "judges say the darndest (and sometimes the most infuriating) things." But such judges' antigay rantings are all the more stark precisely because they belie generally accepted First Amendment principles.

Part I will begin on solid ground with the *inarguable* "free speech" cases, those that request the judiciary to come to terms with the most basic First Amendment values in the most traditional settings, what I refer to as the "access to a forum" cases. Next, we will review the case law on freedom of association (Part II) and the right to engage in symbolic conduct (Part III). Part IV is a discussion of how employment discrimination cases, typically argued on Fourteenth Amendment, equal protection grounds (when federal constitutional provisions are raised at all) should be also seen as relevant to free speech. Within this unit we will identify the special problems posed by gay Americans whose place of employment is the military. In Part V we focus on the constitutionality of sodomy statutes themselves, and their relevance to the study of communication. A concluding section will offer a scenario for future free speech litigation.

I. The "Pure" Speech Cases: Access to a Forum

Toward a Gayer Bicentennial Committee v. Rhode Island Bicentennial Foundation[8] is one of those few cases whose citation alone gives a clear indication of the legal controversy involved. The state of Rhode Island was gearing up to do its part in commemorating the 200th anniversary of the Declaration of Independence. The gay plaintiffs wanted to participate by, among other things, having a parade, a prayer vigil, a town meeting, and a listing in the Foundation's directory as a sponsoring organization. The Foundation refused, citing the state's sodomy statute, arguing they did not want to be put in the position of associating themselves with an organization that advocates illegality (a charge denied by the gay group).[9] Judge Pettine, in ruling that the Foundation could not preclude the gay group's participation without running afoul of the First Amendment, had this to say about the irrelevance of Rhode Island's criminalization of sodomy:

> I cannot help but note the irony of the Bicentennial Commission expressing reluctance to provide a forum for the plaintiff's exercise of their First Amendment rights because they might advocate conduct which is illegal. Does the Bicentennial Commission need re-

minding that, from the perspective of British loyalists, the Bicentennial celebrates one of history's greatest illegal acts?

At issue in *Gay Activists Alliance v. Washington Metro*[10] was whether commuters on the District of Columbia's subway system would have to confront posters provided by GAA that pictured a wide array of Washingtonians of different races and ages with the one-sentence caption, "Someone in your life is gay." The Transit Company refused to display the posters, arguing that some commuters would be upset by the message.[11] Judge Pratt did not find the argument convincing, and pointed out that commuters had already seen posters placed by the Unification Church, the Church of Scientology, and by both pro- and antiabortion rights groups on the Metro system:

> Many riders will undoubtedly take umbrage at the message that "SOMEONE IN YOUR LIFE IS GAY...." Although we are sympathetic to the [transit company's] interests in raising advertising revenue and its natural desire to protect its riders from offensive messages, and to avoid controversy, we are nonetheless compelled to hold that it has run counter to the requirements of the First Amendment in its pursuits of these interests.

One of the forums often sought out by gay rights groups is the ubiquitous "Yellow Pages." Two early cases heard by California's Public Utilities Commission are noteworthy. In the first case—*Council on Religion and the Homosexual v. PT & T*[12]—the gay group had already been advertising in the Yellow Pages under "Religious Organizations," but sought to be listed as a "Homophile Organization." The telephone company denied the request, claiming that the suggested heading was too narrow, too limited; moreover, the word "homophile" did not appear in most dictionaries. The PUC majority deferred to the telephone company's judgment, finding it was not arbitrary or discriminatory.

Commissioner J. P. Vukasin, Jr., wrote a stingingly antigay concurring opinion. After making reference to the "disorders of drug addiction, alcoholism, *and homosexuality*," he admonished the plaintiff organization that their time and effort "would be far better spent in the dedication of time and financial resources to the restoration of their members as respected and dignified citizens of the community."

A similarly antigay result can be found in a second California Public

Utilities Commission case the next year. In *Society for Individual Rights v. PT & T*,[13] a gay group was refused the right to place a display ad in the Yellow Pages. This time the phone company more candidly allowed that it feared the ad would offend some of its subscribers.

Nowadays, of course, "Baby Bells" not only permit gay groups to advertise openly, but even provide such headings as "Gay and Lesbian Services." This reality reflects more a change in political climate than any particular legal precedent that would make the earlier cases inapplicable. Still, it is likely true that courts today would rule in favor of gay litigants in similar cases, *if* the gay groups are able to establish a sufficient connection between the Yellow Pages' publisher and the government to constitute "state action."[14]

Another public forum sought out by lesbian and gay litigants are newspapers. Defendants here tend to be state university newspaper editors,[15] thus at least providing the opportunity to raise the argument that "state action" is involved. That argument was unsuccessful in *Mississippi Gay Alliance v. Goudelock*,[16] wherein the gay group sought to place an ad in the Mississippi State University's *Reflector* to the effect that the group offered "counseling, legal aid, and a library of gay literature." The majority found that student-editor Goudelock functioned with sufficient autonomy to preclude a finding of state action.[17]

The result from Mississippi State is one that gay litigants should not lament. If a student editor truly has functioned independently from the state university administration, the newspaper should legitimately be treated as any privately owned media outlet. If we rally around the right of lesbian and gay litigants to legally force the *New York Times* to publish an ad, or a feature article, or even to use the word "gay" instead of "homosexual,"[18] that same legal principle can be used by various "ex-gay Ministries" to force the alternative gay press nationwide to publish their propaganda.

The public school itself was the forum sought by litigants in *Solmitz v. Maine School Administrative District*,[19] a case with a tragic history and a depressing outcome from the perspective of the gay and pro-gay plaintiffs. Teacher Solmitz, deeply troubled by the killing of a young gay male by three Bangor high-school students, decided to seek support for a "Symposium on Tolerance" to be held during the school day at Madison High School. Representatives of various minority groups—the aged, the disabled, etc., as well as a local lesbian activist—would all take part in the day-long program. When word of Solmitz's invitation to lesbian

Dale McCormick became public, the school received numerous threatening calls from parents and others. There would be a picket, children would be kept home from school, there would be bomb threats. As a result, the School Board canceled Tolerance Day altogether. The trial judge, whose decision was upheld by the state Supreme Court, found it was the Board's genuine and understandable fear of violence, and not its own alleged antigay sentiment, that led to the cancellation.

The decision from Maine is especially troubling in that it represents a judicial failure to apply traditional First Amendment principles with vigor. The state supreme court permitted a classic "hecklers' veto" to prevail. The decision may be an aberration, narrowly tied to its facts. In one of the most celebrated "hecklers' veto" cases of this generation, Nazis were granted a permit to march in Skokie, Illinois,[20] despite the possibility of violence between them and the many concentration camp survivors who live in that Chicago suburb. The potential victims of violence in Maine are distinguishable in two important ways. First, they are children. Second, they are an especially captive audience, governed as they are by mandatory attendance laws.

A final genre of "pure" First Amendment case law involves not so much access to a forum as freedom to utter a specific message. Frequently, litigants with an explicitly gay message have run afoul of obscenity laws and have in so doing prompted the Supreme Court to fine tune accepted definitions of obscenity. More recent controversies concerning the Robert Mapplethorpe exhibits[21] and the "NEA Four"[22] have led to reassessments of the government's obligation to make its financial support of the arts content-neutral.[23] Much concern also has been expressed within the gay community surrounding actions by the Federal Communications Commission that may suggest that even non-obscene gay speech is less protected than heterosexually oriented speech. In one such action, the FCC moved against Pacifica station KPFK-FM of Los Angeles, for broadcasting excerpts from the play "Jerker."[24]

Elsewhere,[25] I have discussed the Supreme Court's regrettably antigay ruling in *San Francisco Arts and Athletics, Inc. v. United States Olympic Committee*,[26] the case that forced the Gay Olympics to change its name. For present purposes suffice it to say that the case points to a need for at least one kind of evolution in First Amendment jurisprudence, i.e., a reconceptualization of the tension between free speech rights and rights to intellectual property (e.g., trademark and copyright). The current Court has shown at least some sensitivity about that tension in its unanimous 1994 decision loosening a bit of the copyright holder's power to deter others' speech.[27]

In recent years, gays have encountered a new obstacle to their freedom of expression in the form of legislative initiatives or referenda seeking to rescind past, and prohibit future, pro-gay legislation. In *Citizens for Responsible Behavior v. Superior Court*,[28] members of the Riverside, California, city council won the right to *not* place such a referendum on the ballot. The First Amendment right to free speech, and to petition the government for redress of grievances, would be hollow indeed if the local government were to be deprived of the power to grant the sought redress. A similar result was reached in Colorado in 1993, when that state's Supreme Court refused to permit "Amendment 2" to take effect.[29]

II. Freedom of Association

Although the phrase "freedom of association" appears nowhere in the United States Constitution, it is incontrovertibly established by the case law that such a right does exist as a corollary First Amendment provision. In its earliest form, this freedom of association was seen as a means to an end only; our right to freedom of speech could most efficiently be exercised if we could freely form political associations. More recent decisions and commentaries recognize a freedom of association that need not be linked to the exercise of political expression. Gay litigants have often had to go to court to seek both kinds of associational freedoms.

A. Political Associations

As we have already seen, the existence of a sodomy statute is often used to deny other rights—including First Amendment rights—to gay litigants. Such an argument was raised by the state of New York in *Gay Activists Alliance v. Lomenzo*,[30] wherein the gay group sought state recognition as a nonprofit corporation. The trial court, whose judgment was eventually reversed, found that

> by identifying themselves as a "homosexual civil rights organization," [plaintiffs] are professing a present or future intent to disobey a penal statute of the State of New York. . . . It would seem that in

order to be a homosexual, the prohibited conduct must have at some time been committed or at least presently contemplated.

The trial judge in the *Lomenzo* case was referring to a sodomy statute then on the books, since found unconstitutional.[31] Yet even the absence of such a statute did not stop the Ohio Supreme Court from refusing to accept the articles of incorporation proposed by the Greater Cincinnati Gay Society.[32] Without explanation, the *per curiam* opinion stated that "although homosexual acts between consenting adults are no longer statutory offenses . . . the promotion of homosexuality as a valid lifestyle is contrary to the public policy of the state."

The plethora of nonprofit gay-oriented organizations in existence today suggests that cases such as *Brown* are mostly of historical interest; indeed, even the Greater Cincinnati Gay Society was granted official status as a nonprofit organization upon resubmitting its articles.[33]

Once granted nonprofit status by the state, an organization's next logical step is often to seek the most favorable tax-exempt status provided by law. As numerous gay-oriented organizations discovered up until at least the late 1970s, the Internal Revenue Service was often a tremendous hindrance. A typical ruling concerned the Lambda Services Bureau of Colorado Springs. In a letter to the organization from the IRS District Director in Austin, Texas, dated March 25, 1976, Lambda was warned:

> The unqualified promotion of the tenet that homosexuality is not a sickness, disturbance, or other pathology in any sense but is merely a preference, orientation or propensity on par with and not different from heterosexuality, carries a serious risk of encouraging or fostering homosexual attitudes and propensities. . . . Therefore, the unqualified promotion of such a proposition would prevent an organization from qualifying for exemption.

This state of affairs apparently came to a halt in 1978 as a result of Revenue Ruling 78-305, 1978-2 C.B. 172, which indicates that "a nonprofit organization formed to educate the public about homosexuality in order to foster an understanding and tolerance of homosexuals and their problems qualifies for exemption."

By far the most litigious situs for politically oriented gay groups seeking to preserve their freedom of association has been the college campus. Student groups at such schools as Virginia Commonwealth University,[34] the University of Georgia,[35] Austin Peay State University in Tennessee,[36] Texas Tech University,[37] the University of South Carolina,[38] the University of Missouri,[39] and Texas A & M University,[40] have all been successful plaintiffs, forcing their host campuses to officially sanction them.

Gay student group cases often presented legal questions that went a bit beyond the simple question of official recognition. In *Department of Education v. Lewis*,[41] the Florida Supreme Court struck down a law denying funding to any state university that permitted approval of sexual relations outside marriage. (The legislative sponsors admitted their aim was to persuade state universities to deny recognition to gay student groups.) A similar statute from Alabama has been challenged by a student group at the University of South Alabama.[42] While these two cases involved the state legislature itself denying funding to gay groups, what about situations in which the campus's own student government members vote to deny such funding? In the Eighth Circuit, such actions are unconstitutional violations of the gay group's freedom of expression, at least if the record shows that personal animus towards the gays' "message" was the primary motivating factor behind the anti-funding vote.[43]

Completing this category of political association cases is a legal controversy so complex that the ACLU engaged in an extended internal debate concerning whose side to support. The national ACLU filed an *amicus* brief in support of the students in *Gay Rights Coalition of Georgetown University Law Center v. Georgetown University*,[44] while the legal director of the organization's local affiliate for the National Capital Area filed an *amicus* brief on behalf of the university. At issue was whether Washington's Human Rights Act could be used by gay litigants to compel the university to grant the group full "university recognition" status. Georgetown argued that such an application of the law would violate the First Amendment in two ways. First, the Free Exercise Clause would be abridged, the university alleged, in that it is a Catholic institution that cannot on religious grounds embrace pro-homosexual advocacy. Second, forcing the university to recognize the group would be tantamount to forcing it to publicly endorse the group, a violation of the institution's right "not to speak." The court held that the university may be compelled to provide the gay group with all the tangible benefits (including a campus mailbox, the use of a computer label service and of mailing services; and the right to apply for, but not necessarily receive, university funding) usually accruing only to groups that have been granted full "university recognition" within Georgetown's by-laws; it also held that the university would not be compelled to officially award the gay groups the status of "university recognition."

A complex postscript to the Georgetown case must be added. The 100th Congress, in a heavily lopsided vote, responded to the court ruling by requiring the District of Columbia to rescind that portion of its Human Rights Ordinance that could apply to religiously affiliated schools. Members of the DC City Council successfully challenged this "Nation's Capital Religious Liberty and Academic Freedom Act" (a.k.a. the Armstrong Amendment) in federal court. The court reasoned that it might have been constitutional for Congress itself to rescind portions of the DC Human Rights Act, but to coerce the DC City Council into doing so, under threat of loss of funding to the District, violated each Council member's First Amendment right *not* to speak.[45]

B. Nonpolitical Associations

In "pre-Stonewall" times, there were few overtly political associations of lesbians and gay males. As such, it is not surprising that the earliest gay rights cases raising freedom of association issues concerned the granting or revocation of liquor licenses to bars with a gay clientele.[46] Freedom of association claims have also been raised by a church-affiliated private gay club seeking to maintain the confidentiality of its membership list[47] and by gay bathhouses seeking to avoid forced closure by local health departments.[48]

No discussion of litigation over nonpolitical associations brought by lesbian or gay male plaintiffs would be complete without at least brief mention of the related issues of same-sex marriage and child custody. Concerning the former issue, suffice it to say that the first wave of cases from the 1970s was unsuccessful,[49] and that a recent decision from the District of Columbia was similarly unavailing. In the more recent case, the court found that, because the legal definition of marriage is restricted to heterosexual unions, denial of that status to two male litigants cannot constitute, again by definition, unequal protection under law.[50] And the Hawaiian Supreme Court has told the state that it must demonstrate a compelling interest in order to prohibit gays from marrying.[51] In a move that may or may not constitute the demonstration of such an interest, the state legislature passed a statute explicitly defining marriage as an *opposite*-sexed pairing.[52]

The issue of child custody is complicated by the truism that custody law is a separate animal entirely, that the "best interests of the child" standard can and often is used to ignore or selectively outweigh what would otherwise seem to be dispositive claims to equal protection or freedom of association. Courts often pay lip service to the notion that one parent's lesbianism should not be treated as an overriding consideration, then in the next paragraph proceed to treat the issue as precisely that. Often, custody or visitation is contingent upon the absence of the same-sex lover, or upon the litigants' relative political *in*activism.[53] Such judicial rulings not only ignore the associational freedoms of the parents; they also work against the best interests of the children, in that clinicians and social scientists who study lesbian and gay communities have shown that the freedom to express affection and to become connected in some way to the larger world of gay politics are signs of positive adjustment.[54]

A cautionary note should be sounded with respect to the child custody issue. Most such decisions are never published, and it is very likely that the number of courts that do, in fact, all but ignore the sexual orientation of the individual parents is on the rise.[55] For the number of such courts to increase does not require a departure from traditional First Amendment theories, but rather a more faithful application of such theories to this area of law.

III. Symbolic Conduct

Consider the wide array of nonverbal actions and artifacts that boldly and omnipresently proclaim heterosexual messages: hand-holding in public,[56] wearing of wedding bands, a good-bye peck at the subway station, the placement of the spouse's photo on one's office desk. Lesbian and gay litigants have frequently had to go to court to win the right to engage in nonverbal expressions of same-sex affections.

Sometimes the very choice of a forum for public expression itself constitutes a powerful symbol. Thus, the AIDS activism group ACT-UP could neither be prohibited from entering the visitors gallery at the State House in Harrisburg nor from wearing t-shirts proclaiming their group membership. "There is an unmistakably symbolic significance in demonstrating close to the center of government," Judge Rambo concluded, namely to let elected officials know "that they are being watched, that their decisions are being scrutinized."[57]

Discussion of one of the student organization cases has been postponed until now, in that the University of New Hampshire was perfectly willing to "recognize" the gay student group, although the group would not be permitted to hold purely social events, especially dances. The court ruled for the Gay Student Organization, finding that the simple act of same-sex dancing can "convey that homosexuals exist, that they feel repressed by existing laws and attitudes, that they wish to emerge from their isolation, and that public understanding of their attitudes and problems is desirable for society."[58] The New Hampshire precedent proved invaluable to Cumberland, Rhode Island, teenager Aaron Fricke, whose own journey to federal district court won for him the right to take a male date to his high-school prom.[59]

The symbolic conduct at issue in *Kristie v. Oklahoma City*[60] was the Miss Gay America Pageant. The event's promoters had contracted with the city for the use of a municipal auditorium, but the city abruptly canceled the contract upon learning the nature of the event, which it saw as an "open expression of homosexuality" in violation of prevailing community standards. The trial judge rejected the city's reasoning, adding with a wink that although the pageant "may not rise to the level of artistic endeavor that *Hair* or *La Cage Aux Folles* represents, it is still expression."

Gay litigants in recent years have been at least as interested in marching as in dancing. In New York, representatives of the gay Catholic organization Dignity won the right to demonstrate peacefully in front of St. Patrick's Cathedral during the annual Gay Pride parade. Judge Motley found that Dignity "sought to convey symbolically its love for the Church and its members' sense of themselves as integral parts of the Church's spiritual body," that "Catholic gays need not choose between their homosexuality and their religion."[61]

Gay groups have not been so fortunate when their goal was to "crash" someone else's parade. A federal judge refused to force the American Legion to permit a group of gay veterans to march with their own banner in New York's Veterans' Day parade (for which the Legion had been given a permit by the city).[62] Gay groups have similarly been denied the claimed right to march under a gay rights banner within the Saint Patrick's Day parade in New York,[63] although the resolution of the same controversy in Boston seems to be more in flux.[64] One cannot help but wonder if the Gay Veterans and Gay Irish contingents may be better off in defeat. Imagine a situation in which a group of religious fundamentalists argue in court that the gay rights parade really raises issues of "family values," and that they should be permitted to participate. These cases are part of that fascinating area of law in which one group's First Amendment right to "associational privacy" may conflict with another's First Amendment right to engage in symbolic conduct.

IV. Employment Discrimination As a Free Speech Issue

Employment discrimination against perceived or actual homosexuals often implicates rights to freedom of speech and association. Generally, employers discover that an employee is lesbian or gay as a result of the latter's "coming out" directly to them or to their coworkers, or as a result of some media attention or at least some modicum of political activity engaged in by the employee.[65] Unfortunately, the judiciary has not always been receptive to gays' free speech claims in this arena. One very notable exception, however, is the bold step taken by one court in 1979. In *Gay Law Students Association v. PT & T,* the California Supreme Court, employing that portion of the state labor code forbidding employment discrimination based on one's political affiliation, held that coming out as openly gay is an act of political speech worthy of protection.[66] A later opinion from the state's Attorney General extended this protection to closeted gay employees as well.[67]

Most of the cases we will mention here concern employment in the public sector.[68] This should not be surprising, of course. The "American Rule" in employment law—that, in the absence of some statutory rule to the contrary, employers are permitted to hire and fire for any reason whatsoever or for no reason whatsoever—still remains a formidable obstacle to plaintiffs. This is true notwithstanding a slowly evolving tendency among courts to question whether a firing is "against the public interest," as in the dismissal of a "whistleblower."

Nonetheless, the literature does reveal a fair number of gay-related employment discrimination cases in the private sector,[69] and some of these raise intriguing First Amendment issues. In *Dorr v. First Kentucky National Bank,*[70] clear associational freedom concerns presented themselves, though Dorr chose to litigate under the Free Exercise Clause, in that he was fired after having assumed a leadership position within a local gay church group.

That lesbians and gays discover "out of the closet" often means "out of a job" is exemplified by the plight of former junior high school teacher Joseph Acanfora, whose homosexuality came to the attention of his employing Maryland school district when an official of the Pennsylvania Department of Education held a press conference to alert the world that the Department had decided, after much consideration, to grant Acanfora a Pennsylvania teaching license.[71] (Acanfora had studied at Pennsylvania State University, where his activism in the gay student group made the state somewhat reluctant to grant him a license; he then moved to Maryland, and obtained a license and a position there.)

Upon learning of Acanfora's sexual preference, his Maryland school board promptly transferred him to non-teaching duties, and eventually fired him. The trial court ruled that the initial reaction by the board—the transfer to non-teaching duties—was unjustifiably arbitrary, but that its later decision to dismiss Acanfora altogether was justifiable. Apparently the trial court was upset at Acanfora's having taken his case to the public—including newspaper interviews and a *60 Minutes* segment—in between the two personnel actions. The Court of Appeals gave Acanfora and later gay litigants a consolation prize in the form of strongly worded dicta[72] in support of the teacher's exercise of his First Amendment rights. Other gay public school teachers, whose sexual orientations were learned similarly as a result of some form of community activism[73] or at least through "coming out" openly on the job,[74] have fared just as poorly as did Acanfora.

Some localities, of course, do not want to even risk that gay teachers' speech will be protected by the judiciary. Oklahoma passed a statute that required the dismissal of any teacher found to have engaged in homosexual acts or even pro-homosexual advocacy. The Court of Appeals for the Tenth Circuit struck down the statute as overbroad, but the Supreme Court's having produced a 4-4 split vote means that such statutes could reemerge in any of the other federal circuits.[75]

Although lesbian and gay teachers seem to comprise a disproportionately high ratio of plaintiffs in employment discrimination cases, they are by no means the only litigants in this area of the law. For example, two of the gay marriage cases from the 1970s prompted related employment discrimination cases. In the one, the firing of a gay male from his job as a Civil Service clerk-typist was upheld by a federal appellate court, even though the dismissal was a direct result of his activism (including his having sought to marry his lover).[76] Employees within the federal civil service are far more protected nowadays from sexual orientation discrimination, but not as a result of any single court decision or Congressional action. Rather, the protection stems from a 1978 civil service directive to the effect that "irrelevant" characteristics should be ignored in hiring decisions. The Carter Administration's Office of Personnel Management treated sexual orientation as one such irrelevant employee characteristic, an interpretation largely ignored by the Reagan and Bush Administrations, but again embraced by the Clinton Administration. The Clinton Administration's policy to date has received mixed reviews from gay activists, in that he has not provided a global executive directive officially ending all antigay discrimination within the federal government, preferring to have each agency review and revise their own equal employment policies.[77]

Among state employees, one successful litigant was a gay man who served as an assistant county treasurer in the state of Texas, a position that provided flexibility in making his own hours. One day he indicated to his superiors his wish to testify in front of a local county commissioners meeting on a gay rights issue. The official response was a written memo effectively restricting him to the office during the hours county commission meetings were held. Upon refusing to sign the memo as received, he was dismissed from his job. The Court of Appeals for the Fifth Circuit overturned the dismissal, holding that the proposed testimony, however offensive to others, "lies at the core of the Free Speech Clause of the First Amendment."[78]

Somewhat less successful was an applicant for a "storekeeper" position in a Dallas police station, who was not hired as a result of his "coming out" during the interview. Although the court recognized that important First Amendment issues had thus been raised, it deferred to the police department claim that its public image would be jeopardized by the presence of an "admitted homosexual."[79]

In 1991, when an earlier version of this essay appeared, I chose not to include a discussion of gays in the military, in that the First Amendment "applies with diminished force" in that setting and would require separate treatment.[80] To an extent that is still true, but the courts have been increasingly reluctant to defer wholesale to the military as employer. Moreover, the pattern of case law, Congressional testimony, and other official public statements concerning lesbian and gay male soldiers demonstrates, more clearly than in any other area of "queer" employment law, that the issue is, indeed, free speech.

The introduction to this essay quoted law professor David Richards for the proposition that the old arguments against gay rights have been largely rejected even by people who do not especially favor the "gay rights agenda." When gays encounter opposition these days, it is not because we are viewed as pederasts, or as psychologically sick, but rather because we present a world view that some do not want to hear, or want their children to hear, or want their tax dollars to support. Similarly, the most defining characteristic of the contemporary debate about gays in the military is the opposition having ceased arguing that lesbians and gay males are incapable of serving with distinction. Instead, the antigay argument in a military context boils down to second-hand prejudice, a classic "hecklers' veto": We cannot afford to let you serve because the unschooled inner-city or country bumpkin recruits won't be able to accept your message.[81]

Not only candidate[82] and later President Clinton,[83] but also Senators Sam Nunn,[84] John Warner,[85] and even Strom Thurmond[86] allowed that gays and lesbians have served "with distinction" for decades. Such statements expose the hypocrisy of the military's assertion that open homosexuality is incompatible with effective military service,[87] a reality not lost on the federal judges in some of the more recent courtroom challenges to the ban.[88]

Supporters of the military ban have effectively been restricted to arguing on the basis of the discomfort presumably felt by heterosexual enlisted men and women who wish not to serve with gays and who especially do not want to know who among their colleagues is gay. Thus, one colonel in the armed forces favors the ban because "a homosexual would be ostracized, excluded, ridiculed, and subjected to cruel, malicious and constant harassment."[89] The executive vice president of the Non-Commissioned Officer Association testified in front of Congress that "recruiting and retention of homosexuals would force upon others tolerance of a lifestyle many consider abnormal and totally unacceptable."[90] And Colonel Fred Peck of the Marine Corps more than earned his fifteen minutes of fame when he testified in favor of the ban despite the gay sexual orientation of his son, Scott. Were Scott to enlist in the Marines, the elder Peck "would be very fearful that his [Scott's] life would be in jeopardy from his own troops."[91]

Free speech issues become paramount, in that the presumably homophobic enlisted men and women will generally not discover who among their colleagues is gay unless the gay soldiers affirmatively reveal their sexual orientation. Although most gay military plaintiffs have been unsuccessful in their attempts to raise First Amendment issues,[92] this new posture of the debate may force the courts to reassess the issue. We will likely know within the next few years the Supreme Court's view of the argument that a government policy permitting speech about sex that reveals a heterosexual orientation while prohibiting speech that reveals a homosexual orientation is violative of the First Amendment.[93]

V. Saying and Doing: Sodomy and the First Amendment

In this essay I have argued that the lesbian and gay rights movement is best conceptualized as a First Amendment issue. No such argument can stand without attempting to articulate the free speech relevance of the chief distinguishing characteristic of gays—what we do in the bedroom. Is sodomy itself a free speech issue?

The legal arguments that gay litigants have traditionally hurled against sodomy statutes are that they violate rights of privacy,[94] equal protection, due process (usually because of allegedly vague wording of the statutory prohibition), and even the Eighth Amendment protections from cruel and unusual punishment (an argument Justice Powell indicated in *Bowers* that he might have entertained had it been raised). When the First Amendment is raised at all in such cases, the Establishment Clause, rather than the Free Speech Clause, tends to be the issue, the allegation being that the only plausible state's interest in criminalizing same-sex lovemaking is an interest in fostering a morality based upon a particular religious ethic, thus "establishing" a state religion.[95]

Still, issues of freedom of expression are plainly implicated by the existence of sodomy statutes. Consider first Justice Douglas's opinion for the Court in *Griswold v. Connecticut*,[96] wherein the Supreme Court first recognized a constitutional right to privacy. In overturning a statute prohibiting the use or counsel of the use of contraceptive devices, Justice Douglas articulated the view that the "right of privacy" was to be found not in any one specific constitutional provision, but in a combination of provisions. Among these was the First Amendment right to freedom of association.

Douglas's opinion describes marriage (Ms. Griswold was convicted of counseling a married couple in the use of contraceptives) as an "association that promotes a way of life, not causes; a harmony in living, not political faiths; a bilateral loyalty, and not commercial or social projects." Despite these distinctions between the institution of marriage and the plainly political associations that were the focus of the early Supreme Court case law, Douglas concludes that marriage "is an association for as noble a purpose as any involved in our prior decisions." As Richards argues,[97] this same freedom of association should extend to "the depth of human significance derived by *lovers* from [their own] association."

Moving for a moment from the realm of judicial discourse to that of common parlance, it is significant that we speak of "sexual *expression*," as if by the use of the phrase we show an awareness that the sexual act *is*, above all, an act of communication. The equating of sexual activity with communication is a threefold equation. First, the act itself can reasonably be seen as the nonverbal equivalent of verbal endearments, and can thus plausibly be considered "symbolic" conduct. A touch, a caress, can say "I love you" as or more effectively than the words themselves. As one commentator put it:

> There is no question that sexual conduct, homosexual or otherwise, qualifies as expressive conduct. . . . Sexual conduct is expressive at its core. While it also serves other purposes, such as carnal pleasure and (increasingly rarely) procreation, sex is one of our most intense ways of expressing our most profound emotions—love, desire, dependency, power, even rage or hatred.[98]

The second part of the equation is that sexual conduct can be seen as a form of "selective disclosure," an imparting of intimate information about the lover to the loved one. Lovers know much about each other simply because of their status as lovers.

Sexual expression may be seen as First Amendment-relevant for yet another reason. In one of the most often-cited treatises on freedom of speech, Emerson[99] enumerates the functions that this freedom serves, the reasons why it is special and deserving of special protection. One of the reasons offered by Emerson is that the freedom to express oneself is a chief means by which humans achieve self-fulfillment. As British philosopher and jurist H. L. A. Hart points out,[100] much the same argument can be made on behalf of sexual expression. Writing in defense of the Wolfenden Report's call for decriminalization of homosexual behavior, Hart argued that "sexual impulses" are "a recurrent and insistent part of daily life." Moreover, Hart continues, any statute calling upon persons to suppress such sexual impulses would damage "the development or balance of the individual's life, happiness, and personality."

VI. Concluding Remarks and a Ridiculously Pollyannaish Prediction

Almost without exception, on those occasions when the Supreme Court has heard a gay rights controversy, First Amendment protections were at stake. Gay rights cases that are currently percolating up through the federal judiciary also include strong First Amendment elements. The very next gay rights case to be reviewed by the Supreme Court will involve the complicated amalgam of associational privacy and symbolic conduct interests at odds in the Saint Patrick's Day parade controversy from Boston. As was suggested earlier (see note 64 and corresponding text), the gay litigants in that case, and the continued vitality of traditional First Amendment freedoms generally, may very well be best served by a defeat.

Beyond the Boston case, the Court has also decided to hear the *Romer* case involving the antigay Amendment 2 from Colorado. These "citizens' referenda" cases carry important First Amendment implications, in that they are designed to prevent elected representatives from passing pro-gay legislation. As such, they require jurists to deal not only with the First Amendment's free speech/press clauses but also the often-ignored petition clause. The wording of the petition clause (which grants us the right to "petition the government for redress of grievances") presupposes a representative form of government rather than pure, unchecked majoritariansim. Why would we need a right to "petition" ourselves, after all? Citizen referenda whose effect (whether by statute or through amendments to state constitutions or city charters) is to remove whole categories of political issues from the petition clause's scope are almost certainly unconstitutional.

Precisely because the issues raised by the antigay citizen referenda are so clear, they will likely continue to produce a pattern of pro-speech, pro-gay case law. It is doubtful that four members of the current Supreme Court will feel moved to review such a body of law.

So many gay military cases are winding their way through the federal judiciary that it is unlikely the Court will be able to avoid the issue for much longer. Such a case will almost certainly be decided on Fifth Amendment, equal protection grounds, turning on what burden of proof the Court places upon the government to justify its policy of treating gays in such a blatantly discriminatory fashion. The Equal Protection arguments, however, are inextricably intertwined with free speech issues:

> The very name given to the military's policy—"don't ask, don't tell"—reveals that it is designed to regulate expression. The military expressly disclaims any concern with whether an individual is in fact homosexual; its concern is specifically with those individuals who "tell" that fact to others.... The military has conceded that homosexual identity does not affect a soldier's ability to perform in the military, *except to the extent that the identity is expressed to others.*[101]

That the gay military cases are fraught with First Amendment issues is apparent from a careful reading of the federal appellate panel decision finding that Navy Academy Midshipman Joseph Steffan's rights had been violated by his dismissal.[102] Steffan did not raise First Amendment claims, and Judge Mikva's opinion is based on Fifth Amendment grounds.

Still, the court could not avoid the First Amendment "texture" of the case. Judge Mikva quotes from such First Amendment landmark decisions as *Stanley v. Georgia*[103] and *Terminiello v. Chicago*.[104] He reminds us of the Court's handling of World War II–era Smith Act instances of proscribed speech. More crucially, he drives home the fact that the military's chief argument—that openly gay soldiers cannot be permitted to serve because many heterosexual soldiers will feel threatened by their presence—has a clear First Amendment analogue.[105] It is a classic "hecklers' veto," Mikva reminds us:

> The First Amendment forbids the government to silence speech based on the reaction of a hostile audience, unless there is a clear and present danger of grave and imminent harm. Otherwise, a vocal minority (or even majority) could prevent the expression of disfavored viewpoints—a result contrary to the central purpose of the First Amendment's guarantee of free expression.[106]

Before going further I should make clear that the Mikva decision, although written for a unanimous three-judge panel, stands virtually alone. Indeed, as we were preparing to go to press, the *en banc* ruling of the federal appellate court in *Steffan* was handed down and, as expected, it overturned the lower court's decision.[107] It should also be admitted that most courts that have dealt with the gay military issue have similarly deferred to the government.

Still, what if the First Amendment implications of the military issues surface more clearly, and what if the Supreme Court embraces them? Admittedly, a complete victory on equal protection grounds is unlikely to be granted gay litigants in a military case. It is more plausible that the Court majority will continue to defer to the military, if not on the issue of overall threat to morale, then at least on the point of the need for heterosexuals' privacy when living in close quarters with gay soldiers. But if such a decision includes strongly pro-gay First Amendment language, it may then open the door to an eventual undoing of the great harm caused by the Court's 5-4 sodomy decision.[108] Free speech arguments were not raised, thus not explicitly rejected, in the *Bowers* case. The Court's ruling in *Bowers* did include clear rejections of the Mr. Hardwick's equal protection and privacy arguments, however. A new Court could thus effectively overturn *Bowers* on First Amendment grounds without having to criticize its own earlier reasoning. (It is very unusual for the Court to overturn its own decisions without a fairly lengthy passage of time intervening.)

This scenario may seem absurdly naive, but we already have witnessed events in the gay movement that few would have predicted. As recently as five years ago, it was unthinkable that the gay military issue would be taken so seriously, and that even our fiercest opponents would concede in front of Congress that the only reason for continuing to support the ban is the irrational prejudice of others.

Or move beyond the military issue, and turn the clock back further, say twenty years or so. Suppose that back in the mid-1970s some unnamed but highly reliable psychic were to see in her crystal ball that a new and deadly virus would come on the scene in a few years, that it would kill millions of people, and that the epidemiology of the virus would be such that homophobes would be able to blame gays plausibly for spreading the disease. While our governmental response to AIDS has not been a source of pride, any of us who took the psychic's words seriously would have predicted the reopening of concentration camps.

The sense of guarded optimism I am trying to convey here has been stated more eloquently by Congressman Barney Frank. You can tell how far the gay movement has come by comparing the under-the-breath mutterings of House members whenever a gay vote is scheduled. These used to be the "No way!" votes, the ones where members absolutely had to vote no, or fear losing their seat. For the past several years, these have been instead the "Oh shit!" votes, the ones that members—even those from fairly conservative districts—would really like to avoid altogether, because they recognize that many constituents will be angered no matter how they vote. This ability to offer a counterposing threat is a major step forward. Needless to say, the strength of that threat depends upon our willingness to speak out, to show our recognition that we are, in fact, a free speech movement.

Notes

Portions of this chapter appeared in an essay entitled "Lesbian and Gay Rights as a Free Speech Issue: A Review of Relevant Caselaw," in Michelle Wolf and Alfred Kielwasser, eds., *Gay People, Sex and the Media* (New York: Haworth Press, 1991).

1. Brent Hunter Allen, "The First Amendment and Homosexual Expression: The Need for an Expanded Interpretation," *Vanderbilt Law Review* 47 (1994), 1073-1106.

2. David A. J. Richards, "Constitutional Privacy and Homosexual Love," *New York University Review of Law and Social Change* 14 (1986): 895-905.

3. Amia Lieblich and Gitza Friedman, "Attitudes toward Male and Female Homosexuals and Sex Role Stereotypes in Israeli and American Students," *Sex Roles* 12 (1985): 561-570; A. P. MacDonald and Richard G. Games, "Some Characteristics of Those Who Hold Positive and Negative Attitudes toward Homosexuals," *Journal of Homosexuality* 1 (1974): 9-27; Paul Siegel, "Androgyny, Sex Role Rigidity and Homophobia," in James W. Chesebro, ed., *Gayspeak: Gay Male and Lesbian Communication* (New York: Pilgrim Press, 1981), 142-152; L. Weinberger and James Millham, "Attitudinal Homophobia and Support of Traditional Sex Roles," *Journal of Homosexuality* 4 (1979): 237-245.

4. Richards, "Constitutional Privacy," 905.

5. *Board of Education v. NGTF*, 470 U.S. 903 (1985); *Jacobson v. United States*, 112 S. Ct. 1535 (1992); *Manual Enterprises v. Day*, 370 U.S. 478 (1962); *Mishkin v. New York*, 383 U.S. 502 (1966); *New York v. Uplinger*, 467 U.S. 246 (1984); *Pope v. Illinois*, 481 U.S. 487 (1987); *San Francisco Arts and Athletics v. United States Olympic Committee*, 483 U.S. 522 (1987).

6. William B. Rubenstein, "Since When Is the Fourteenth Amendment Our Route to Equality?: Some Reflections on the Construction of the Hate Speech Debate from a Lesbian/Gay Perspective," *Law and Sexuality* 2 (1992): 19-27.

7. *Bowers v. Hardwick*, 478 U.S. 186 (1986).

8. 417 F. Supp. 632 (U.S. Dist. RI, 1976). See also, *Alaska Gay Coalition v. Sullivan*, 578 P. 2d 951 (Sup. Ct. Alaska, 1978).

9. Making reference to the existence of a sodomy statute in order to deny gay litigants other rights is an all too common theme in gay rights law. Antigay litigants and judges have argued that student associations should not be recognized and/or should not receive funding because such official sanctions will lead to increased sodomy violations. No further findings need be made to support the contention that a lesbian teacher is immoral if she works in a state that makes her lesbianism a crime. And surely one of the reasons the military has considered homosexuality "incompatible with military service" is the existence of a sodomy statute within the military code. (That same code would outlaw both oral and anal heterosexual sex, of course, but since the only kind of genital sexual expression the code permits is the one gays cannot engage in—penile-vaginal intercourse—the military's argument seems impenetrable.) To the extent that this essay offers an argument for the primacy of the First Amendment, that argument is in no way intended to devalue the importance of ridding the statute books nationwide of all sodomy statutes.

10. 78-2217 (U.S. Dist. Ct., DC, 1979).

11. During the author's tenure as Executive Director of the American Civil Liberties Union's affiliate for Kansas and Western Missouri, the *Washington Metro* case proved an invaluable precedent for an ACLU case involving a local Kansas City gay group that wanted to advertise on that city's transit system. The proffered poster in the latter case—perhaps a reflection of Midwestern vs. Eastern sensibilities—more tentatively asserted that "SOMEONE IN YOUR LIFE *MAY BE* GAY."

12. 70 Cal. PUC 471 (1969).

13. 71 Cal. PUC 662 (1970).

14. Gay litigants in *Loring v. Bellsouth Advertising and Publications Company*, 339 S.E. 2d 372 (Ct. App. Ga., 1986) lost on these grounds.

15. But see *Hatheway v. Gannett Satellite Information Network*, 459 N.W. 2d 873 (Ct. App. WI, 1990) (gay business unsuccessfully tries using state public accommodation law to force privately owned newspaper to accept its advertising).

16. 536 F. 2d 1073 (Cir. 5, 1976), cert. den., 430 U.S. 982 (1977).

17. Judge Coleman was not content to leave the issue there, however. In an almost comic exchange of dicta with dissenting Judge Goldberg, he expressed concern about the ad's offer of "legal aid": "Such an offer is open to various interpretations," he claimed, "one of which is that criminal activity is contem-

plated, necessitating the aid of counsel." Judge Goldberg's reply: "The suggestion ... that the criminal taint in the ad is demonstrated by the offer of 'legal aid' implies a presumption of illegality whenever lawyers are involved—surely the level of respect for the profession has not reached this nadir."

18. It was perfectly reasonable for activists to *persuade* the *Times* to change its editorial policy in this regard. The cautions here are addressed only toward attempts to use courts as a vehicle to distort traditional First Amendment doctrine concerning freedom of the *press*.

19. 495 A. 2d 812 (Sup. Ct. Maine, 1985).

20. *Collin v. Smith,* 578 F. 2d 1197 (Cir. 7, 1978).

21. Sam Walker, "Arts Agency Still in the Hot Seat," *Christian Science Monitor,* August 6, 1993, 12.

22. *Finley v. National Endowment,* 795 F. Supp. 1457 (C.D. CA, 1992).

23. See also *Gay Men's Health Crisis v. Sullivan,* 792 F. Supp. 278 (S.D. NY, 1992) (Centers for Disease Control may not censor the explicit sexual references and depictions of AIDS educational materials for which it subcontracts through its grant-making process unless the resulting pamphlets would meet the legal definition of obscenity). These kind of results are highly relevant to a recent U.S. Senate vote that, had it become law, would cut off federal funding to any public school district whose curricula teach acceptance of "the homosexual lifestyle." Bettina Boxall, "Gay Activists Downplay Senate School Bill," *Los Angeles Times,* August 4, 1994, A20.

24. *In the matter of Pacifica Foundation,* 2 FCC Rcd. 2698 (1987).

25. Paul Siegel, "On the Owning of Words: Reflections on *San Francisco Arts and Athletics v. United States Olympics Committee,*" in R. Jeffrey Ringer, ed., *Queer Words, Queer Images: Communication and the Construction of Homosexuality* (New York: New York University Press, 1994), 30-44. See also, *MGM-Pathe Communications v. The Pink Panther,* 774 F. Supp. 869 (S.D. NY, 1991) (gay self-help, self-defense organization not permitted to use the Pink Panther trademark, which its owner had painstakingly associated over the years with "comedic, non-political fun.")

26. 483 U.S. 522 (1987).

27. *Acuff-Rose Music v. Campbell,* 114 S. Ct. 1164 (1994).

28. 1 Cal. App. 4th 1013 (4th App. Dist., Div. 2, 1991).

29. *Evans v. Romer,* 854 P. 2d 1270 (Sup. Ct. Colo., 1993), cert. den., 114 S. Ct. 419 (1993). As we were going to press, the Supreme Court decided to hear the *Romer* case in its 1995–1996 term. 1995 U.S. LEXIS 1571 (1995). See also *Equality Foundation of Greater Cincinnati v. City of Cincinnati,* 838 F. Supp. 1235 (S.D. Ohio, 1993) (temporarily enjoining enforcement of the antigay "Issue 3" referendum result). A permanent injunction was issued in August of 1994 (D.C. S. Ohio, No. C-1-93-0773, 1994).

30. 341 N.Y.S. 108 (Ct. App. NY, 1973).

31. *People v. Onofre*, 415 N.E. 2d 936 (Ct. App. NY, 1980).

32. *State, ex rel., v. Brown*, 313 N.E. 2d 847 (Sup. Ct. Ohio, 1974).

33. Rhonda Rivera, "Our Straight-Laced Judges: The Legal Position of Homosexual Persons in the United States," *Hastings Law Journal* 30 (1979): 799-955, at 911, n. 674.

34. *Gay Alliance of Students v. Matthews*, 544 F. 2d 162 (Cir. 4, 1976).

35. *Wood v. Davison*, 351 F. Supp. 543 (N.D. Georgia, 1972).

36. *Student Coalition for Gay Rights v. Austin Peay State University*, 477 F. Supp. 1267 (M.D. Tennessee, 1979).

37. *Student Services for Lesbians/Gay v. Texas Tech University*, 635 F. Supp. 776 (N.D. Texas, 1986).

38. *Gay Students Association v. University of South Carolina*, #82-3030-0 (U.S. Dist. Ct., SC. 1983).

39. *Gay Lib v. University of Missouri*, 538 F. 2d 848 (Cir. 8, 1977), cert. den., 434 U.S. 1080 (1978).

40. *Gay Student Services v. Texas A & M University*, 737 F. 2d 1317 (Cir. 5, 1984).

41. 416 So. 2d 455 (Sup. Ct. Fla., 1982).

42. *Gay, Lesbian and Bisexual Alliance v. Evans*, 843 F. Supp. 1424 (M.D. Ala., 1994). As of this writing, the court has not ruled on the merits, but has held that Attorney General Jimmy Evans cannot be dismissed as a defendant. Mike Smith, "Around the South," *Atlanta Constitution*, June 18, 1994, A3.

43. *Gay and Lesbian Students Association v. Gohn*, 850 F. 2d 361 (Cir. 8, 1988). This precedent proved helpful to ACLU attorneys in California, whose threat of legal action against the State University's Fresno campus resulted in restoration of funding to that campus's Gay and Lesbian Students Alliance. See "Out on Campus," *The Advocate*, August 30, 1988, 32.

44. 536 A. 2d 1 (Ct. App. DC, 1987).

45. *Clarke v. United States*, 705 F. Supp. 605 (D.C., 1988), aff'd., 886 F. 2d 404 (Cir. DC, 1989); vacated, 915 F. 2d 699 (Cir. DC, 1990). In response to the court rulings, Congress did indeed itself modify the DC Human Rights Act.

46. Rivera, "Our Straight-Laced Judges," 913-924; *Stoumen v. Reilly*, 213 P. 2d 969 (Sup. Ct. CA, 1951); *Vallerga v. Dept. of Alcoholic Beverage Control*, 347 P. 2d 909 (Sup. Ct. CA, 1959); *111 Wines and Liquors v. Division of Alcoholic Beverage Control*, 235 A. 2d 12 (Sup. Ct. NJ, 1967).

47. *Freeman v. Hittle*, 747 F. 2d 1299 (Cir. 9, 1984).

48. *New York v. St Mark's Baths*, 130 Misc. 2d 911 (Sup. Ct. NY, 1986).

49. *Baker v. Nelson*, 191 N.W. 2d 185 (Sup. Ct. Minn., 1971); *Singer v. Hara*, 522 P. 2d 1187 (Ct. App. Wash., 1974).

50. *Gill v. District of Columbia*, 1995 D.C. App. LEXIS 8.

51. *Baehr v. Lewin*, 852 P. 2d 44 (Sup. Ct. Haw., 1993); George de Lama,

"Hawaii May Lead the Way in Same-Sex Marriages," *Times-Picayune*, May 22, 1994, A14. Extrapolating from the Hawaii example, we might surmise that the gay marriage issue will ultimately be resolved by one, then several, states finding the right in their own state constitutions, thus freeing the United States Supreme Court from having to address the issue as a matter of federal constitutional law. While strong arguments can be made for viewing marriage as an associational freedom protected by the First Amendment, the Supreme Court's analogous decision overturning Virginia's miscegenation statute was based squarely on Fourteenth Amendment grounds. *Loving v. Virginia*, 388 U.S. 1 (1967). This would be more difficult for gay litigants, who are not viewed by the Court as a "suspect class" and upon whose rights states may therefore differentially infringe without incurring the Court's "heightened scrutiny."

52. Craig de Silva, "Hawaii May Become First State to Legalize Gay Marriages," *National Public Radio Morning Edition*, May 16, 1994.

53. *Chicoine v. Chicoine*, 479 N.W. 2d 891 (Sup. Ct. South Dakota, 1991); *L. v. D.*, 630 S.W. 2d 240 (Ct. App. S.D. MO., 1982); *M.P. v. S.P.*, 404 A. 2d 1257 (Sup. Ct. NJ, 1979); *Scarlett v. Scarlett*, 390 A. 2d 1331 (Sup. Ct. PA, 1978); *Woodruff v. Woodruff*, 260 S.E. 2d 775 (Ct. App. NC, 1979).

54. C. Rand, D. Graham, and E. Rawlings, "Psychological Health and Factors the Court Seeks to Control in Lesbian Mother Custody Cases," *Journal of Homosexuality* 5 (1982): 27-39.

55. Susan Chira, "Gay Parents Become Increasingly Visible," *New York Times*, September 30, 1993, A1.

56. Interestingly enough, same-sex hand-holding is one of the pieces of conduct that military officers are told they may interpret as a clear enough pro-gay message to commence an investigation of a soldier's sexual orientation. See David Cole and William N. Eskridge, Jr., "From Hand-Holding to Sodomy: First Amendment Protection of Homosexual (Expressive) Conduct," *Harvard Civil Rights-Civil Liberties Law Review* 29 (1994): 319-351.

57. *ACT-UP v. Commissioner*, 755 F. Supp. 1281 (M.D. PA, 1991).

58. *Gay Student Association v. Bonner*, 367 F. Supp. 1088 (N.H., 1974), aff'd, 509 F. 2d 652 (Cir. 1, 1974).

59. *Fricke v. Lynch*, 491 F. Supp. 381 (R.I., 1980).

60. 572 F. Supp. 88 (W.D. Okla., 1983).

61. *Olivieri v. Ward*, 637 F. Supp. 851 (S.D. NY, 1986), aff'd as modified, 801 F. 2d 602 (Cir. 2, 1986), cert den., 480 U.S. 917 (1987).

62. *Gay Veterans Association v. American Legion*, 621 F. Supp 1510 (S.D. NY, 1985).

63. *Irish Lesbian and Gay Organization v. New York State Board of Ancient Order of Hibernians*, 788 F. Supp. 172 (S.D. NY, 1992); *New York County Board of Ancient Order of Hibernians v. Dinkins*, 814 F. Supp. 358 (S.D. NY,

1993); Deborah Pines, "Saint Patrick's Day Parade Settlement Approved; City Will Not Deny Permit to Hibernians," *New York Law Journal*, February 3, 1994.

64. *Irish-American Gay, Lesbian and Bisexual Group of Boston v. City of Boston*, 418 Mass. 238 (Sup. Ct. Mass., 1994); Jeff Jacoby, "A Glib Excuse to Crash the Saint Patrick's Day Parade in Southie," *Boston Globe*, March 10, 1994, 19. As we were going to press, the Supreme Court decided to review the Saint Patrick's Day parade controversy from Boston. 115 S. Ct. 714 (1995).

65. William B. Rubenstein, "Since When," 1992.

66. 595 P. 2d 592 (Sup. Ct. CA, 1979).

67. Op. Atty. Gen. Cal. 80 (1986).

68. See, for example, *Webster v. Doe*, wherein the Supreme Court held that even the director of the CIA was not immune from the judicial review of a fired employee's constitutional claims. 486 U.S. 592 (1988).

69. Rhonda Rivera, "Queer Law: Sexual Orientation Law in the Mid-Eighties, Part I," *University of Dayton Law Review* 10 (1985): 459-540.

70. 41 FEP Cases 423, pet. for reh. granted, 796 F. 2d 179 (1986). See also *Madsen v. Erwin*, 481 N.E. 2d 1160 (Sup. Ct. Mass., 1984), wherein the *Christian Science Monitor* argued successfully that *its* freedom to act on its religious beliefs permitted it to fire reporter Christine Madsen when her lesbianism became known.

71. *Acanfora v. Board of Education*, 359 F. Supp. 843 (MD, 1973), aff'd on other grounds, 491 F. 2d 498 (Cir. 4, 1974), cert. den., 419 U.S. 836 (1974).

72. The words are only dicta because the appellate court ruled against Acanfora on other grounds.

73. *Gaylord v. Tacoma School District*, 559 P. 2d 1340 (Sup. Ct. Wash., 1977).

74. *Rowland v. Mad River School District*, 730 F. 2d 444 (Cir. 6, 1984), cert. den., 470 U.S. 1009, reh. den., 471 U.S. 1062 (1985).

75. *Board of Education v. National Gay Task Force*, 729 F. 2d 1270 (Cir. 10, 1984), aff'd by 4-4 vote, 470 U.S. 903 (1985).

76. *Singer v. U.S. Civil Services Commission*, 530 F. 2d 247 (Cir. 9, 1976), vacated, 429 U.S. 1034 (1977). A second potential gay marriage partner found a job offer in the University of Minnesota system rescinded, a move the courts upheld lest plaintiff be permitted to "foist tacit approval of the socially repugnant concept upon his employer." *McConnell v. Anderson*, 451 F. 2d 193 (Cir. 8, 1971).

77. David Tuller, "Defeating Discrimination Step by Step: Gay Rights in the Federal Workplace," *San Francisco Chronicle*, February 10, 1994, A1.

78. *Van Ooteghem v. Gray*, 628 F. 2d 488 (Cir. 5, 1980), aff'd en banc, 654 F. 2d 304 (1982), cert. den., 445 U.S. 909 (1982).

79. *Childers v. Dallas Police Department*, 513 F. Supp. 134 (N.D. Texas, 1981), aff'd mem., 669 F. 2d 732 (Cir. 5, 1982).

80. The First Amendment also applies with diminished force in the context of immigration and naturalization cases, and when the gay plaintiffs are inmates. Concerning the latter, the Court of Appeals for the Sixth Circuit has recently reaffirmed the judiciary's tendency to defer to prison authorities who deny prisoners the opportunity to read any literature depicting "homosexual activity." *Kobe v. Mcginnis*, 21 F. 3d 428 (Cir., 6 1994).

81. Cole and Eskridge, "From Hand-Holding to Sodomy," 327-328; Paul Siegel, "Second Hand Prejudice, Racial Analogies, and Shared Sorrows: Why 'Don't Ask, Don't Tell' Won't Sell," Notre Dame Journal of Law, Ethics and Public Policy 9 (1995): 185–213.

82. "President-Elect Clinton News Conference," *Reuters Transcript Report*, November 12, 1992.

83. "Statement by President Bill Clinton," *Federal News Service*, July 19, 1993.

84. "Capitol Hill Hearing," *Federal News Service*, March 29, 1993.

85. "Senate Armed Services Committee Hearing," *Reuter Transcript Record*, March 31, 1993.

86. "Hearing of the Senate Armed Services Committee," *Federal News Service*, July 20, 1993.

87. William B. Rubenstein, "Don't Ask, Don't Tell: Don't Believe It," *New York Times*, July 20, 1993, A19.

88. *Cammermeyer v. Aspin*, 850 F. Supp. 910 (W. D. Wash., 1994) (striking down the old exclusionary policy as violative of Equal Protection and Due Process); *Able I v. United States*, 847 F. Supp. 1038 (E.D.N.Y., 1994) (granting preliminary injunction against enforcement of the new, "Don't ask, Don't tell policy); *Able II v. United States*, No. CV 94-0974, 1994 U.S. Dist. LEXIS 13519 (E.D.N.Y., Sept. 14, 1994) (rejecting government's motion to dismiss complaint).

89. Douglas B. Routt, "Should Homosexuals Be in the Military?" *Buffalo News*, December 3, 1992 (letter to the editor), 2.

90. "Capitol Hill Hearing," *Federal News Service*, December 9, 1992.

91. "Gays in the Military: One Family's Dilemma," *Larry King Live*, May 13, 1993, CNN, Transcript #826.

92. The six plaintiffs in *Able v. U.S.* (1994) constitute a notable exception to this pattern.

93. William B. Rubenstein, "Day of Judgment for Gay Ban," *Legal Times*, August 2, 1993, 21.

94. Ever since the Supreme Court's 5-4 decision in *Bowers v. Hardwick*, 478 U.S. 186 (1986) (refusing to extend the federal right of privacy to same-sex

conduct), such arguments must be based upon *state* constitution privacy provisions.

95. *Baker v. Wade,* 553 F. Supp. 1121 (N.D. Texas, 1982), rev'd, 769 F. 2d 289 (Cir. 5, 1985), cert. den. 478 U.S. 1022 (1986).

96. 381 U.S. 479 (1965).

97. David A. J. Richards, "Unnatural Acts and the Constitutional Right to Privacy: A Moral Theory," *Fordham Law Review* 45 (1977): 1281-1348.

98. David Cole, "Sexual Conduct and the First Amendment," *Legal Times,* August 30, 1993, 23.

99. Thomas Emerson, *The System of Freedom of Expression* (New York: Random House, 1970).

100. *Law, Liberty, and Morality* (Stanford, Calif.: Stanford University Press, 1963).

101. Cole and Eskridge, "From Hand-Holding to Sodomy," 332 (emphasis in original).

102. *Steffan v. Aspin,* 8 F. 3d 57 (Cir DC, 1993), overturned *sub nom Steffan v. Perry,* 1994 U.S. App. LEXIS 33045.

103. 394 U.S. 557 (1969).

104. 337 U.S. 1 (1949).

105. The same argument would suggest, of course, that since many women in the armed forces have legitimate reason to fear men—especially in light of the Tailhook and similar incidents—perhaps it would be wise to forbid heterosexual males from serving in the military.

106. 8 F. 3d at 68.

107. *Steffan v. Perry,* 1994 U.S. App. LEXIS 33045. Mr. Steffan has decided not to appeal the new ruling to the Supreme Court. See "Ex-Midshipman Ends Discharge Fight," *Baltimore Sun,* January 4, 1995, 1A.

108. *Bowers v. Hardwick,* 478 U.S. 186 (1986).

TWELVE

The Reality and Ideology of First Amendment Jurisprudence: Giving Aid and Comfort to Racial Terrorists

ROBIN D. BARNES

I. INTRODUCTION

I first learned of Ku Klux Klan-style violence from my beloved great-grandmother, Mrs. Ada Mae Hopkins, who now rests in peace. At age 13 I heard her account of what still strikes me as the most heinous crime imaginable, by South Carolina Klansmen, against a black woman in their hometown. Lynching seems almost humane by comparison. The 10-year-old child in John Grisham's best-seller, *A Time to Kill*, must have experienced a similar degree of terror. Memories of my great-grandmother's report, involving an adult kidnapping and a large animal, were triggered by Grisham's depiction of the crime:

> She was ten, and small for her age. She lay on her elbows, which were stuck and bound together with yellow nylon rope. Her legs were spread grotesquely with the right foot tied tight to an oak sapling and the left to a rotting, leaning post of a long-neglected fence. The ski rope had cut into her ankles and the blood ran down her legs. Her face was bloody and swollen, with one eye bulging and closed and the other eye half open so she could see the other white man sitting on the truck. She did not look at the man on top of her. He was breathing hard and sweating and cursing. He was hurting her.
> ... For two six-packs now they had thrown their half-empty cans at her and laughed. ...

The warm beer mixed with the dark blood and ran down her face and neck into a puddle behind her head. She did not move.

Willard asked Cobb if he thought she was dead. Cobb opened another beer and explained that she was not dead because niggers generally could not be killed by kicking and beating and raping. It took much more, something like a knife or a gun or a rope to dispose of a nigger.[1]

These men, like the South Carolina Klansmen, were vicious white supremacists who acted in concert against members of a targeted population. Across the United States, equally heinous crimes occur in many jurisdictions on a weekly basis.

Violence motivated by hatred or intolerance is steadily increasing in the United States.[2] Moreover, general use of harassment and intimidation as a means of silencing those with whom we disagree appears to be among the dominant social trends in the United States today. This trend has been encouraged by a legal regime that relies upon rather tenuous assumptions about democracy and tolerance as demonstrated by its efforts to uphold freedom of political expression at seemingly any cost. Theoretically, strenuous efforts to avoid the "slippery slope of runaway censorship" and protecting freedom of (public) expression for the "idea we hate" are laudable when the expression does not join group hatred and advocacy of violence. Otherwise, such protection is squarely at odds with fundamental notions of justice and our commitment to human rights. In reality, these ideals serve to impose hyperneutral standards upon governmental policy-makers, who are severely burdened, at the outset, by certain structural elements in our criminal justice system that converge to thwart effective punishment of crimes motivated by hatred. Issues of tacit endorsement or governmental complicity are central to any just resolution of the problems surrounding hate-crime because in many jurisdictions there are still significant obstacles, such as a lack of investigative resources, which thwart the consistent and effective punishment of racially motivated violence. There are, however, several intervening factors that converge to create and perpetuate this dilemma. The most important factors relate to policies governing police, prosecutorial, and judicial discretion.

Recent applications of free speech principles demonstrate that the law, as it currently stands, is balanced in favor of violent hate-mongers against other more compelling individual and societal interests. Patterns of Klan-style violence demonstrate that their crimes are inextricably linked to hate-speech activity.

When hate-mongering occurs in public fora, the Klan's goals of recruitment, retention, and agitation of violent activity wreak havoc upon the communities in which they are active. Residents of Skokie, Illinois, where the majority were Holocaust survivors, endured a series of harassing incidents throughout the litigation process, which eventually allowed neo-Nazis to march through their town. The tears and nightmares of those who are targets of hateful speech, along with the breakdown in community relations and the threat of violence, suggest that perhaps confining hate-mongering activity to private fora would lessen its deleterious effects. Just short of banning paramilitary extremist organizations altogether, there is room for recognition of the complex nature of associational rights, which are as unique to this nation's history as its legacy of racial violence.

A regulation that forecloses the use of public space for concerted hate-mongering activity would afford substantial deference to and consideration of the painstaking evolution of the speech and association principles to which we have pledged our allegiance, while giving identical consideration to the harms caused by hate-speech activity and our constitutional commitment to ensuring liberty and justice for all.

Comparing the three major cases dealing with hate-mongering activity—*Brandenburg v. Ohio*[3] (*Brandenburg*), *Collin v. Smith*[4] (*Skokie*), and *R.A.V. v. City of St. Paul*[5] (*R.A.V.*)—provides a view of the public versus private interests of American citizens that were and/or should have been considered by the Court in those cases. Adequate consideration of these interests would produce results identical to the ruling of the Court in *Brandenburg*, and the opposite results in both *Skokie* and *R.A.V.*

With the initial thesis summarized above, part two of this chapter proceeds to further define hate-mongering speech activity and review the current debate over the legitimate scope of free speech principles from an academic and lay person's perspective. Part three describes the rejection of violent tyranny by the majority of American citizens, even as race-related conflicts rage unrelentingly. Part four acknowledges the extent to which racism is a fact of life, emphasizing that public speech that merely reflects racist attitudes would not be affected by the proposal outlined above.

Part five examines the three landmark cases in which courts have addressed hate-mongering activity. Noting the public-private distinctions that are relevant in all three cases, this section argues in favor of the decision to permit hate-mongering activity in private forums consistent with the majority opinion in *Brandenburg*. The hate speech activity in this case, though concerted, occurred on privately owned property and was not plainly directed at any group other than the Klan's own sympathizers. The facts of *Skokie* and *R.A.V.*, on the other hand, demonstrate that the hate-speech activities were concerted or targeted, or both. Considering the violent and coercive nature of such speech, allowing violent hate-mongering in public space represents a qualitatively different kind of injury to individual members of the target group as well as the community. The widespread injury suggests that public hate-mongering activity should be banned on that basis.

Given the level of harm that Klan-type groups generate throughout the nation, and the rising level of danger that they pose to the public welfare, part six examines the constitutional principles related to freedom of conscience articulated in originalist theories of constitutional rights. Arguably, these principles tip the balance in favor of allowing right-wing extremists to meet in private forums. Part seven analyzes the alleged need for societal tolerance, and concludes that the desired balance between the safety and welfare of individuals and the communities in which they live, can only be struck by establishing meaningful standards for legitimate use of public fora.

II. Hate-Mongering and the Current Debate over Speech

The public activities of Klan, neo-Nazi, and Skinhead groups are designed to harass, intimidate, and threaten victim populations with impending violence. The threat resounds in the language of persecution, degradation, recruitment, and provocation, all while advocating violent or illegal means for depriving target group members of life, liberty, and civil and property rights.

The Klan invariably operates in a twofold manner: hate-mongering or hate-speech activity and the wholesale violence, harassment, and intimidation that follows. According to the definition provided by the Federal Bureau of Investigation, terrorism is a violent act or an act dangerous to human life in violation of the criminal law of the United States or of any individual state to intimidate or coerce a government, the civilian population, or any segment thereof, in furtherance of political or social objectives. Thus, violent white supremacists are an indigenous terrorist organization. Our failure to treat them as such places the citizens of the United States in the rather precarious position of condemning terrorism abroad while appearing to safeguard it at home.

As the law currently stands, rights to engage in public spectacles of the most extreme forms of hate-mongering activity appear to be firmly, albeit inadvertently, endorsed by judges, lawyers, and government officials. The discernable effects of the tacit endorsement of hate-speech activity in public fora, viewed by some legal scholars as legitimate political speech and therefore "off regulatory limits," have been observed by Professor Mari Matsuda:

> The constitutional commitment to equality and the promise to abolish the badges and incidents of slavery are emptied of meaning when target group members must alter their behavior, change their choice of neighborhood, leave their jobs, and warn their children off the streets because of hate-group activity. When the presence of the Klan deters employers from hiring target-group members, prevents citizens from socializing freely, and keeps parents from sending their children to integrated schools, the goal of nondiscrimination is moved farther away from present realities.[6]

Several lines of argument in the current debate over the legitimate scope of protection for freedom of speech is based on distortions in the historical record. The prevailing myth is that the realization of public protest rights played a pivotal role in securing civil rights for black America. It was, in fact, the protection guaranteed to the press which had a crucial impact upon the efforts toward constructive engagement, that led to significant changes for blacks and other Americans. News reports,[7] stinging editorial columns, and paid advertisements that doubled as fundraising mechanisms, similar to that featured in *New York Times v. Sullivan*,[8] had a far more discernable impact upon the life of the Civil Rights Movement. Statements that suggest that freedom of expression has done more for blacks than any other group reflects the distorted view that it was the enforcement of public protest rights by Southern federal judges (of all people) that erected some kind of fortress around the movement. As noted by Professor Steven Smith, "[T]he earlier view that free speech was a threat to those in power and a blessing to those who wanted to challenge the existing order somehow got things backwards; and the interesting question is why it took us so long to realize this."[9] Public perception that widespread judicial enforcement of rights to public protest over three decades laid the foundation for successful initiatives toward civil and human rights for black Americans is inconsistent with the record of the Warren Court during that period, and rests heavily upon casually informed historical assumptions.

Perhaps with the exception of the order of Federal District Court Judge Frank Johnson authorizing the march led by the Rev. Martin Luther King, Jr. from Selma to Montgomery, public protest rights rarely "saved" civil rights workers from the wrath of local government officials. And on those occasions when the Supreme Court "came through," the damage had already been done. To argue otherwise is to present a caricature of lofty principles and elevated "rights," which have only existed prospectively for the group or individual in legitimate need—rights many argue must now be defended on behalf of racial terrorists, reflecting a distorted equal-protection ideology.

Efforts to invoke an equal-protection standard on behalf of "unpopular beliefs" have almost completely restructured the debate so as to label racial minorities who demand greater preventative measures against hate-crime as advocates of an unacceptable double standard. The allegation is that blacks, in particular, seek back-door remedies to the problems of inequality. A trend has developed among proponents of First Amendment absolutism of alleging that undue sensitivity, coupled with misguided "perceptions" of white exclusion, are reflected in black demands for regulation while they defend the use of racist language during their own expressions of political protest. In astonishingly simplistic fashion, critics warn racial minorities that the regulation of spoken words will not yield changes in underlying attitudes. The reality, however, is that Skinhead activity is much less a reflection of "attitude" than the acting out of a vicious hatred; blacks and other minorities understand firsthand that words *do* wound and that violent action and official inaction often kill. The tendency to characterize the issue as relating purely to speech and ideas minimizes the mass violence that the Klan represents. For example, after Klan firefighters were charged with allowing two black children to burn to death in fires in Blakely County, Georgia, the question that needs to be asked is: Upon what ideological basis could the targets of Klan activity in that jurisdiction be labeled overly sensitive?[10] The accusation that members of groups targeted by hate-mongers are suffering from paranoia or sensitivity in a dialogue about racial terrorism suggests a fundamental lack of understanding of the issue. In some quarters it demonstrates a lack of intelligence, and in others, it points to a callous disregard for those who do not have the luxury of remaining indifferent to such a vicious assault upon human rights.

This tendency to mischaracterize the issue provides a paradigmatic example of how the requisite legal response to the inhumanity of domestic terrorism has been attenuated by the same ideological and rhetorical distortions that accompany almost every discussion of larger social and racial issues. The conflict over so-called speech rights is the functional equivalent of the stage upon which dramatic debates over race-based affirmative action, crime, black nationalism, miscegenation, and "Black-Jewish relations" are being played out. There is no justification for the influence these issues have exerted upon our manifest resolve to provide relief for those who are perpetual targets of hate-mongering activity.

In present reality, the extent to which hate-speech activity destroys equality of opportunity for racial minorities without adequate redress remains buried beneath the dogma surrounding race relations generally and the nature and scope of First Amendment freedom in particular. Those who defend public protest rights for hate-mongering activity sometimes compare it to the Labor Movement's battle against oppressive, ruling-class minorities. The Labor Movement's struggle, however, is not analogous to that of those concerned with the lack of official response to racial terrorism. Such arguments dismiss the deep and lasting injury caused by hate-speech activity and the resulting harm inflicted upon its victims and their communities. They ignore the culpability of government agents, particularly law enforcement officials, for the ineffective punishment of these crimes. On those occasions where the injury is obvious and official insouciance is undeniably clear, advocates of protection for hate-mongering shift to factual and ideological manipulation. According to this self-appointed garrison, it is a group of self-interested, hypersensitive minorities who now pose the all-consuming threat to free expression. The recurring context in which hate-crimes are encouraged is routinely dismissed, the crimes themselves are portrayed as mere isolated incidents, and the dangers of despotic government have risen to yet another level. Racial minorities are warned that since government can never be counted on to "get it right," minorities are certain to head the list of those wronged. Tragically, the distortion in our understanding of the impact that racial terrorism continues to exert across socioeconomic and geographic boundaries has yet to be fully realized by legal academics.

From a constitutional perspective, it is worth noting that there are certain guarantees and policy objectives that afford a breadth and depth of freedom to the individual that were never deemed appropriate for groups. During the early Civil Rights Movement, the opportunities afforded those engaged in concerted activity were granted in contexts where the aggrieved parties sought to peacefully petition the government for redress of grievances. While this experience provides compelling reasons to afford heightened protection for public protests in a democracy, none of those apply to the hate-mongering of Klan and neo-Nazi type groups.

The ideals under which public protest rights were deemed suitable for checking arbitrary exercise and abuse of governmental powers are far removed from current notions that terrorism—in the form of public threats of violence, harassment, and intimidation—must be tolerated in the name of democracy. Under current theoretical models, the speech-related activities of Klansmen, neo-Nazis, and their confederates have served as a license to promote terrorism under the guise of political expression.

What is needed is a constitutional paradigm that promotes human dignity, harmony, and order in our nation, while increasing legitimate access to the marketplace of ideas through civic awareness and personal responsibility. As stated by Professor Kathryn Abrams, "The absolutist tendencies of the First Amendment legal regime have contributed to a climate where expression is overprotected, and members of the intellectual community are deterred from thinking systematically about how to reconcile [free] expression with other norms."[11] Racist hate-speech activity in public fora not only promotes harassment and intimidation, but jeopardizes safety, feeds the collective frustrations of the community, and thwarts prospects for meaningful initiatives toward open and productive dialogue by lowering the quality of public discourse.

Even in the absence of standards for evaluating the "quality of public dialogue," some regulation of the public fora is deemed crucial for mediating the tension between our collective needs and individual rights.[12] Collectively, we need a governmental process that provides a license to enjoy certain liberties, privileges, and immunities within boundaries that ensure this freedom for all on an equal basis. The development of mechanisms for resolution of disputes that respect the individual's sovereign autonomy are central to the pursuit of liberty and happiness.

III. THE CONSENSUS SURROUNDING RACIAL TERRORISM

As we approach the 21st century, debate about the persistence and/or measurable force of "structural racism," and the future of race-relations generally, competes with the debate over abortion rights to top the short list of most controversial and divisive issues. The toll of collective frustration has left fewer initiatives toward meaningful discussion. Most people have little interest in participating in race-related dialogue. Those who are willing often lack the communication skills, and/or courage, to carry it off effectively. Those who are both willing and able to jump-start the dialogue must guard against the passions of those who deify rhetorical gaming. In the contest for absolute control and power, some people place little value on harmony, equality, and personhood. Drive-by debate with steel-jacketed half-truths are their *modus operandi.*

Against this backdrop, an exceptional circumstance has developed during the thirty years since government-sponsored violence against black Americans was nationally televised during Mississippi Freedom Summer. A consensus has formed around the issue of racial terrorism. The overwhelming majority of Americans oppose the use of such violent threats because they invite the deaths and injuries of those who are victimized by it, while jeopardizing the safety and order of entire communities.

IV. ACKNOWLEDGING RACISM AS A FACT OF LIFE

In order to implement an effective ban on public hate-mongering activity, meaningful distinctions between concerted activity designed to terrorize a target group (which would be prohibited in public) and everyday racist speech (which would be fully protected in public or private) must be clearly identified. Everyday racist speech is fully entitled to First Amendment protection and distinguishable from hate-speech activity. Racist speech may well be directed at racial minorities and motivated by the desire to publicly insult or otherwise offend members of a particular race or to mobilize one group of citizens to oppose another with respect to legislative policies. However, when the expression is neither concerted, nor targets one group with threats of violence, harassment, or intimidation, it has few of the characteristics that give rise to the harm noted above.

The category of "valued political speech" must embrace racist speech that is (1) an honest reflection of an individual's conscience, which manifests in varying degrees throughout his lifetime, and/or (2) deliberately injected into the national dialogue, even as a tool of public manipulation. Such manipulation permeates the political arena, where rhetorical gaming by self-interested people with partisan loyalties and specific agendas is the order of the day.

A. Individual Conscience

Banning groups or expression of certain ideas altogether has been rejected as a policy alternative to a great extent because governmental suppression of an idea may increase its appeal. Embodied in this view is the recognition that formation of personal and political views is an ongoing process, which is both fluid and changing. According to Professor David Richards, the goal of First Amendment protection is "to provide freedom of expression because it nurtures a basic sense of self-respect, a belief in the competent independence and integrity of one's person."[13]

Dialogical rights are thought to enhance the individual in two ways. Exposure to numerous perspectives is thought to assist in the goals of sorting out ideas, which promotes informed political participation. Simultaneously, the formation of values, character, maturity, and human reason are perceived as products of liberty as a means and an end, serving to subsidize healthy interdependence. Value choices in the ideal world will always be left to the individual.

Jurisprudentially, free speech would ensure that, along the journey to self-realization, no citizen is compelled or restrained in the quest for knowledge about whatever religion, discipline, philosophy, or ideology holds her interest. The dissemination of ideas, the right to challenge those presented by others, to hold government accountable, and unite with others in furtherance of common social and political agendas is a major conduit for self-realization.[14] To a large extent, self-actualization is achieved as we gain greater awareness of our purpose and goals in relation to other individuals and the larger social order. Invariably, some individuals carry the process too far by presuming that their ability or inability to find meaningful experiences are solely influenced by other individuals or social conditions, without any regard for the values of justice and equality.

Scapegoating may be prompted on a number of levels by different stimuli. There are times when either a series of incidents or even one emotionally charged event causes an otherwise free-thinking and tolerant person to damn an entire group based on experience with an individual. For example, in the course of a private discussion one could express the view that Asians are worthless. The exact same sentiments expressed to a friend from a public telephone booth, along the jogger's path in a city park, or in a letter addressed to fellow sympathizers are all certainly entitled to First Amendment protection. Those wishing to attend a lecture at Madison Square Garden where a speaker vilifies, degrades, and criticizes members of even a discreet and insular minority should have that option under the free speech doctrine. Such action may, in fact, represent a temporary blowing off of steam (for the speaker or members of the audience) that has no long-lasting or residual effects, or it could represent a deeply felt, long-lasting commitment to racial segregation. This distinction is irrelevant for purposes of the First Amendment.

What is vitally important, as Professor Richard Delgado has argued, is that we have lost much of our moral imperative on the free speech issue because of our failure to acknowledge how the movement from the expression of racist attitudes in what is essentially private space, to public display of hate-mongering activity constitutes a qualitatively different kind of threat.[15] White supremacist hate-mongers are not simply "disaffected" youths blowing off steam.[16] They are habitual criminals committing random as well as studied acts of violence against target-victim populations.

B. Politics As Usual

The use of racially inflammatory rhetoric is most often evident during political campaigns, where issues of employment, crime, and social welfare legislation are usually the focus of public debate.

The 1992 campaign to reelect U.S. Sen. Jesse Helms certainly had racist overtones. His opposition to laws widely perceived as necessary to protect minority rights was featured in his regionally televised ads, during which a white male crumples up a rejection letter from an employer while announcing that "the job went to a minority." Helms won the election by a comfortable margin and stated during a victory speech that night that "there is no joy in Mudville," a phrase from the popular poem "Casey at the Bat" and a thinly veiled reference to the campaign headquarters of his black opponent. (Although a Helms defender could argue that his Mudville comment was a reference to dirty campaign tactics, a variant on "mud slinging.") Likewise, the 1988 campaign promoting the election of George Bush for president featured Willie Horton, a black male prisoner who held a white couple hostage and raped the wife while on a weekend furlough, which was signed into legislation by his opponent.

Both ads contain arguably racist speech, but also valued political speech. Both feature public officials speaking on matters that affect the application and enforcement of public policy, laws, and government. And we should not be surprised when public officials link race and the public's fear of crime to achieve their political ends. The content, though offensive, has none of the characteristics of hate-speech activity.

If Helms or Bush had joined with others and issued violent threats, their actions might not be entitled to First Amendment protection. Such speech denies black Americans and neighboring communities the sense of safety, security, and liberty to which they are entitled under the Constitution. The recent murders and violence against abortion clinic doctors, who along with other members of their families had been repeated targets of harassment and intimidation at home, school, work, and in the course of carrying on social and civic activities, speaks volumes about governmental interests in clearly defining the scope of legitimate public protest.[17] What is required is a careful delineation of the legal line at which such activity evolves into overt threats of violence. Effective intervention is necessary at the very point at which public hate-mongering activity, with its attendant dangers of violence, becomes the primary goal, though perpetrated under the guise of legitimate public protest.

Concerted acts that amount to public threats of violence against families, and that throw communities into turmoil, exact a social and financial cost to the individual and society, which Americans are no longer willing to bear. Freedom of conscience under the First Amendment has always held that the right of belief will be protected against the imposition of orthodoxy, but it has never provided license to practices, however consistent with belief, that contravene existing laws. The physical and psychological threat of hate-group activity is greater than individual acts of racist manipulation. As noted by Professor Mari Matsuda, "[the presence of Skinheads] and the active dissemination of racist propaganda means that [a substantial number of Americans] are denied personal security and liberty as they go about their daily lives."[18]

Brandenburg, Skokie, and R.A.V.

Regulation of hate-mongering activity is a complex area of constitutional jurisprudence, where the dangers of getting it wrong (for example, a legal regime that supports public advocacy of racial violence) are precisely the opposite of those argued by absolutists (such as fears of a despotic government). The International Court of Justice details recent examples of near-successful attempts of race genocide as horrifying as that of Nazi Germany, which teach powerful lessons about public imprimatur and its deleterious effects.[19]

From the standpoint of those who have been victimized by right-wing extremists, legal or doctrinal support for the public display of Klan-type activity appears to clothe the message of hatred in a garment of legitimacy.[20] This response is mirrored by the majority of lay people. Average Americans view the law as operating largely to sanction harmful hate-mongering activity to the detriment of the community. The Jews of Skokie experienced the communal impact of a uniformed parade of American Nazis as representing something significantly more than expression of "a point of view."

When Klansmen or neo-Nazis are granted certificates of incorporation, licenses to march or rally, and are then surrounded with armed National Guardsmen for protection, government must take responsibility for the resulting injury and escalating violence. According to Canadian journalist Barry Brown, the responsibility of the government goes above and beyond the protection of civil liberties at the expense of human rights:

> [W]hen the United States Supreme Court allowed the American Nazi Party . . . to march in a suburb of Chicago known as Skokie where many Holocaust survivors live, it undoubtedly brought new members to the Jewish Defense League. These new members were probably convinced with arguments that ran like this: if society is not going to protect us from racial attack now, why would they

protect us if these madmen ever came to power? ... Extremism breeds extremism.[21]

The problems of escalating violence are substantially diminished when adequate consideration is given to the appropriate standards and their communal impact in our efforts to identify and promote legitimate uses of public resources. Hate-speech activity of the nature described in *Brandenburg v. Ohio*, where Klan leaders held a cross-burning ceremony on a privately owned farm, has a different impact overall than if the same events had taken place in a public park on the holiday honoring the birth of the Rev. Martin Luther King, Jr. The Court in *Brandenburg* recognized that the message of the Klan expressed on private property did advocate violence and was directed to inciting lawlessness, but held that such would be protected lest abstract teaching and discussions surrounding the moral propriety or necessity for resort to violence become confused with an actual call-to-arms.

The Court in *Brandenburg* must have deemed criminal conspiracy statutes and other provisions of the penal code sufficient to punish the violence perpetrated by the Klan on the heels of a rally on private property. There are numerous accounts of the harm and injuries that occur after militant white supremacists ban together in private space.[22] In many instances, where police, prosecutors, and judges uphold their oath and seek justice for all, the full force of the criminal law is brought to bear upon the perpetrators.

But when Klan groups seek to advocate such views in public arenas, there is a twofold rationale for denying that opportunity, and neither element has ever been deemed antithetical to existing constitutional principles. First, organizations with a history of terrorist activity pose a qualitatively different kind of threat to the public order. Thus, governments are authorized to regulate accordingly. Secondly, the harms attending the public display of hate-mongering activity extend far beyond those that occur in the aftermath of private meetings, resulting in circumstances to which the criminal justice system and government officials are incapable of responding.

The increased conflict resulting from public displays of hate-mongering activity is not unlike the kerosene-soaked cloth that burns even upon the surface of a pool of water. In the most widely reported incident, the neo-Nazi speech activity in Skokie, Illinois, was designed to promote hatred of and incite violence against the Jews of that village, representing the first part of the Nazi's general plan. Appearing in full Nazi regalia and displaying the swastika also enabled them to simultaneously achieve part two of their general plan, which was violent confrontation. The speech activity perpetrated psychological violence, while the men and their sympathizers perpetrated physical violence, harassment, and intimidation. Thus, the conditions that led to harassing phone calls throughout the nights, and distribution of life-threatening flyers, in addition to the specter of a community in utter chaos and its attendant loss of security, were whipped up by five or six neo-Nazis. Had they been legally confined to a private farm outside of Chicago, the harms generated would have been far less substantial. In that case, a decision to enter the village as they did would have been at their own risk. Instead, they received widespread media attention, a court-mandated license for the march issued by local government officials, and armed police protection. All of which encouraged fellow sympathizers to anonymously join in the threats of violence, thereby magnifying the perceived as well as actual threat and attendant injury.

In the most obvious sense, the fact pattern of *R.A.V.* was entirely different, but the injury was exactly the same. In 1990, one of many crosses burned nationwide was on the lawn of a black couple living in a predominantly white neighborhood in St. Paul, Minnesota. General knowledge of the facts surrounding the impact of the juvenile cross-burner in St. Paul is minuscule, leading to the assumption that his actions were less disruptive than the events in Skokie. In fact, we know little about the case because an individual acting under the veil of darkness provokes less media attention than live coverage of a blazing cross. Nevertheless, whether the individual terrorist was an adult or minor, acting alone or in concert, the act of burning a cross on someone else's lawn (or even one's own, though targeting another) provides more than enough fuel for all of the smoke damage and fire that was ignited in Skokie, Illinois. Professor Charles Lawrence describes a circumstance where a member of his family experienced similar threats and the harm to the victims was more than evident and disruption of the community just as great, though less well publicized until his article appeared in the *Duke Law Journal*.[23]

In *R.A.V.*, Minnesotans recognized the true nature of the dilemma. The perpetrators of racist hate-crimes usually do not target behaviors, but rather they advocate race genocide and challenge the existential validity of the target group. By banning the public display of hate-mongering activity, government officials were addressing the problem with the specificity required to reach the desired result. Ensuring safety and order in that community, in their view, warranted a content-specific measure, which would communicate to minority groups that the group-hatred aspect of this kind of speech is not condoned by the majority of Minnesota citizens.[24] No doubt the citizens of that jurisdiction felt well within their rights, consistent with constitutional mandates, given the level of violence that has historically and perpetually been the hallmark of Ku Klux Klan, neo-Nazi, and Skinhead activity.

According to the reasoning of the U.S. Supreme Court in *R.A.V.*, the speech element of the cross-burning activity was entitled to constitutional protection under First Amendment principles. Justice Scalia, writing for the majority, reasoned that although expression of the "message" could be banned under the traditional fighting words exception to free speech, the ordinance at issue proscribed only racist fighting words. Such regulation was deemed a content-based restriction and, hence, official suppression of a point of view.

Since the Court's tacit affirmation of the holding in *Skokie*, hate-speech activity, "steeped in [a] centuries-long tradition of violent attacks," has sprung up in many areas of the country as right-wing extremists have victimized groups beyond African-Americans and Jews.[25] Hispanics, Native Americans, Asian-Americans, lesbians, and gay men have been subject to violent attack. The spread of terrorist behavior suggests that the imprimatur of overt and public displays of hate-mongering activity lifts the veil of shame. The hate-monger perceives public acquiescence, in the midst of both affirmation and opposition to the message, which often results in physical and psychological injury for those who are scapegoated as objects of their contempt.

Those proposing guidelines governing hate-speech activities in jurisdictions where the Klan is active are cognizant of the unique dangers presented by hate-speech activity in the current social and economic climate, as well as the correlation between public display and violence. The legislative, judicial, and executive branches of state and federal governments have a shared obligation to ensure peace, tranquility, and public order on behalf of all Americans. In this context, the three branches of government must examine the relation between public and private advocacy of racial violence and the resulting injury to victims and communities. Professor Richard Kay notes that while the constitutional distinction between the public and the private as essential qualities of conduct cannot be maintained, it nonetheless appeals to a powerful intuition about constitutional law. That intuition is the idea that the rules of the Constitution make up a separate and exceptional body of law with its own subject matter and its own limits.[26]

Examining the body of judicial opinions where the nature and scope of the defendant's hate-mongering activity is a central issue, the courts refuse to interpret the Constitution as imposing affirmative responsibilities on the state. And yet according to Kay's analysis, "The enforcement of such duties [wherever they reasonably exist would] effectively hold the state accountable for the privately inflicted injuries its positive actions might have prevented."[27]

With doubtless assurance that public hate-mongering activity leads to widespread violence and severe community disruption, restricting such activity to the private realm appears to be the sole means of balancing rights to be free from government-imposed orthodoxy against our commitment to civil and human rights.

V. Freedom of Conscience in an Ideal World

There are any number of circumstances for which the principles ensuring freedom of conscience can be reasonably applied. For example, a local group of Boy Scouts, led by a dedicated environmentalist, publicly protesting the dumping of hazardous wastes into a community reservoir by a regional manufacturer has all the earmarks of political speech. Public protest opportunities for Boy Scouts acting in environmental interests serve the highest purpose for which speech and association rights were developed.

Compare that hypothetical situation to the actions of a Ku Klux Klansman and convicted felon who taught youngsters from an Explorer Scout Post in Texas how to fire semiautomatic weapons, decapitate enemies with a machete, and use the *garrote*. The group's charter application for membership in the Boy Scout Council was denied when an investigation revealed that young boys between the ages of 13 and 19 were granted permission by their parents to go on weekend camping trips that turned into guerrilla-warfare training expeditions. One mother recalls that her son reported a plan to "go on a mission to the Mexican border to watch for illegal alien crossings."[28]

The question surrounding parental and community involvement in the lives of the children is crucial. If a lawsuit had arisen because of these facts, few would be likely to object to the effective ban on the Klan-Scout organization because minors are involved. Few would accuse the Boy Scout Council of engaging in censorship or using its membership policy as a means of eliminating critical perspectives from public dialogue. On the contrary, an argument can be sustained that in cases where speech activity presents a threat to the public welfare and individual citizens there ought to be a compelling justification for *not* regulating speech.

Scholars attempt to articulate the basic values to be enhanced through protection of the speech elements of Klan, neo-Nazi, and Skinhead activity. A survey of the most current literature demonstrates that none of the scholars advance a plausible argument that Klan-style activity is valuable because it leads, however indirectly, to verifiable truth.[29] None have argued that it contributes to the range and quality of public discourse, nor has it been readily identified as valued political speech because of its contribution to our system of checks and balances.

Nevertheless, Martin Redish would argue that it doesn't matter that Klan speech activities achieve none of these lofty goals, for all of the important benefits derived from free speech are found in a version of self-realization.[30] Redish contends that no matter where one finds the greatest degree of theoretical and intellectual comfort, the nest itself is feathered by virtue of the First Amendment's ultimate value of self-actualization, which Redish views as the natural by-product of all other reasoning.

Klan/Nazi activity, as expressed by former Klansmen, affirms the existential validity of violent white supremacists. Understanding the mindset that drives their behavior is simple, although it is rarely discussed by white Americans unless the topic relates to conditions attributable to extreme bigots.

The phenomena was quite accurately highlighted in the movie *Mississippi Burning*, a fictional account of events leading to the federal prosecution of the Klan, Mississippi sheriffs, and local police officers for conspiracy in the murder of three civil rights workers in the mid-sixties. Based upon a true story, the film made clear that racial terrorism was a way of life in the South, passed on from one generation to the next. The movie depicted agents working to enforce federal civil rights law, in direct conflict with abuses of state police, who encouraged and participated in the mass torture, arson, and lynchings of blacks by white mobs during that period. The agent of the FBI's state office was asked to explain how the people in the region could condone what has become known as a reign of terror. He provided this explanation to his northern counterpart:

> They believe that some things are worth killing for. When I was a little boy, there was an old negro farmer who lived down the road from us by the name of Monroe. He was a little luckier than my daddy was. He bought himself a mule; that was a big deal around that town. Well my daddy hated that mule 'cause his friends were always kidding him about how they saw Monroe out plowing with his new mule, and that Monroe was gonna rent another field now that he had a mule, and one morning that mule just showed up dead. They'd poisoned the water. And after that, there was never any mention of that mule around my daddy—it just never came up. One time we were driving down the road and we passed Monroe's place and we saw that it was empty—he just packed up and left. ... I looked over at my daddy's face and I knew he'd done it, and he saw that I knew and he was ashamed. I guess he was ashamed 'cause he looked at me and said if you ain't better than a nigger, then who are you better than?

From a free speech and association perspective, hardly anyone would argue that the agent's father had moved beyond the rights guaranteed him by the constitution because he believed that being "less than a nigger" was an intolerable condition for which violence was justified. Nor would anyone object to his sharing such beliefs with his son, or even his association with others who held similar views. He would be within his rights even if he chose to act in concert with others peacefully marching in the public thoroughfare in order to deliver a petition to the secretary of state seeking repeal of the Thirteenth, Fourteenth, and Fifteenth Amendments. Acceding the full value of self-realization in this context, community and governmental responses to the protest would undoubtedly be hearty and robust. The "more speech" paradigm could be effectively employed to counter such a message. These are the circumstances for which the clause insuring freedom of conscience was insisted upon during the constitutional convention of 1791.

Redish argues that self-actualization is the core value for which the First Amendment was developed and which, in and of itself, provides a powerful rationale for protection of most speech, assembly, and association. Freedom of conscience has been persuasively presented as precisely what the First Amendment is all about: protecting the rights to formulate, develop, and express one's point of view individually, collectively, in private, or in public. And yet, domestic terrorists marching in Klan regalia and displaying swastikas before Holocaust survivors provide a paradigmatic exception to the rules governing public protest and should therefore be restricted to private space. Expression allowed in public fora under state licensing authority carries the sanction of government officials as to its form, if not to its content; as to its method, if not its madness; and as to its worth, if not its value.

VI. Ideological Servitude or the "Need" for Public Tolerance?

Much of the resistance to regulating any kind of speech is centered on our sense that it would be counterintuitive to insist that particular ideas cannot be imposed upon the citizenry as the only true or most virtuous, while censoring others as totally false. Quotes declaring that the discovery of truth is aided, rather than hindered, by public testing abound.[31] Justice Holmes offered the "marketplace" metaphor, expounding upon his theory that inclusion of all opinions in the marketplace of ideas will ensure selection of "true" ideas. While many Americans recognize that various demagogues throughout history have skillfully manipulated public opinion and in so doing greatly harmed the interests of minorities, there is a pocket of resistance to the total abandonment of "searching for truth" as a methodology. It still partially serves as a justification for tolerance.[32]

Adherents of Holmesian jurisprudence operate under the assumption that the ability of a society to tolerate the advocacy of race genocide, for example, is the best protection against its acceptance. Thus, a Jewish community invaded by men in Nazi regalia—advertising free transportation to a specially crafted gas chamber on Hitler's birthday—is expected to tolerate such expression because it has been deemed antithetical to the views of so many, so patently absurd that it would yield little, if any, persuasive force. However, the capacity of such speech to strike a chord with "a few crazies" fails to articulate the primary concern. Public expression of extreme ideas fortifies the speaker, mobilizes the hate-group toward actualization, and results in substantial injury. The terror and harassment of racial minorities is followed by deaths and physical violence, and the community is left without an effective means of response.

According to Professor Paul Chevigny, there is a special reason to carefully consider our willingness to tolerate the opinion we hate in the public context:

> It will be connected, through fantasy or linguistic meaning or both, to opinions that some people in the society find attractive; it is essential to come to grips with those fantasies and meanings, to try to explain and answer them. Even though we cannot conceive of the opinions as "true" as a matter of policy, it may be a reflection of social or psychological conflicts that cannot be touched except through a response to those fantasies.[33]

Chevigny's view provides ample justification for widespread tolerance of the individual biker who walks into a gas station with a t-shirt that exposes his swastika tatoo. Yet, a fully outfitted parade of Klansmen strikes an entirely different blow to the safety and order of the community. Moreover, while the concerted activities of the group may be distinguished upon the basis of greater likelihood of injury or violence, other antiviolence ordinances have recognized those instances where similar distinctions necessarily apply to individuals. For example, Shade Miller, an individual member of the Invisible Empire of the Knights of the Ku Klux Klan emerged from a pick-up truck in Lawrenceville, Georgia, wearing the traditional hood of the Klan, and was arrested for wearing a mask so as to conceal his identity while on public streets or property.[34] Few of the concerns addressed by the Georgia statute are relevant when such outfits are donned in private space. As the Georgia court noted:

> Legislatures enacted anti-mask laws to eliminate a form of terroristic threat, discourage the violence that anonymity encourages and aid the apprehension of criminals, certainly these represent signifi-

cant government interests. Laws which prohibit wearing masks with intent to conceal identity in public places serve these interests, for the dangers posed may all be traced to concealment.... "[A] nameless, faceless figure strikes terror in the human heart. But, remove the mask, and the nightmarish form is reduced to its true dimensions."[35]

That which we allow in public fora carries with it a judgment about its desirability, legitimacy, and appropriateness, otherwise there would be no need to distinguish between public and private activity.

VII. Conclusion

Over a period of several years, legal scholars have gone into earnest deliberation and on to defensible justification for tolerance of the harsh consequences of providing heightened protection for hate-speech activity. Freedom of conscience in the broadest sense, buttressed by near-absolutist construction of First Amendment principles, is at the core of our national identity. Unfortunately, many scholars have summarily concluded that there is no room for regulation of hate-mongering activity that could be reconciled with our fundamental beliefs in individual freedom to be an idiot or not, particularly in a country where freedom in the realm of ideas has been hailed as the great cornerstone of our success.

Nonetheless, we've established some core values and principles upon which we base our current free speech doctrine. Thus, if we reach a collective finding that there is little truth in the malicious display of the swastika before Holocaust survivors, that burning a cross on the lawns of interracial families serves no useful role in the exposition of ideas, that threatening to kill blacks and Asians cannot be construed as petitioning the government for redress of grievances, then the only principle that prevents us from banning hate-groups altogether, is the hate-monger's entitlement to autonomy and self-fulfillment in an atmosphere free from government imposed orthodoxy.

Nothing embodied in our constitutional principles prevents a regulatory scheme that restricts the vile and debased tenets of militant white supremacists to the private realm, while allowing criminal conspiracy and other relevant statutes to serve as the primary means of punishing the violence in which they glory. Society's interest in protecting the victims of racial violence and harassment, social equality, community security and civility, and the symbolic significance of law as a teacher, places an affirmative obligation upon government to restrict hate-speech activity to the private realm.

In concluding that we need to regulate hate-mongering, a comprehensive restatement of First Amendment principles is in order. Klan and Nazi-type activity, under a tightened regulatory scheme, could not be displayed in public fora. Such a proposal would not affect purely private activity, such as intimate gatherings or cross-burning rallies on isolated farmland, nor would it impact directly upon the privately directed speech of your everyday bigot or racist ideology disseminated under the guise of pseudo-scientific eugenic theories.

Admittedly, some cases will arise where a public display of hate-mongering activity will only present a few of the dangers outlined. There may be artistic performances that use offensive and threatening words, for example, that we can tolerate. Where the activity is neither concerted, nor targets a victim population with an actual threat, such activity would fall outside of the realm contemplated in this recommendation. A Nazi rally held in the middle of town, on privately owned land but plainly visible to the public, presents the opposite dilemma. When hate-mongering activity is publicly directed at a target population it should be restricted on that basis. The regulation would focus exclusively upon concerted acts of targeted vilification and seek to abolish First Amendment protection of open conspiracies to engage in harassment, intimidation, and obvious threats of violence.

Making law, in view of collective value judgments surrounding the character and quality of community interaction, is a function of duly elected government officials. Citizens of the United States have made clear, through decades of legislation, that harassment and intimidation form no essential part of the public dialogue. Thus, terrorism abroad cannot be condemned while domestic terrorism motivated by racial hatred continues apace at home.

Notes

Funding for the research upon which this article is based was provided by the William H. Hastie Fellowship Program at the University of Wisconsin School of

Law. Substantial portions of the research were gathered during my enrollment in the Intensive Research Program at the University of Buffalo, Faculty of Law and Jurisprudence.

1. John Grisham, *A Time to Kill* (New York: Wynwood Press, 1989), 1–2, 1989.

2. See generally, *Brief Amici Curiae in Support of Respondent*, by the Center for Democratic Renewal, in *R.A.V. against City of St. Paul*. This source contains a fairly comprehensive list of national surveys, studies, and reports that detail the rising levels of violence in the last decade.

3. 395 U.S. 444 (1969).

4. 578 F. 2d 1197 (7th Cir. 1978).

5. 112 S. Ct 2538 (1992).

6. Mari Matsuda, "Public Response to Racist Speech: Considering the Victim's Story," 87 *Michigan Law Review*, 2320, 2377–78 (1989).

7. For an example of the news reports, see *United States v. Price*, 383 U.S. 787 (1966), which chronicles the events leading up to the conviction of Klan-cops in the Mississippi case.

8. 376 U.S 254 (1964).

9. Steven D. Smith, "The Politics of Free Speech: A Comment on Schauer," 64 *University of Colorado Law Review*, 960 (1993).

10. "Blacks Claim Victory in Georgia Suit on Fire Department Racism," *New York Times*, April 4, 1991, A14.

11. Kathryn Abrams, "Creeping Absolutism and Moral Impoverishment: The Case for Limits on Free Expression," in *The Limits of Expression in American Intellectual Life* (New York: American Council of Learned Societies, 1993), 1.

12. Abrams.

13. David A. J. Richards, "Free Speech and Obscenity Law: Toward a Moral View of the First Amendment," 123 *University of Pennsylvania Law Review*, 45, 63 (1974).

14. *NAACP v. Alabama*, 357 U.S. 449 (1958) (the nature of the belief sought to be advanced is irrelevant, and state action that effectively curtails association will be strictly scrutinized).

15. Richard Delgado, "Campus Antiracism Rules: Constitutional Narratives in Collision," 85 *Northwestern University Law Review*, 343, 384–85 (1991).

16. Tamara Jones, "Neo-Nazi Hate Groups: Violence by Skinheads Spreads across Nation," *Los Angeles Times*, Dec. 19, 1988. (Skinheads have been responsible for the growth of racist violence around the country. They were responsible for three deaths within an 11-month period during 1988.)

17. See *e.g., Van Duyn v. Smith*, 527 N.E. 2d 1005 (1988).

18. Matsuda, "Public Response," 2320.

19. Official Document, "International Court of Justice: Case Concerning

Application of the Convention on the Prevention and Punishment of the Crime of Genocide," 97 *A.J.I.L.*, 505 (1993).

20. Charles Frye, ed., *Values in Conflict: Blacks and the American Ambivalence toward Violence* (1980).

21. "Language as Violence v. Freedom of Expression: Canadian & American Perspectives on Group Defamation," 37 *Buffalo Law Review*, 337, 369 (1989).

22. Gregory L. Padgett, "Racially Motivated Violence and Intimidation: Inadequate State Enforcement and Federal Civil Rights Remedies," 75 *Journal of Criminal Law and Criminology*, 103–139 (1984).

23. Charles R. Lawrence III, "If He Hollers Let Him Go: Regulating Racist Speech on Campus," *Duke Law Journal*, 431, 476–77 (1990).

24. *R.A.V.*, 2548.

25. Amici Curiae Brief in *R.A.V.*, 41.

26. Richard S. Kay, "The State Action Doctrine, the Public-Private Distinction, and the Independence of Constitutional Law," 10 *Constitutional Commentary*, 329, 337 (1993).

27. Kay, 330–331.

28. "Paramilitary Actions Irk Neighbors of Texas Camp," *New York Times*, Nov. 30, 1980, at 67.

29. Mary Ellen Gale, "Reimagining the First Amendment: Racist Speech and Equal Liberty," 65 *St. John's Law Review*, 119, 136–153 (1991); see generally, J. M. Balkin, "Some Realism about Pluralism: Legal Realist Approaches to the First Amendment," *Duke Law Journal*, 375 (1990).

30. See Martin Redish, *Freedom of Expression: A Critical Analysis* (Charlottesville, Va.: Michie, 1984), 13. (The author explicitly rejects all authorities to the contrary.)

31. John Milton, *Areopagitica* (1644), reprinted in *II Complete Prose Works of John Milton*, 485, 561 (Milton is alleged to have stated the original version of this theory: "Let [truth] and falsehood grapple, who ever knew [truth] put to the worse, a free and open encounter.")

32. Lee C. Bollinger, *The Tolerant Society: Freedom of Speech and Extremist Speech in America* (New York: Oxford University Press, 1986).

33. Paul Chevigny, *More Speech: Dialogue Rights and Modern Liberty*, 121 (Philadelphia: Temple University Press, 1988).

34. Wayne R. Allen, "Klan, Cloth and Constitution: Anti-Mask Laws and the First Amendment," 26 *Georgia Law Review*, 819 (1991).

35. Allen, 845 (quoting *State v. Miller*, 260 Ga. 669, 671–72 (1990)).

THIRTEEN

Speaking the Corn into Being

DIANE GLANCY

There was a time when what you said actually happened. If you needed to hunt, you spoke the herd into the woods or prairie. You spoke your arrow into the animal. You gave thanks to the Great Spirit for the reciprocal process of word and "happening." You gave thanks to the animal for its life. It was a time when the word was ceremony. Not so much a chronological time, such as "long ago," but a conditional sense of the word pushed through to Word.

Speech had the power to became physical property. Maybe still does. Nobody knew how it happened, but that's the way it was. It seemed to be connected with oral tradition. When there were no books or written laws or any way to write them. When everything was carried in the belief system of the tribe and was a matter of the heart and head. When this word/object relationship was intact.

The word also could be transferred at times just by thinking. Without sound. In fact it's not really the words but the thought, the spirit or energy behind what is said. Putting into being the vital life-force of which words are only the carriers.

We've lost those times. They hardly exist in memory even among the old ones. Ask Cherokees on the streets of Tahlequah, Oklahoma, about the meaning of their language and they'd probably say, "What?" They talk about the things people talk about. They might say that "words making things" sounds like the ancestors talking. They'd probably say, "Go away."

But somehow there's still the sense of the word as a creative force. The power of the word is to be respected. Words are a tribe with different "duties." There's the word as sacred, as holy, as ceremony. There's ordinary words of conversation. There's silence, which is a powerful internal structure. Even the land has a voice. And the animals. Once they spoke, too, but gave up their language. According to legend, they didn't want to be like us.

My concept of the word, the spoken word, is an image I have. It goes back to the time before we killed the word. Before we put it in its little coffin which the written form is. When the word was alive. When it was spirit. When what we spoke coordinated conditions (brought into harmony arrow and animal). Or what we spoke actually served as a causal function. Words as transformers. As makers of things that happened.

I want to remember what it was like. Those times before the alphabet aren't here anymore, but neither are they gone. They wake now and then at moments when something stirs them. Or when, for an instant, I catch a peripheral glance of something which must have been like them. Though I have changed from what the ancestors were, and language and the world in which that language operated have changed as well. And in the end, what does it matter? That way of life, despite all its power, was defeated.

Now this is the Cherokee understanding of the spoken word, the voice, anyway. In our tradition, people do not simply speak about the world, they speak the world into being. What we say is intricately intertwined with what we are and can be. To the Cherokee people, all things in the world have a voice—and that voice carries life. Storying gives shape to meaning. This concept of speech and voice is based on a notion that the voice does not speak alone, but generations of voices speak. They must be heard and understood by others and added onto by them. When we speak we take the power of the spoken word and infuse it with new breath. We add our voice to story so it shifts, changes, renews with the multiplicity of meanings and the variables of possibilities. To keep words alive and elastic. To keep them the shape-changers they have to be for our survival.

The voice and the thought that rides upon the voice is the challenge. What you speak is spoken into an energy-field or field-of-force that has consequence. The breath forming words is holy. The sound and shape of them breathed into being.

The Cherokee knew their words had the power to create. That's also the guardian, the check and balance, of the word. Its power to generate force. What you said could last for generations. Therefore you guarded your words. You made them count in the oral tradition. You spoke them responsibly. You kept in mind what the speaker says also affects the speaker as much as the spoken to.

Now this is what I have to say about speaking the corn into being.

In the old days the farmers did not know the day of planting. It was announced by the holy men. Then the orators would come and sing the seed-corn into the field and the field into the form from which the corn would rise in the process of the seeds breaking. Then someone, usually the grandmother, would sit on her platform speaking the crows away from the seeded fields until the seeds were established in stalks and corn tassels waving and the corn itself could speak the crows away. The corn was mixed with words all summer. The fields were never without sound. Even after harvest, a green-corn ceremony honored the new crop. During the storing process. Even during baking or cooking, a woman would speak to the corn. Tell it stories.

There was an interconnectedness of things.

And it shall come to pass in that day, I will hear, saith the Lord, I will hear the heavens, and they shall hear the earth; And the earth shall hear the corn . . . and [the corn] shall hear [the people]. (Hosea 2:21–22)

Some of the Cherokee were evangelized by Christian missionaries. They found similarities in Yahweh and the Great Spirit because the Judeo-Christian God also spoke the world into being. He had the power to join mind and word. He knew the wholeness of being. In fact, there are stories the Great Spirit made us because he wanted to share that power. He mixed us with the dust of the ground and his breath. It's breath which gives us kinship with the Great Spirit. Breath is in the sacredness of the spoken word. In turn, we are creators when we speak.

We are accountable for our words.

But the spirit of the word is often smothered under papers and documents and files and debates and laws and libraries and books. There also should be a category for indifference and ignorance of the power of words. Just as denominations smother the spirit of the Great Spirit. I'm not against the new world. But it gave up a lot. Mainly without knowing what it lost.

Sometimes I speak my *corn* into being. I speak to my words. I say to them, you will talk in the old way.

My son is a teacher, my daughter an attorney. I say to them, your words speak your path into being.

But the Cherokee lost their way of life in the coming of the new. Yet it's in the stillness sometimes I see a word come to life. It's an ancient power.

This is what I have to say.

Over spring break I traveled for the United States Information Agency to a country where there was no freedom of expression. What a person was to believe was broadcast into the streets over loudspeakers several times a day. There were armed soldiers at check-points. That's what you have to do to guard against a politically and morally fractured, pluralistic society which the United States is. Full of diversity and discord and messiness and life.

But where do you stop regulating once you begin?

In the old way of speaking, the speaker always remembers he connects not only to others (this includes the unseen past and future generations who surround him), but also to the original creator of speech himself, the Great Spirit, from whom this process was given and learned. I'm not looking back and saying that then was good and now is bad. That's not true at all.

Things aren't as simple as absolutes.

There is never a lone voice which can be judged true or false. The voice always connects to the something it speaks into being, and brings with it not only the thought or spirit of the speaker, but the accumulated voices that ride upon any single voice, and in turn, that something-brought-into-being affects other voices that speak with others and so forth. Without the polarity of truth and falsity. Without that concept. In fact, the same words can be both "good" and "bad" depending on the circumstance and the speaker. An "alive" word can travel both ways at once.

Language should be a ceremony changing the way we think. It operates in conditions which allow it to operate. Language doesn't work with a harness. It has to move with the changing sameness it always has.

The same changeableness. Those subtle differences or inferences that change the context. That shift the meaning of the text. So that we are renewed and not tied to circumstance. Meaning with changeable consistency. We have to reflect it in our words. And in turn we are reflected.

Language has a holy-clown element which goes backward or contrariwise. To give possibilities. To lose the bonds. So the tribe isn't stuck with hunger. Or unalterable, negative situations. Yes, that's something like it.

Because all sorts of words set all sorts of energy fields into being, our words light a match to the dark, and the dark has a substance. Or if not, then darkness is a void which becomes something according to our words.

And you see in the end we're going to talk in circles which the true migration path is. So that the process of the journey is more important than the arrival point. Inconclusiveness and open-endedness are also a part of native thought. Which irritates the western mind. But it's been around a long time. It just hasn't been recognized by the present dominant culture. Many voices, many points-of-view, full of contradictions and moving variables and kinetic energies which keep a civilization breathing its life-breath. Take away a language and all its possibilities and you extinguish a people, or at least the spirit of a people.

Because meaning has to be multi-placed as it speaks, which reflects the multi-placement of the Great Spirit and his relationship to otherness.

Our language, and ourselves for that matter, are basically spiritual according to Cherokee belief. The world-that-is doesn't usually consider that to be a point. So maybe it will also miss the Cherokee concept of words.

The nature of meaning is moving. Words changing by intonation or the circumstances in which they are spoken. Words changing in combination with other words. Kinetic beings rolling around like marbles. There are many variables. Even punctuation. It's in our voice. Our nation. Which is language.

I would like to hear the Cherokee grandfathers with their long-stemmed pipes and turbans sitting around the brush-arbor talking about these matters. Speaking the corn into being. Speaking the corn beings.

There are some stories that take seven days to tell. There are other stories that take you all your life.

PART VI
Conclusion

FOURTEEN

Embracing Uncertainty/Facing Fear

ROBERT JENSEN

This volume is eclectic by design. The contributors come from a variety of disciplines, and the styles of the chapters vary widely. Some writers are reformist in tone and within the mainstream free-speech tradition, while others argue for more radical change and reject basic premises of liberalism. There is common ground among the authors on some issues, but no uniform agreement on much of anything, from the nature of constitutional interpretation to the nature of speech. However, all are committed to rethinking the First Amendment and freedom of expression, and to considering critical ideas that may violate tenets of the established order or apply traditional doctrine in new ways.

So, this volume is more a series of questions and tentative proposals that are sometimes contradictory than it is a manifesto of critical approaches or a coherent statement of a single approach to theory and policy. This open-ended perspective is particularly evident in Diane Glancy's exploration of Cherokee notions of expression and the power of the word. Taking us outside the familiar framework of Western legal thought, Glancy opens up what may be for many readers a new way of thinking about words and meaning. Her essay comes at the end of the book to remind us that our own ontological assumptions—things we think we know about the way the world is—are only assumptions, that other people rooted in other traditions have different ideas not only about religion or social practices, but about the nature of the world and the word. This is, then, an uncertain volume, but one that celebrates its uncertainty. It suggests that we have had far too much certainty—or, more accurately, the pretense of certainty—in free expression theory, and what we need is more imagination. As Christine Delphy reminds us:

> [T]o understand reality, and hence eventually to have the power to change it, we must be prepared to abandon our certainties and to accept the (temporary) pain of an increased uncertainty about the world. Having the courage to confront the unknown is a precondition for imagination, and the capacity to imagine another world is an essential element in scientific progress.[1]

We need to abandon certainties about freedom of expression and the First Amendment. The liberal/libertarian approach to free speech and press law, which has been widely accepted in the U.S. legal system and intellectual community for decades, is no longer sacrosanct; the struggle over the meaning of the First Amendment can no longer be contained within safe boundaries. This kind of call for change can be unsettling and often creates fear. But no growth comes without change, and change rarely comes without uncertainty, and uncertainty almost always sparks fear.

I conclude this volume with a story that touches on this fear. I think this story suggests how complicated freedom of expression can be, even in settings explicitly dedicated to the celebration and protection of free speech. It is a story about law and power, about words and actions, about reason and emotion.

A couple of years back I was invited to sit in on the private portion of a First Amendment conference. A number of constitutional law scholars gathered together for a weekend bull session to toss around ideas about the future of free-speech law. As a young scholar of meager reputation, I was flattered at the invitation, and I listened and learned much from these professors. On the second of two days, the discussion turned to hate speech and pornography. One participant threw out a hypothetical that involved feminist legal scholar Catharine MacKinnon, who teaches at the University of Michigan and is active in the movement to end violence against women.[2] Would the university, this man asked, be right in prohibiting a student from wearing to MacKinnon's class a button that said, "Fuck Kitty MacKinnon" (a nickname of MacKinnon used by friends, but which also is widely known)? The discussion bounced around the room, and each speaker seemed to make sure he repeated the hypothetical slogan before addressing the legal issues. Some appeared to speak it with a certain relish. And each time those words were spoken, I became more uncomfortable. After several repetitions of the phrase, I entered the conversation. I told the group that before rendering a scholarly opinion, I wanted to tell them that I felt bad listening to them repeat those words over and over. I am not a woman, I said, but still it felt assaultive to me; I felt scared by the power, the violence of those words, and the hatred behind them. At the time there was only one woman in the room with a dozen or so men (there had been one other female participant the day before), and I looked to her as if to say, "Join my dissent if you like; I don't want to speak for you." She made it clear from body language and a quick comment that she would prefer to stay out of it. I pressed on, trying to explain that those words had power, that they made me feel a certain way and that I didn't like it. My comments dropped on the table like lead; the men were mostly mute, some looking away from me to avoid my eyes. Finally one of the men ended the episode by asking how I would respond if he suggested that I was just overly sensitive. I said I understood how that conclusion would seem reasonable to many, and I made it clear that I would press the point no further. As a man I could live with such talk without really feeling threatened; after all, they weren't talking about violating me. And the discussion moved on. Everyone seemed relieved to put the issue to rest without further questioning or exploration.

I often ponder that incident and what it means. My first reaction was that it was a boys-will-be-boys problem: The men who lingered on the hypothetical just liked getting away with talking dirty. I had to admit to myself that I sometimes feel very adolescent and enjoy the sound of such words. But I think there is much more to the incident than the pleasure of occasional vulgarity. In that story, I think, are examples of some of the central problems of the contemporary free-speech debate. If there ever was a place where free speech should be lived out in all its glory, a meeting of intellectuals discussing free speech should be it. And, certainly, there was considerable latitude for expression in that room. But in my expression of dissent are reminders of some of the problems we face.

First, I was clearly marked as an equal-but-not-quite-equal in the room. I was the youngest person with the least amount of teaching experience, and I don't publish in law journals. I was a communications Ph.D. in a meeting of mostly law professors, and while I have studied media law I am not as conversant in constitutional case law as the others. The currency in that room was the ability to spin constitutional theory and cite precedent; on that score, I clearly had less facility and, hence, less power. (Of course, this doesn't begin to deal with the obvious point that countless people have no access to such rooms and such discussions in the first place.) While the participants were polite and gracious, it was clear that, in that room, ideas that did not come carrying that currency were of lesser interest to the group. So, when I expressed my concerns about the nature of their conversation—when I suggested that their exercise of their freedom to speak was constraining me—my remarks did not get the automatic consideration that others' comments received. I had no power in that room to demand that they listen to me. I had the freedom to say anything I wanted, within the rules set up for the conversation, but I had no power to make them take me seriously and hear my concerns; it was easy for them to ignore me. While I can't know exactly what each person in the room thought, my guess is that many of them simply did not hear me.

The woman in the room, in some ways, was even more silenced than I. After talking to her briefly at the end of the meeting, I got the feeling that she had survived and been tenured in a relatively conservative law school by avoiding arguments such as this. While I respect her decisions and choices about coping with institutionalized sexism, it seems likely that those choices have, in certain situations, silenced her; patriarchal institutions' threats of punishment for certain kinds of speech—through the mechanisms of hiring and firing, tenure and promotion, and professional rewards—often are successful. This isn't to suggest that I know for sure this woman agreed with my assessment of the men's remarks or would have supported me if she had joined the discussion, but only to point out that she felt constrained from speaking in that gathering. Part of my willingness to raise the issue no doubt came from my own sense of male privilege; no matter how junior I was in the room, I took for granted my right to speak.

But perhaps the most important point to make about that incident concerns the inability of the participants to acknowledge and deal with my expression of emotion. Here were some of the brightest constitutional law scholars in the country, who have written volumes on speech and the First Amendment, and had been speaking eloquently for two days about crucial issues concerning expression. But when I took the question out of the intellectual stratosphere and brought it down into my body, no one could respond to me at that level. (Looking back, I have to take some responsibility for the way in which the discussion went after my comments. I set up my remarks as not-scholarly, as something I wanted to say about a personal matter before I made my real comments, the disembodied intellectual assertions. By doing that, I invited the others to ignore my reaction. I had accepted and invited the devaluation of my own emotions; not surprisingly, the others were happy to agree with me.)

No one in the room asked me to elaborate on my reaction; there were no questions about why such words would make me feel that way. What would such a discussion have produced? Perhaps I would have talked about some of my questions and confusions about sexuality, intercourse, and violence—about fucking. Perhaps I would have confided to them that I am a survivor of sexualized childhood abuse and find certain kinds of talk about sex threatening. Such disclosures by me might have changed the nature of the discussion, leading to talk about how certain kinds of speech affect people with certain kinds of experiences, about how the routine abuses of power in our culture position people differently to speak and to be affected by speech. That discussion didn't take place, at least partly because traditional legal scholarship (and Western scholarship in general, especially before the challenges of feminists, critical race theorists, and other nontraditional scholars) stays so locked in the abstracted mind, divorced from the body and emotional life. The result is an impoverished discussion of crucial issues. Antipornography feminists and critical race scholars, for example, have been asking others to understand the complex ways in which pornography and hate speech affect people, at the intellectual, emotional, and physical levels. Traditional free-speech libertarians usually treat such assertions as irrelevant; a common response is that the law cannot worry about hurt feelings. But more than hurt feelings are at issue; these kinds of coercive and hateful speech are part of a system that constrains people, injures people, keeps people from living their freedom. They are, in some sense, more than speech. As MacKinnon's own work points out, those words spoken around the table were not just speech but a form of sex, a kind of verbal gang rape, a way for the men to assert power in sexualized form. To understand all that, we have to work to understand beyond disembodied intellectual arguments. We have to struggle to feel, to have empathy, to be truly alive to others and to ourselves.

So, was the speech in that room free? On many levels, of course, it was a paradigmatic example of free speech. But at other levels, discrepancies of power silenced some speech, constrained some speech, and left other speech unheard. As this book suggests, the questions about free speech are always complex. Speech is never free in a pure sense. That doesn't mean we don't have commitments to fostering the freest possible speech, or shouldn't protect some kinds of speech. It means we can't accept simplistic conceptions and should be wary of simple solutions.

Perhaps the most important question to leave this volume pondering is a simple one: How seriously do we take our words? Several contributors to this volume have raised, either explicitly or implicitly, this issue. Professor Glancy's essay offers one clear assessment, one in which the word is understood as having great power. In the law, and society in general, it seems to me that we have a somewhat schizophrenic view on this question. I return to my story:

I think the men at the table were taking words seriously. They gave great thought to what they said. As influential scholars and teachers, they knew their words had impact. But when I pressed my objection to a way they were speaking, their response was that I was making too much of just words; denying the power of the words was their first line of defense. This may be the central tension in the ongoing debate about freedom of expression: We can't decide if we believe words are incredibly powerful or ultimately powerless. We take all sorts of words very seriously (such as the words in the First Amendment when we debate free expression), and yet we often defend the right to say things that hurt others because they are, after all, just words. It takes us back to the phrase "sticks and stones may break my bones, but words can never hurt me," which Julia Penelope has called a "desperately hopeful incantation" from childhood that all children know to be a lie.[3] Penelope points out that it is not only words that hurt us, but languages and their systems of rules, tied to systems of power. Words have enormous power, a power we acknowledge at times but often run from.

Answering this question about words does not make it clear exactly how First Amendment doctrine should be written, but it is a good place to start. And it reminds me that the Western view of speech and power and law is a particularly fragile construct, one that—through the manipulation of words—tries to hide from the power of the word.

Notes

1. Christine Delphy, "Rethinking Sex and Gender," *Women's Studies International Forum* 16:1 (1993): 1.

2. Before publishing this account, I sent a draft to Professor MacKinnon to ask her permission to use her name in this fashion and to offer the option of substituting a pseudonym. I would not have circulated the story that follows without her permission, and even with it I have misgivings about putting the words into print. My thanks to Professor MacKinnon for her gracious response to my query and also for her thoughts on the meaning of the incident.

3. Julia Penelope, *Speaking Freely: Unlearning the Lies of the Fathers' Tongues* (New York: Pergamon Press, 1990), xiii.

CONTRIBUTORS

DAVID S. ALLEN (Ph.D., Journalism and Mass Communication, University of Minnesota) is an assistant professor in the Department of Communication at Illinois State University, where he teaches courses in mass media law, mass communication theory, and journalism. Allen worked as a newspaper reporter for six years before completing his Ph.D. Allen's research focuses on how the Supreme Court defines the press's role in society and the connection between democratic theory and the practices of the professional press.

ELVIA R. ARRIOLA (J.D., University of California at Berkeley; M.A., History, New York University) is an assistant professor in the School of Law at the University of Texas at Austin, where she teaches courses in employment discrimination, civil rights law, legal ethics, and gender theory. She has published articles on sexual harassment, discrimination against lesbians and gays, and feminist legal theory. Arriola was a practicing civil rights lawyer as an assistant attorney general for the state of New York before becoming a professor.

ROBIN D. BARNES (J.D., University of Buffalo; LL.M., University of Wisconsin Law School) is an associate professor in the School of Law at the University of Connecticut. She teaches courses in wills, trusts, and estates, constitutional law, and legal ethics. Barnes has published a number of articles dealing with race consciousness in legal scholarship and is completing work based on a long-term research project on white supremacist groups in the United States.

SANDRA BRAMAN (Ph.D., Journalism and Mass Communication, University of Minnesota) is a research assistant professor of communication at the University of Illinois at Urbana-Champaign. She worked several years in public relations before her academic career. Braman is the author of a book, *The Information Regime* (Sage, forthcoming) and numerous articles on information technology, policy, development, and law. Braman also is a poet, short-story writer, storyteller, and performance artist who has practiced those arts since the early 1970s in print and public.

OWEN M. FISS (LL.B., Harvard Law School) is Sterling Professor of Law at Yale University, and he also has taught at the University of Chicago and Stanford law schools. Fiss, an active scholar for nearly three decades, is one of the country's preeminent constitutional authorities. He has published dozens of articles in legal and philosophical journals on constitutional law and legal theory, and is the author or coauthor of books on legal procedure, injunctions, and, most recently, the history of the Supreme Court.

DIANE GLANCY (M.F.A., University of Iowa) is a poet, short-story writer, and novelist, who teaches Native American literature and creative writing as an associate professor at Macalester College in St. Paul, Minnesota. Glancy has won several awards and prizes for her writing, including the 1990 Native American Prose Award from the University of Nebraska Press for her collection of essays, *Claiming Breath*. Her fourth book of poetry, *Lone Dog's Winter Count,* was published in 1990. Glancy, who is of Cherokee and German/English descent, also has published three collections of stories, *Trigger Dance* (Charles Nilon Fiction Award, University of Colorado), *Firesticks* (University of Oklahoma Press), and *Monkey Secret* (TriQuarterly/Northwestern University Press). A collection of plays, *War Cries,* is forthcoming from Holy Cow! Press in Duluth, Minnesota.

VICTORIA SMITH HOLDEN (Ph.D., Journalism and Mass Communication, University of Minnesota) is an assistant professor of communication at the University of North Dakota, where she teaches courses on media law, history, and sociology. Smith's recent research has focused on freedom of expression and U.S. labor unions. She also has written on media history, race and culture, and underground newspapers. In addition to her scholarly work, Smith has been a writer, editor, and manager for a variety of alternative publications.

ROBERT JENSEN (Ph.D., Journalism and Mass Communication, University of Minnesota) is an assistant professor of journalism at the University of Texas at Austin. Before coming to Texas, he worked for 10 years as a writer and editor for a variety of publications and institutions. Jensen's work in media law and ethics focuses on issues of gender, race, and sexual identity.

NORMAN ROSENBERG is DeWitt Wallace Professor of History and Legal Studies at Macalester College. He is the author of *Protecting the Best Men* (University of North Carolina Press, 1990) and coauthor of *In Our Times* (Prentice-Hall, 1995) and *Liberty, Equality, Power: A History of the American People* (Harcourt Brace, 1995). He is also the author of numerous articles in historical and legal journals, including "Hollywood on Trials: Courts and Films, 1930–1960" in *Law and History Review* (Fall 1994). He is currently working on a study of free speech discourses during the 1940s and 1950s.

FREDERICK SCHAUER (J.D., Harvard Law School) is Frank Stanton Professor of the First Amendment in the John F. Kennedy School of Government at Harvard University. He also has taught at the law schools of the University of Michigan, College of William and Mary, and West Virginia University. Schauer is the author of *Playing by the Rules: A Philosophical Examination of Rule-Based Decision-Making in Law and Life* (Oxford University Press, 1991) and *Free Speech: A Philosophical Enquiry* (Cambridge University Press, 1982). He has written extensively on judicial decision-making, constitutional law, and the First Amendment.

PAUL SIEGEL (Ph.D., Communication Studies, Northwestern University) is an associate professor in the Department of Communication Arts at Gallaudet University in Washington, D.C., and an adjunct professor at American University and George Mason University. He has written extensively on gay rights and other First Amendment issues in law reviews and in other academic book chapters. His edited collection of readings on the Hill/Thomas hearings, entitled *Outsiders Looking In,* is forthcoming from Hampton Press. Siegel is also an associate editor of the *Free Speech Yearbook,* published by the Southern Illinois University Press.

THOMAS STREETER (Ph.D., Speech Communication, University of Illinois at Urbana-Champaign) is an assistant professor of sociology at the University of Vermont and has previously taught at the University of Wisconsin-Madison. Streeter has published articles on cultural theory, broadcast policy, and critical legal studies. His book, *Selling the Air: A Critique of the Policy of Commercial Broadcasting,* is forthcoming from the University of Chicago Press.

CASS R. SUNSTEIN (J.D., Harvard Law School) is Karl N. Llewellyn Professor of Jurisprudence in the Law School and Department of Political Science at the University of Chicago. Sunstein, one of the country's leading constitutional law scholars, is the author of *Democracy and the Problem of Free Speech* (Free Press, 1993), *The Partial Constitution* (Harvard University Press, 1993), and *After the Rights Revolution* (Harvard University Press, 1990), as well as numerous articles, essays, and reviews.

INDEX

Abrams, Floyd, 5, 6, 16
Abrams, Kathryn, 260
absolutism, free-speech, 80
advertising, influence on news content, 67–68
AIDS, 234, 244
American Civil Liberties Union, 43, 47, 232
anti-mask laws, 273–74
Arendt, Hannah, 94, 97, 101, 103, 110
Atleson, James, 119
at-will-rule in employment, 117–18, 236
Austin, J. L., 38

Bachrach, Peter, 100
Baker, C. Edwin, 124–25, 131
Balkin, J. M., 4
Barthes, Roland, 40
Baudrillard, Jean, 170–74
Bentham, Jeremy, 99
Bernstein, Basil, 48
Black, Hugo, 80–81
Blackstone, William, 131
Bollinger, Lee, 17
Bourdieu, Pierre, 49
Bowman, Cynthia, 216–17
Boyte, Harry, 98
Brandeis, Louis, 205
Breen, Joseph, 146

Brennan, William, 106
broadcast regulation, 58–59, 62–66, 68–69, 72–73
Brown, Barry, 265–66
Bush, George, 264

Cable TV Act of 1992, 58
Campos, Paul, 158–59
Capra, Frank, 145
Carey, James, 49
Center for Democratic Institutions, 15
Chafee, Zechariah, 143
Cherokees, 278–82
Chevigny, Paul, 273
children's television, 68–69, 72
chilling effect, 20
Chomsky, Noam, 40
Civil Rights Movement, 258–61
Clinton, Bill, 239
codetermination, 116, 130
Cohen, Felix, 44
Cohen, Joshua, 102
Colby College, 213–15
collective bargaining, 121
communicative action, 102
company towns, 101
consciousness raising, 202
consumer sovereignty, 70–71
Convention on the Elimination of All Forms of Racial Discrimination, 14

corporate interests and First Amendment, 4, 37
cross burning, 79, 266, 268, 274–75

"decision authority," 124, 127, 130
Delgado, Richard, 5, 263
deliberative democracy, 100–102
Delphy, Christine, 286
democratic elitism, 99, 100
Douglas, William, 93, 105, 108, 240–41
draft card burning, 96
Dworkin, Andrea, 214–16

Edelman, Martin, 98
effective voice, 115–16, 130, 133
Emerson, Thomas, 95–96, 144, 241
enablement/enabling rights, 126–27, 130
equality and liberty, tension between, 55, 84, 88
Evans, Sara, 98
Ewing, David, 114

facticity, 170–71; and labels, 185–87, 189
fairness doctrine, 62–63, 65–66
Federal Communications Commission (FCC), 43, 62–64, 66, 68, 72
Fifteenth Amendment, 271
fighting words, 81, 84–85, 268
File on Thelma Jordan, The, 150–53, 157–58
film noir, 148–150
"First Freedom," 143
Fish, Stanley, 37, 39, 41, 44
Fiss, Owen, 123
flag burning, 36–38, 47
Force of Evil, 150, 153–58
formalism: legal, 37, 43–45, 117–19; and speech, 5, 46
Fourteenth Amendment, 118, 132–33, 271
Fowler, Mark, 68
France, Anatole, 118
Frankfurter, Felix, 117
fraternities and sexual violence, 213–14
Frye, Marilyn, 198

Gates, Henry Louis, 32–35, 50–51
gays. *See* lesbians and gays

Ginzberg, Ruth, 199–200
Great Spirit, 278, 280–81
Greene, Nathan, 117
Grisham, John, 253–54

Habermas, Jürgen, 4, 94, 100–103, 110
Hackney, Sheldon, 7
Hale, Robert, 55
Hand, Learned, 10–11, 23
Hart, H. L. A., 241–42
hate speech, 79–80, 87, 255–58
hecklers' veto, 86, 229, 243
Held, David, 99
Heldke, Lisa, 211
Helms, Jesse, 22–23, 263–64
Holmes, Oliver Wendell, 19, 65, 105, 118, 186, 272
Holocaust, 37, 255, 272, 274
homosexuals. *See* lesbians and gays
hooks, bell, 201
Horkheimer, Max, 6
Horton, Willie, 264
Hutchins, Robert, 15
hyperreality, 170–74

ideology, 11–12
incest. *See* sexual violence
individualism, 94

Jacobs, Lea, 146
Johnson, Barbara, 36

Kairys, David, 110
Kalven, Harry, 86–87
Kay, Richard, 268–69
Kendall, Willmore, 23
King, Martin Luther, Jr., 258, 266
Ku Klux Klan, 253–58, 260, 265–66, 268–75

labor unions, 114–15; and picketing and boycotting, 120
laissez-faire, 54, 215
Lakoff, Robin, 144–45
language, indeterminacy of, 34–36
law noirs, 150–51
Lawrence, Charles, 16–17, 267
Lazarsfield, Paul, 97–98

"legal reelism," 144
lesbians and gays: and child custody, 234; and employment discrimination, 236–40; forums for, 226–30; and Gay Pride parades, 235–36; and the military, 238–40, 242–44; and non-political associations, 233–34; and political associations, 230–33; and sexual expression, 241–42; and sodomy laws, 240–42, 244
Levy, Leonard, 15–16
Lewis, Anthony, 5, 6
libel and defamation, 14, 57, 61, 206–7
liberty of contract, 117, 118
Liebling, A. J., 47
linguistic style, 33–34; and class, 47–48
linguistic turn in philosophy, 31–32, 40
Lugones, Maria, 201–2

MacKinnon, Catharine, 5, 16, 41, 215, 286–87, 289
Macpherson, C. B., 127–130
Madison, James, 71, 99
mail, right to receive from foreign countries, 105–6
Mapplethorpe, Robert, 229
Marcuse, Herbert, 23
Margolis, Michael, 99
marketplace of ideas, 10, 32, 34, 39, 106, 205, 272
markets for speech, 56, 65
Marvin, Carolyn, 49–50
Matsuda, Mari, 39, 41, 51, 202–3, 257, 265
McCluksey, Martha, 213–14
McLuhan, Marshall and Eric, 172
Meiklejohn, Alexander, 45, 57, 81, 86, 143
Merton, Robert, 97–98
Mill J. S., 11, 18–22, 99
Miranda warning, 34
Mississippi Burning, 270–71
more-speech principle, 4, 143, 205
movies, legal regulation of, 146, 148
Murdoch, Rupert, 48

National Endowment for the Arts, 229
National Endowment for the Humanities, 7

National Labor Relations (Wagner) Act, 119–20
national security, 14
Nazis, 36–37, 46, 80, 82, 85, 205, 256, 260, 265–70, 272, 275
neutrality, content/viewpoint, 74, 204–5
New Deal, 19, 54–59
"new journalism," 170
news: local, 66, network, 67
Nunn, Sam, 239

oppression, 198–201

Penelope, Julia, 290
political action, 94, 97, 110
pornography, 31, 37, 41, 205, 212, 215–17
Post, Robert, 86
Powell, Lewis, 108–9
prisons, right of access to, 107–9
Production Code Administration (PCA), 146–47
property rights, 45, 116–17, 123–24, 127, 129–30, 134; employer's, 119, 123, 131; as a right of access, 129; and worker protection, 115, 131, 133
"protective democracy," 99
public good, information as, 70
public sphere, 7, 101–3, 106

racist speech, 14, 16, 32, 212, 253–75
rape. *See* sexual violence
realism, legal, 44
Redish, Martin, 270, 272
referentiality: and commodification, 188; and postmodernity, 170
Richards, David, 224–25
rights, positive/negative, 60
Rockwell, Norman, 144
Roosevelt, Franklin, 80

Scalia, Antonin, 79–82, 179, 268
Schauer, Frederick, 210
Schumpeter, Joseph, 99–100
Sennett, Richard, 97
sexual harassment, 196, 216–17
sexual violence, 195–200, 203–9, 214–17
simulation and dissimulation, 173
Skokie, Illinois, 14, 36, 46, 255, 266–67
slippery-slope argument, 21, 254

Smith, Steven, 257–58
soap box speakers, 46
sociolinguistics, 33
speech-conduct distinction, 38, 81, 95, 106
Spelman, Elizabeth, 201
Stephen, James, 23
Stewart, Potter, 107–9
Stock, Wendy, 203–4
Strossen, Nadine, 17
suffrage, 42
Sunstein, Cass, 45
survivors' wall, 195, 203

television and law, 144–45
Telotte, J. P., 148
Thirteenth Amendment, 114–15, 117, 131–34, 271

Thurmond, Strom, 239
trademarks, 174–79
travel to foreign countries, restriction of, 104–6

Universal Declaration of Human Rights, 14

Warner, John, 239
West, Robin, 210–12
White, James, 103
women: and defamation, 206–8; media portrayals of, 208–9; and silencing, 195, 199–206, 209
Women Against Rape, 206–7
workers' expression rights, 116, 119, 121–22, 126, 130, 134; and collective bargaining, 121

KF 4722.F744 1995